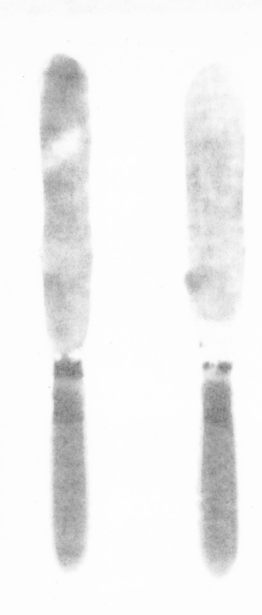

Texas Vistas: Selections from the
            Southwestern Historical Quarterly

The publication of this book was made possible by a grant from the Texas Educational Association.

TEXAS VISTAS:
SELECTIONS FROM THE SOUTHWESTERN HISTORICAL QUARTERLY

Compiled by
RALPH A. WOOSTER
and
ROBERT A. CALVERT

THE TEXAS STATE HISTORICAL ASSOCIATION
in Cooperation with the
CENTER FOR STUDIES IN TEXAS HISTORY
UNIVERSITY OF TEXAS AT AUSTIN

Austin

1980

Copyright © 1980 Texas State Historical Association
All rights reserved
Library of Congress Catalog Card No. 80-52706
Hardcover. ISBN: 0-87611-047-2
Paperback. ISBN: 0-87611-048-0

Preface

Since 1897, for over eighty years, the finest articles on Texas history have appeared in the pages of the *Southwestern Historical Quarterly*. Published by Texas's oldest learned society, the *Southwestern Historical Quarterly* originally bore the name *Quarterly of the Texas State Historical Association*. In Volume XIV, published in July, 1910, that name was changed to *Southwestern Historical Quarterly* in an attempt to broaden the geographic coverage of the journal. From time to time editorial policy regarding geographic coverage of the *Quarterly* has changed, but since 1910 the name has remained unchanged.

Over the years the Texas State Historical Association has been most fortunate in its choice of editors for the *Quarterly*. George P. Garrison, Eugene C. Barker, Herbert E. Bolton, Charles W. Hackett, Walter P. Webb, H. Bailey Carroll, Joe B. Frantz, and L. Tuffly Ellis have all at one time or another served as editor and/or managing editor. All have left a definite imprint upon the *Quarterly* and upon the history of their state. In particular, Barker, editor for twenty-seven years (1910–1937), and Carroll, editor for twenty-four years (1942–1966), played major roles in establishing the *Quarterly* as the premier

publication in its field. Recent editors Frantz (1966–1977) and Ellis
(1977–   ) have continued this tradition of excellence while
modernizing the physical appearance of the *Quarterly*.

The present volume, *Texas Vistas*, is a collection of eighteen articles
originally published in the *Quarterly*. In selecting this particular
group from over one thousand articles that have appeared in the
Quarterly, the editors have attempted to cover the broad range of
Texas history from the earliest Spanish exploration to the present. In
making our selections we also tried to include examples of political,
social, economic, and military history. We do not claim these are the
BEST studies which appeared in the *Quarterly;* but we do believe they
represent a balanced sampling of the articles.

This collection has been designed primarily as a collateral reading
book for college and university classes in Texas history; but it is hoped
that the work will have appeal to all readers who are interested in the
history of Texas. Some minor corrections and emendations have been
incorporated in the present edition, and footnotes which accompanied the articles as they originally appeared have been omitted.

RALPH A. WOOSTER, Beaumont
ROBERT A. CALVERT, College Station

Table of Contents

SECTION IV.   TWENTIETH CENTURY

SECTION I.

THE COLONIAL ERA

The Spanish Occupation of Texas, 1519-1690

Herbert E. Bolton[*]

In 1519 the Spanish explorer Alonso Alvarez de Piñeda sailed along the Gulf Coast from Florida to Mexico, observing the land and making a map. He landed at the mouth of the Rio Grande, which he called the "Río de las Palmas," or "River of Palms." Although he did not explore the interior of Texas, he recommended that the Spaniards establish settlements in the new land. The Spaniards, however, were involved and busy in other parts of New Spain and did not settle in Texas until nearly two centuries later.

During those two centuries the Spaniards did explore much of Texas. In the article which follows, Herbert Eugene Bolton (1870–1953), perhaps the greatest historian of the Spanish Southwest, traces the various Spanish approaches to Texas. Bolton notes that the Spaniards used four approaches in exploring the region: they came from the east and south by way of the Gulf of Mexico, from the east by way of Florida, from the west by way of New Mexico, and from the south through the expansion of Nuevo León and Coahuila.

Bolton points out that Spanish interest in Texas was well established before the Frenchman René-Robert Cavalier, Sieur de la Salle, built a fort on the Texas coast in the 1680s. The French settlement, Bolton

*Herbert E. Bolton, "The Spanish Occupation of Texas, 1519–1690," *Southwestern Historical Quarterly*, XVI (July, 1912), 1–26.

argues, did not cause but merely quickened the Spanish desire to occupy Texas. This, he believes, explains why the first Spanish outpost in Texas was placed not on the coast where the French built their fort but several hundred miles to the northwest, among the Indians whom the Spaniards had always hoped to reach.

I. INTRODUCTORY

For a century and a half before they made definite attempts to occupy the region now called Texas the Spaniards gradually explored it, proceeding step by step from the borders toward the interior, and slowly formed ideas concerning its geography and its suitability for settlement. Viewed in this light, the final occupation of Texas at the end of the seventeenth century was by no means the sudden event—brought about by the chance settlement of the French on the Gulf Coast—which is was once thought to be.

Though it is not commonly known, Texas had its share in the romance, and myth, and fable which everywhere attended the Spanish conquest in America. In Florida the Spaniards sought the Fountain of Youth; in South America the Gilded Man (El Dorado); on the west coast of Mexico the Isle of the Amazons; in Arizona and New Mexico the Seven Cities of Cíbola; on the California coast the Strait of Anian. Likewise, in Texas they searched for the Kingdom of Gran Quivira, where "everyone had their ordinary dishes made of wrought plate, and the jugs and bowls were of gold"; for the Seven Hills of the Aijados, or Aixaos, where gold was so plentiful that "the natives not knowing any of the other metals, make of it everything they need, such as vessels and the tips of arrows and lances"; for the Sierra (or Cerro) de la Plata (Silver Mountain), somewhere north of the Rio Grande; for the pearls of the Jumano country; and for the "Great Kingdom of the Texas"—a people who (like the Jumanos) had been miraculously converted by the woman in blue, who lived next door to the kingdom of Gran Quivira, and who were ruled by a powerful lord, had well-built towns (each several miles in length), and raised grain in such abundance that they even fed it to their horses. All these various quests and beliefs had made the Texas country an object of interest to the

Spaniards long before it became a field for political contest with France.

II. FOUR LINES OF APPROACH TO TEXAS, 1519–1678

There were four lines of approach to Spanish Texas, through the development of which a knowledge of the region was gradually unfolded: (1) from the east and south, by way of the Gulf of Mexico; (2) from the east, by way of the vast region known in early days as La Florida; (3) from the west and southwest, by way of New Mexico and Nueva Vizcaya; and (4) from the south, through the expansion of Nuevo León and Coahuila.

1. By Way of the Gulf

In the course of the exploration of the Gulf Coast and the search for a strait through the newly found land mass to the East Indies, Alonso Alvarez de Piñeda, in the employ of Francisco Garay, governor of Jamaica, in 1519 ran the coast from Florida to Pánuco (Tampico) and back, and made a map which shows with substantial accuracy the entire shoreline of Texas. Two years later, on the basis of this exploration, Garay was granted a province, called Amichel, comprising the whole Gulf Coast from modern Alabama to Tampico, which he attempted to colonize at its southern extremity. In this he was forestalled by the master conquistador himself, Hernando Cortés, who in 1522 founded a villa at Pánuco. By 1528 two expeditions from this place explored the coasts northward beyond the Río Bravo, or Rio Grande. On a later expedition, made in 1544 it is said, Father Olmos took back and settled at Pánuco the tribe of the Olives, thought by some to have been secured on Texas soil. In 1553 more than three hundred survivors of a wrecked treasure fleet were cast on the Texas shore five days' march north of the Rio Grande, and escaped toward Pánuco. In 1558 an expedition destined to colonize Florida was led from Vera Cruz by Bazares. In latitude 27°30′ he landed on the Texas shore; coasting eastward, in latitude 28°30′, he discovered and took possession of a bay which he called "San Francisco" and which may have been the modern Matagorda Bay. Thereafter occasional voyages were made along the northern shores of the Gulf; but the Texas coast, instead of being one of the first portions of the Gulf shore to be colonized, as it would have been had Garay succeeded, was destined to be nearly the last, its settlement being deferred till two centuries after Garay's day.

2. By Way of Florida

Incident to the early attempts to explore and conquer La Florida from the east, the survivors of two shattered expeditions, seeking refuge in the settlements of Mexico, entered what is now Texas, crossed large stretches of its territory, and gained the first knowledge sent to Europe of the southern and northeastern interiors. As has been intimated, so far as the crossing of Texas is concerned, both of these explorations were accidental.

Reference is made, of course, to the well-known journeys of Alvar Núñez, Cabeza de Vaca and Luis de Moscoso de Alvarado. In 1528 Cabeza de Vaca and some two hundred companions, survivors of the Florida expedition led by Pánfilo de Narváez, were cast on the southeastern shore of Texas. After spending six years on Texas soil, and enduring the hardships of enslavement by the Indians, Cabeza de Vaca and three others made their way westward across the whole southwestern border of the present state of Texas, entered northern Chihuahua, and finally reached Culiacán, in Sinaloa. In 1542 Moscoso led the survivors of the Hernando de Soto expedition into Texas near the northeastern corner, westward or southwestward to a point thought by Theodore H. Lewis to have been on the upper Brazos, and back across the Red River by essentially the same route. This journey gave the Spaniards some knowledge of the geography of northeastern Texas and of the Caddoan group of Indians then, as later, inhabiting the region. It is remarkable, in this connection, that a map based on Moscoso's exploration shows the Nondacau, Nisone, Ays, and Guasco tribes in the same general location as that in which they were found a century and a half later.

3. By Way of New Mexico

The third line of approach, that from the west and southwest through New Mexico, was till the late seventeenth century the principal one, and for this reason until 1685 western Texas was much better known than the southern portion, lying nearer Mexico, or than the eastern portion, commonly regarded as "old" Texas.

The Coronado expedition—Just before the Moscoso party entered northeastern Texas, another band, led by Francisco Vásquez de Coronado, entered its northwestern border. Coronado had come, by way of the Pacific Slope, to New Mexico in search of the Seven Cities of Cíbola. Disappointed at what he found, and hearing while in the upper Rio Grande valley of a great kingdom called Quivira to the northeast, he set out in search of it across the Llanos del Cíbolo (Buffalo Plains), going, it is believed, from the upper Pecos River southeastward to the upper Colorado, thence north across the Brazos, Red, Canadian, and Arkansas rivers, eastward into central Kansas, and directly back to the Pecos. In the course of the expedition, northwestern Texas was traversed in four distinct paths, and the Spaniards learned of the Llanos del Cíbolo and of the wandering tribes of Plains Indians who followed the buffalo for subsistence.

Incidental crossing of southwestern Texas—After the Coronado expedition interest in our Southwest lagged for nearly four decades, when the Spaniards again gave it their attention, this time approaching it by way of the central Mexican plateau, across what is now northern Chihuahua and up the Rio Grande or the Pecos. In the course of the renewed exploration and the colonization of New Mexico, in the last two decades of the sixteenth century, several expeditions incidentally crossed the western extremity of Texas, between the Pecos and the Rio Grande. Of these expeditions the ones best known are those made by Father Agustín Rodríguez in 1581, Antonio de Espéjo in 1582, Gaspar Castaño de Sosa in 1590, Francisco Leyva de Bonilla and Antonio Gutiérrez de Humaña about 1595, and Juan de Oñate, the colonizer of New Mexico, in 1598. All this region was then a part of New Mexico, and the exploration of it was made chiefly incident to the development and exploitation of the more interesting Pueblo region in the upper Rio Grande valley.

The search for Gran Quivira—But the subjugation of the Pueblos did not exhaust the energies of the conquistadores, and they turned again from time to time with all their old fire to exploit and explore. To the east there were several points of interest. Gran Quivira was still to be sought somewhere across the Llanos del Cíbolo; adjacent to it were the Aijados, in whose country were the Seven Hills supposedly rich in gold; southeast of Santa Fe, on the upper Colorado River, were the Jumano Indians, who welcomed missionaries and afforded trade in hides, and in whose streams were found pearls. Finally, in the pursuit of these objects, still another, more remote, rose above the horizon in the east, the great kingdom of the Texas.

Concerning the expeditions made in search of Quivira after Coronado's day, our information is exaggerated and unsatisfactory, but the general outline of events is fairly clear. As the record has it, about 1595 Antonio Gutiérrez de Humaña and a party of soldiers were destroyed by the Indians while returning from a search for Quivira, at a place some two hundred leagues northeast of Santa Fe, afterward known in tradition as La Matanza [La Mantanza?] (the death place). It was said that they were returning laden with gold. In June, 1601, Juan de Oñate, governor of New Mexico, made the opening expedition of the seventeenth century. Accompanied by two friars and eighty men, and with a survivor of the Humaña expedition as guide, he went east-northeast and north two hundred leagues from Santa Fe, reached La Matanza, received ambassadors from Quivira, engaged in a terrible battle with the Escanjaques Indians, and returned home. In 1629, when Father Juan de Salas of New Mexico was on the eastern plains among the Jumanos, messengers from the Aijados and Quiviras were sent to see him and accompanied him to Santa Fe to ask for missionaries. In 1634 Alonso de Vaca went three hundred leagues east from New Mexico, possibly in response to the call of 1629, to a great river across which was Quivira. Finally, don Diego de Peñalosa, an evicted and discredited governor of New Mexico, later claimed that in 1662 he had made an expedition several hundred leagues east and north, and succeeded in finding the city of Quivira. That Peñalosa made such a journey at all is doubted by most scholars, but the news that he was telling the tale at the court of France, for the purpose of getting up an expedition against Spain's possessions on the Gulf, aroused Spain in 1678 to take a livelier interest in Texas than she had before manifested, and to renewed talk of searching for Gran Quivira.

Father Benavides's proposal—In 1630, when Quivira was attracting so much attention, Father Alonso de Benavides, *custos* of the missions of New Mexico, made a most interesting suggestion regarding the eastern country, and one which later bore fruit. Writing of the "kingdoms" of Quivira and Aixaos, he described them as rich in gold; and, as a means of subduing them, restraining the English and the Dutch, and providing a shorter route from Cuba to New Mexico, he suggested the occupation of a place on the Gulf Coast known as the Bay of Espíritu Santo, shown on the maps as somewhere between Apalache and Tampico, and, as Benavides thought, less than a hundred leagues from Quivira. In 1632 Benavides published another memorial urging the same plan. It will be seen that nearly half a century later the Spanish government took the proposal under consideration, and had set about putting it into effect before the La Salle expedition occurred.

Expeditions to the Jumanos: News of the Texas—Much more satisfactory is our information concerning a similar series of expeditions made in the seventeenth century to the Jumano Indians of the upper Colorado River, in the interest of missionary work, pearl hunting, trade in skins, and exploration.

The Jumanos left a most interesting and, on account of the numerous localities in which people of that name were encountered at different times, a somewhat puzzling record. They were found, for example, on the Rio Grande below El Paso, in eastern New Mexico, in Central Texas on the Colorado, in southeastern Texas, on the Arkansas, and on the Red. This ubiquity of the Jumanos is to be explained in part, no doubt, by the migration of the tribe to and from the buffalo plains at different seasons of the year; but it seems equally clear that there were at least two distinct divisions of people known to the Spaniards by the same name. The division of particular interest here is the one which, in the seventeenth century, frequented or lived upon the buffalo plains of west-central Texas and was often visited there by the Spaniards of New Mexico for the purposes indicated.

The first recorded journey to these eastern Jumanos was made in 1629. Previous to that time Father Juan de Salas, of Isleta (old Isleta, near the present Albuquerque), had worked among the Tompiros and Salineros in eastern New Mexico and had come in contact with Jumanos living east of these tribes and hostile to them. In the year mentioned, the Jumanos sent a delegation to Isleta to repeat a request previously made that Salas go with them to their homes to minister to their people. On being asked why they desired missionaries, they told the story, now a classic in the lore of the Southwest, of the miraculous conversion of their tribes by a beautiful woman wearing the garb of a nun, and later identified as Mother María de Agreda, abbess of a famous convent in Spain, who declared that she had converted these tribes during a visit to America "in ecstacy."

Setting out with the petitioners, accompanied by Father Diego López and three soldiers, Salas went to a point more than 112 leagues eastward from Santa Fe, where he found a multitude of Indians, wrought miraculous cures, received messengers from the Quiviras and Aixaos, and returned to Santa Fe for aid in founding missions among the people he had visited. There is evidence that a part of the Jumanos followed the missionaries to New Mexico and were for a time ministered to in a separate mission. But the period was short, and in 1632 Father Salas went again to the Jumanos on the plains, accompanied by Father Diego de Ortega and some soldiers. When Salas returned, Father Ortega remained with the Indians six months.

From now on the location of the Jumanos comes into clearer light. The place where they were found this time was described as two hundred leagues southeast of Santa Fe, on a stream called the Nueces, because of the abundance of nuts *(nueces)* on its banks. This description corresponds essentially with those of all subsequent journeys made in the seventeenth century. The stream, as we shall see, was clearly one of the branches of the Colorado River, and not improbably the Concho.

What occurred in the interim does not appear, but eighteen years later an expedition led by Captains Hernando Martín and Diego del Castillo visited the Jumanos on the Nueces and remained with them six months. While there two things of greatest interest occurred. The first was the gathering of a large quantity of shells *(conchos)* from the river, which, on being burned, disclosed pearls. The other was the approach of a portion of the party, after passing fifty leagues beyond the Jumanos through the country of the Cuitaos, Escanjaques, and Aijados, to the borders of a people called "Tejas." "They did not enter their territory," our chronicler tells us, "as they learned that it was very large and contained many people," but a "lieutenant" of the Tejas "king" went to see Castillo. This, so far as I know, is the first information acquired by the Spaniards unquestionably concerning the people from whom Texas got its name.

The arrival of Martín and Castillo at Santa Fe with pearls, at a time when the pearls of California were proving to be a disappointment, now created a new interest in Central Texas. The samples were sent to the viceroy in Mexico, who at once ordered another expedition to the Nueces. It was made in 1654 by Diego de Guadalajara, with thirty soldiers, among whom was Juan Domínguez de Mendoza, thirty years later the leader of a more important expedition to the same place. Guadalajara found the Jumanos in the same region where they had been encountered in 1632 and 1650. Thirty leagues farther on they had a hard fight with the Cuitaos, of whom they killed many, besides taking two hundred prisoners and rich spoils in the way of buckskins, elkskins, and buffalo hides. Still another interest in the country had arisen—that of commerce in peltry.

No other specific expedition to the Jumanos is recorded till that of Juan Domínguez de Mendoza in 1684, the records of which settle all doubt as to the location of the tribe to whom these visits were directed. But in the interim many journeys seem to have been made to them for the purpose of trade, evidence of which has just come to light in the Mexican archives. In 1683, when a delegation of Jumanos from the eastern plains visited the Spanish refugees then at El Paso, the authorities declared in writing, as evidence of the friendship of the tribe, that before 1680, when the Pueblo Revolt had occurred, trade and friendship had been maintained with the Jumanos "with such security that the Spaniards, six, eight, and ten, went to their lands and villages every year to trade with these Indians" in buckskins, *teocas*, and buffalo hides. We shall see that the Mendoza party in 1684 brought back nearly five thousand buffalo skins. It was later asserted that some time before this event, two Franciscan missionaries, inspired by the Venerable Mother María de Agreda, had gone to the Texas and baptized many of their number, "their very prince" being the first to receive the faith. This allusion may have been to the visits of Father Salas and his companions to the borders of the Texas early in the century, for no other record of a missionary visit to these people before 1689 is known.

4. From the South, by Way of Nuevo León and Coahuila

While there had thus been definite progress eastward from New Mexico during the first three-fourths of the seventeenth century, and considerable contact between that province and what is now the western half of Texas, from the south, the natural line of advance from Mexico to Texas, progress was slow.

The outposts of northeastern New Spain—In the sixteenth century, nevertheless, northeastward expansion from the valley of Mexico had been rapid. It has already been stated that as early as 1522 Pánuco had been founded by Cortés himself, and that by 1528 two expeditions from that point had explored the coasts north of the Rio Grande. For half a century Pánuco remained the northeasternmost outpost, but meanwhile progress was more rapid along the central Mexican plateau, where, following the line of the most promising mineral deposits, by 1565 conquests were extended as far as Parras, Saltillo, and perhaps Monterrey.

Advance was now made again along the Gulf plain. In 1576 Luis de Carabajal pursued Indians into the country north of Pánuco, and in 1579 was commissioned to conquer and settle it. The province assigned to him was called Nuevo León, and was to extend two hundred leagues north from Pánuco, a jurisdiction reaching nearly or quite to the mouth of the Colorado River. For a few years Carabajal's headquarters were at Pánuco, but in (or by) 1583 he went inland with a colony, opened the mines of San Gregorio, and founded there the city of León, now Cerralvo. This place, situated about 150 miles from the coast and only some 40 from the Rio Grande (near modern Mier), was for a long time the principal settlement and the capital of the province, and was for a century, with some intervals, the northernmost outpost on the Rio Grande frontier. Shortly after founding León, Carabajal established the villa of San Luis, farther south, which in 1596 became or was succeeded by the villa of Monterrey. Subsequently various intermediate points were occupied.

Temporarily a more northerly outpost than León was established. Hearing of rich mineral deposits toward the northwest, in the district called Coahuila, about 1590 Carabajal took from Saltillo supplies and a colony, opened mines, and founded the villa of Almadén where Monclova now stands. While there he was arrested by the Inquisition on the charge of Judaism and thrown into prison in Mexico, where he died. A few months after Carabajal's arrest, Gaspar Castaño de Sosa, left in charge of the colony, abandoned the place and led the settlers off to attempt the conquest of New Mexico, crossing the Rio Grande at the Pecos and following that stream to the Pueblo region. In 1603 and again in 1644 Almadén was temporarily reoccupied, but without success, and after this León (Cerralvo), where a mission was founded in 1630 and a presidio in 1653, remained the northern outpost till 1673.

Frontier explorations, 1590–1665—By the middle of the seventeenth century explorations beyond the frontier had been made on a small scale in all directions. That they were not more extensive was due to Indian troubles and the feebleness of the frontier settlements. From Cerralvo an expedition was sent eastward in 1638 to verify the report that Europeans, thought to be Dutch, were trading with the Indians near the Gulf. The party was impeded by the swollen "Camalucanos" River, had a battle with the Indians, and failed to reach the coast. A direct route to the Gulf would have taken them across the Río Bravo, but that stream was apparently not reached, unless it was the Camalucanos. By 1653 a regular line of trade had been established between Cerralvo and Pánuco, the Río de las Palmas (Santander) had been re-explored, and the country twenty leagues beyond that stream traversed.

To the north the Spaniards were led short distances by a desire to establish connection with La Florida, by rumors of the silver deposit called El Cerro (or La Sierra) de la Plata, and in pursuit of Indians. Soon after Castaño de Sosa's expedition up the Pecos, a party of eight men from Saltillo is said to have crossed the Río Bravo into what is now Texas, but no details of the event are known. Interest in Florida is shown by the fact that in 1613 two citizens of Nuevo León, Captains José Treviño and Bernabé Casas, offered the viceroy "their persons and their property to undertake the conquest of the interior provinces of the Kingdom of León, helping thereby to expel the English from La Florida." Perhaps they had heard of the settlement of Jamestown six years before. To discover the Cerro de la Plata two attempts were made in 1644 and 1648 by General Juan de Zavala, but both of them were frustrated by Indian revolts. Writing of this mineral deposit in 1648, Alonso de León said, "It is unknown to those now living . . . and must have been to those in the past." Summarizing in 1650 what he had accomplished by way of exploration since 1626, when he became governor, Martín de Zavala said of himself:

he has made a beginning of northern discovery, whereby he has explored more than fifty leagues with the purpose of continuing till communication is established with La Florida, and has almost certain knowledge of the Sierra de la Plata, which he intends to reach, a feat which has so often been attempted by the governors of Nueva Vizcaya and Nuevo León, but which has been abandoned because of Indian troubles.

It is not clear whether the fifty leagues explored toward La Florida were those covered in search of the mine or not; but in either case, the Río Bravo was in all probability passed.

Pursuit of the Indians was a constant occupation on this frontier. From the outset slave catching for the markets and for the *encomiendas,* which in Nuevo León were generally established, had been a favorite occupation at Cerralvo, more attractive than mining. In retaliation, the savage tribes made frequent raids upon the settlements, and were as often pursued beyond the frontiers by such doughty warriors as Alonso de León, Juan de Zavala, Juan de la Garza, and Fernández de Azcué. In 1653, for example, a campaign led by Garza was made jointly by soldiers of Saltillo and Nuevo León against the Cacaxtles, who were found more than seventy leagues northward from Monterrey. Two years later another joint campaign was made by the soldiers of Saltillo and Monterrey against the same tribe. The troop of 103 soldiers, equipped with 800 horses, and led by Fernández de Azcué, were supported by more than 300 Indian allies of the Coahuila region. Going north from Monterrey, at a place twenty-four leagues beyond the Río Bravo they encountered the enemy within a wood, surrounded them, fought all day, slew 100 men and took 70 prisoners, themselves suffering the loss of 20 wounded. This campaign of Azcué, made against the Cacaxtles, is the first expedition to cross the lower Rio Grande of which we have definite record.

Thus, by 1670 the Spaniards had barely broken over the Rio Grande frontier below the Pecos. Now, however, another forward step was taken on this border, the frontier of settlement pushed northeastward, and missionary activity extended across the Rio Grande, a movement that brought other important developments in its train. As was often the case, the pioneers in this advance movement were the missionaries; their leader was Juan Larios, a native of Nueva Galicia and a friar of the Franciscan province of Santiago de Jalisco.

The founding of Coahuila: the Larios-Bosque expedition—In 1670 Father Larios began missionary work on the troubled Coahuila frontier, where he seems to have remained alone for some three years.

Returning to Guadalajara, in 1673 he went again to Coahuila, accompanied by Father Dionysio de Peñasco and Fray Manuel de la Cruz, a lay brother. Aided by soldiers sent by the governor of Nueva Vizcaya, they founded of the roving tribes two Indian settlements, one on the Río Sabinas and one to the north of that stream. On one of his missionary trips made at this time Fray Manuel de la Cruz crossed the Rio Grande to visit the interior tribes, and barely escaped capture by the Yerbipiames, a people who from that time till the day of their extinction gave untold trouble on this border. In the next year, 1674, Antonio de Valcárcel, appointed *alcalde mayor* of the Coahuila district, founded on the site of the thrice-abandoned Almadén a "city" called Nuestra Señora de Guadalupe, and assisted Father Larios in transferring thither his temporary missions, which included numerous Indians from across the Rio Grande. Meanwhile the friars had been joined by Father Dionysio de San Buenaventura. In 1675 Valcárcel sent Alférez Fernando del Bosque, accompanied by Fathers Larios and San Buenaventura, across the Rio Grande to explore the country and reconnoiter the tribes. As a result of the report brought back, four missions were soon established in the Coahuila district, one for each of the four groups or confederacies, which embraced tribes to the north as well as to the south of the Rio Grande.

News of the Texas—Now the Texas arose above the Coahuila horizon, just as they had appeared above that of New Mexico a quarter of a century before. In 1676 the bishop of Guadalajara visited Coahuila, and one of the reasons which he gave in his report for favoring the four missions recommended by Bosque was the opportunity which they would afford to reach and convert a more important people beyond—the Texas, of whom he gives a most interesting account. "Coahuila," he says,

has as a neighbor on the north, inclining somewhat to the east, a populous nation of people, and so extensive that those who give detailed reports of them do not know where it ends. These [who give the reports] are many, through having communicated with the people of that nation, which they call Texas, and who, they maintain, live under an organized government *(en policía)*, congregated in their pueblos, and governed by a casique who is named by the Great Lord, as they call the one who rules them all, and who, they say, resides in the interior. They have houses made of wood, cultivate the soil, plant maize and other crops, wear clothes, and punish misdemeanors, especially theft. The Coahuiles do not give more detailed reports of the Texas because, they

say, they are allowed to go only to the first pueblos of the border, since the
Great Lord of the Texas does not permit foreign nations to enter the interior
of his country. There are many of these Coahuiles who give these reports, and
who say that they got them through having aided the Texas in their wars
against the Pauit, another very warlike nation. The Coahuiles once pacified,
the Spaniards can reach the land of the Texas without touching the country
of enemies.

This account of the Texas is of special interest as being the earliest
extant, so far as is known, although, as we have seen, reports of [for
some unexplained reason, two lines are missing in the original text.]
jective points of the Spaniards both of New Mexico and Coahuila was
thenceforth the kingdom of the Texas.

Summary—By 1676 some advance had been made into Texas from
all directions. Sixteenth-century explorers coming by way of the Gulf,
Florida, and New Mexico had run its coasts and traversed its southern,
northern, and western borders. In the seventeenth century the
continued search for Gran Quivira had led to further explorations in
the west and north; frequent visits to the Jumano country had made
better known the country between Santa Fe and the middle Colorado,
while some beginnings had been made of missionary work and
settlement in the Rio Grande valley between El Paso and the mouth
of the Río Conchos. In addition to interest in Quivira, the Aixaos, the
Jumanos, the pearls of the Nueces (Colorado), and trade in peltry and
captives on the plains, there had arisen a desire to reach another land
reputed to be rich but as yet untrod, the great kingdom of the Texas.
From the south, meanwhile, the frontier had slowly expanded across
the lower Rio Grande through the search for the Cerro de la Plata,
pursuit of hostile Indians, efforts to establish communication with
Florida, and missionary work among the tribes of the Coahuila
frontier. In the pursuit of this last object, interest was aroused, here as
in New Mexico, in the Texas Indians.

It is clear that all these forces were leading slowly but surely to the
occupation of central and eastern Texas, even in the absence of the
stimulus of foreign aggression. But the old interests were now all
quickened by rumors of foreign encroachment, and thenceforth the
various lines of advance rapidly converged and led to the settlement
of the country beyond the Trinity. At the same time the El Paso
district, at the other extreme of Texas, became definitely settled as a
result of a counter movement from New Mexico.

III. THE CONVERGENCE OF THE LINES

1. Peñalosa and Plans to Occupy the Bay of Espíritu Santo

In 1678 news was received at the Spanish court that Peñalosa, the discredited governor of New Mexico already mentioned, had proposed at the court of France an expedition against New Spain. Incident to the investigation of the report, the royal secretaries brought forth Benavides's memorial of 1630, and noted his recommendation that the Bay of Espíritu Santo be occupied as a base of operations in New Mexico and Quivira and as a defence against the encroachment of foreigners. Thereupon, the king asked the viceroy for a report on the geography of the country east of New Mexico and on the feasibility of Benavides's plan—

what advantages would come from Christianizing the kingdoms of Quivira and Tagago [Teguayo]; what means would be needed to effect it; whether it could be done better by the way of Florida than through the Bay of Espíritu Santo; and whether any danger was to be feared from the proposals of Peñalosa.

Sometime before August 2, 1685, Martín de Echegaray, pilot major and captain at Pensacola, reported to the king the danger that the French might occupy the Bay of Espíritu Santo and enter thence to New Mexico. He accordingly repeated the suggestion of Father Benavides, and offered to explore the bay with a view to its occupation and to prepare a map of the coast. A *junta de guerra* approved the proposal, and on August 2 the king ordered the governor of Florida to cooperate with Echegaray. At the same time, he repeated the request for the report from the viceroy, which had not yet been made,

in order that from all directions may be had the desired notices with respect to all the foregoing, for the greater security and certainty of the achievement of the discovery of the said Bay of Espíritu Santo and the kingdoms of Quivira and Tagago, and of their settlement and conservation, in order thereby to make the said provinces of Florida secure from the menaces in which they stand from the corsairs and pirates who commonly infest them.

2. The Settlement of the El Paso District

Meanwhile, the center of the province of New Mexico had been transferred to the El Paso district, where it remained till near the end of the seventeenth century. This change of base not only resulted in the planting of considerable establishments on what is now Texas soil, but also served to increase interest in the country toward the east.

In 1659 a mission, Nuestra Señora de Guadalupe, was begun at El Paso, on the south side of the river, and a small civil settlement grew up there. Before 1680 another mission, San Francisco de los Sumas, was founded some twelve leagues down the river. In 1680 the colony received a large accretion through the revolt of the Pueblo Indians of New Mexico. As a result of this event all the Spanish inhabitants and the Indians of three pueblos retreated down the river and settled at the Pass and at different points below that place on both sides of the river for a distance of twelve or more leagues. There were now in or near the valley six missions (Guadalupe, San Francisco de los Sumas, Senecú, Socorro, Isleta, and Santa Gertrudis); four Spanish villages or pueblos (San Lorenzo, San Pedro de Alcántara, San José, and Isleta); and the presidio of El Paso.

In 1683 and 1684 missionary work was temporarily extended from El Paso to the junction of the Río Conchos with the Rio Grande, a point then known as La Junta, among the Julimes and their allies. Already two Franciscans, Fray García de San Francisco, founder of the mission of Guadalupe at El Paso in 1659 and guardian there till 1671, and Fray Juan de Sumesta, had separately visited the Indians at La Junta, but had not remained. Requests for missionaries at Parral proving without avail, the Indians turned in 1683 to the settlement of El Paso. In response to their appeal, Fray Nicolás López and Fathers Juan Zavaleta and Antonio Acevedo went in December, 1683, to La Junta, and before the end of 1684 seven churches had been built for nine tribes, living, apparently, on both sides of the Rio Grande, and five hundred persons had been baptized. Father López tried to secure a settlement of Spaniards for the place, but failed, and within a short time the missions were abandoned on account of an uprising.

3. *The Mendoza-López Expedition to the Jumanos, 1684*

The same appeal that led Father López to undertake missionary work at La Junta resulted in the expedition made in 1684 by Juan Domínguez de Mendoza and Father López to the Jumano Indians of the Nueces; this event, in turn, greatly increased interest in the eastern tribes, especially the Texas and Quiviras.

The principal bearer of the request for missionaries in 1683 was a

Jumano Indian known to history as Juan Sabeata, who appeared before Governor Domingo Jironza Petriz de Cruzate in October. According to his story he and some of his people lived with the Julimes at La Junta. Part of his tribe lived six days to the eastward, on the Nueces River, which was three days beyond the place where the buffalo herds began. Among more than thirty tribes which he named as living toward the east were the "extended nation of the Humanas," the "great kingdom of the Texas," and the "great kingdom of Quivira." He told particularly of the "great kingdom of the Texas." This populous realm, which was fifteen days eastward from La Junta, was ruled by a powerful king. As for the man who had visited Castillo in 1650, he was not king, "but only the king's lieutenant." The Texas were a settled people, raised crops in abundance, and were neighbors of La Gran Quivira, so close, indeed, that they visited back and forth almost daily. From what he had heard, they would gladly welcome settlers and missionaries, for ever since Castillo's day they had been wishing for and expecting them. Even now two messengers from the Texas were waiting at La Junta for a reply to their request sent through Sabeata. A touch of interest was added to the story by the statement, on the authority of the two Texas messengers, "that in that part of the east Spaniards enter by water in Houses made of trees, and maintain trade with the said Nation of the Texas." It was easy for the authorities, after the menace offered by Peñalosa, to transform these "Spaniards" into encroaching Frenchmen.

Governor Cruzate was enthusiastic at the prospect of a new field for exploration, and forwarded Sabeata's declaration to the viceroy with a letter in which he stated that he would consider it a great triumph if "another New World" and "two Realms with two more Crowns" should be added to the kingdom. In answer to Sabeata's request, Father López went to La Junta, as we have already seen. Shortly afterward he was followed by Maestre de Campo Juan Domínguez de Mendoza and a small band of soldiers, destined to "the Discovery of the Orient and the Kingdom of the Texas." On January 1, 1684, the party, accompanied by Father López, and leaving Father Acevedo to minister to the Indians at La Junta, set out for the country of the Nueces, which they found after going seventy leagues northward to the Pecos and thence forty leagues toward the east. Mendoza kept a diary of the expedition which identifies the Nueces with one of the branches of the upper Colorado, probably the Concho, and with the stream visited by the expedition of 1654, for Mendoza had himself been on that journey and recognized the place. Moreover, he had with him Hernando Martín, who had been one of the leaders of the expedition of 1650. Forty leagues from the head of the Nueces, at a stream called the San Clemente, apparently the Colorado, a temporary fort and chapel were built. During the stay of several weeks a number of Indians were baptized and nearly five thousand buffalo hides secured. The Indians asked for missionaries and settlers, and before returning Father López and Mendoza promised to return within a year prepared to grant the request.

Writing to the king of this expedition, Father López said:

Penetrating and mapping out their lands, both to the north and the east, I was in sixty-six other nations [besides those at La Junta], all docile and friendly toward the Spaniard, and asking also for the water of baptism, and that we should settle where it should seem convenient. . . . We were in their lands six months, sustained by the said heathen solely on the fruits of the soil. . . . Their mineral hills offer much; there are many rivers, all with different kinds of fish and abounding in nacre, from which years ago many pearls were secured. . . . And besides these nations we had ambassadors from the Texas, a powerful kingdom, where Mother María de Agreda catechized many Indians, as she relates in her writings. . . . And we came to tread the borders of the first settlements of this nation. . . . We succeeded also in treading the lands of the Aijados nation, next to the great kingdom of Quivira, of whom Fray Alonso de Benavides makes mention, but because the said Aijados were at war with the tribes which we had in our friendship, I did not communicate with them, although they were already planning to make friends with us. It [the Aijados tribe] is less than seventy leagues distant from La Gran Quivira.

4. Proposals for the Occupation of the Jumano Country, 1685–1686

This expedition of 1684, coupled with news of Peñalosa's doings, now became the basis of an attempt to occupy the Jumano country with missionaries and soldiers, and of renewed talk by the New Mexico officials of Gran Quivira, Gran Teguayo, and the great kingdom of the Texas.

On their return to El Paso, Father López and Mendoza both went to the city of Mexico. In a memorial of June 7, 1685, López urged, besides support for the settlements about El Paso and the missions at

La Junta, the occupation of the recently explored country of the Jumanos. Sixty-six tribes, he said, northeastward from La Junta, had given obedience, and twenty additional missionaries were needed to serve them. He was backed in this request by his order, for the commissary general advertised the new field in the various monasteries, and forty-six friars volunteered to go. López's petition being negatived by the authorities at Mexico City on account of the bad situation at El Paso, in March, 1686, he urged anew "the manifest peril threatened by delay." At present two hundred men would suffice to avert the danger, at little cost, because of the richness of the country; but later it would "be impossible to repair it with millions." He now asked, not for twenty but for fifty-two missionaries. In another memorial he requested one hundred soldiers, even from the jails, and offered, on the promise of his two wealthy brothers of El Rosario, to furnish for the undertaking five hundred fanegas of maize, three hundred beeves, and two hundred horses. His proposals were pronounced by the *fiscal* as "fantastic, and ideas meriting no consideration"; but he had already turned to the king, repeating his request, and urging especially the nearness of the country to be occupied to the Aijados, Texas, and the great kingdom of Quivira.

About the same time Mendoza also addressed a memorial to the viceroy, saying that Peñalosa, under whom he had served in New Mexico, really possessed detailed information regarding Teguayo, the Sierra Azul, and the kingdom of the Texas. "And if this Peñalosa should carry out his intention, great ruin of this New Spain is to be feared, since these lands are the most fertile and fruitful of this New World." But in Mendoza lay the remedy. To avert the danger he offered, if the king would only supply him with two hundred men from the jails, to enter the eastern country again, explore as far as the North Sea, reconnoiter Gran Quivira and the kingdom of the Texas, make maps and reports, plant two presidios in the country of the Nueces, and reduce the Indians to settled life. The only expense to the crown would be that incident to arming the men and maintaining them till they should reach the Nueces, since, once there, the country would support, not two hundred, but two million; "for, besides these advantages, we have immediate recourse to the settlement of the Texas, which nation plants maize, calabashes, and beans." This memorial was perhaps written by Father López, for, besides bearing

internal marks of that friar's authorship, it was sent by him to the king
with "hearty commendation."

5. The La Salle Expedition and the Occupation of Eastern Texas, 1685–1690

By this time news had been received in Mexico of the La Salle
expedition to some point on the Gulf Coast, and in 1686 began the
series of explorations, four by sea from Vera Cruz and five by land from
Monterrey and Monclova, in search, not of the French alone, but (1)
of the French, (2) the Bay of Espíritu Santo, and (3) the country of the
Texas, which had not yet been reached.

The events of this period have been so well told by Clark and George
P. Garrison that they need no more than the merest summary here. But
from what has gone before, some of them will now take on a new
meaning. In 1689, on the fourth of these land expeditions, Alonso de
León and Father Damián Massanet found the remains of the French
settlement on Matagorda Bay, to which the name of Espíritu Santo
thenceforth became attached for a reason which is now obvious.
During the same expedition de León and Massanet went as far east as
the Colorado River, where they were met by the chief of the
Nabedache, the westernmost of the Hasinai, or Texas, tribes. After a
short conference they arranged to return in the following year to found
a mission for his people.

Again the country of the Texas had been approached but not
reached, and again was recorded a description of that promised but
unseen land. On the basis of this conference, preconceived notions,
and the reports made by some rescued Frenchmen who had been
farther east, de León wrote in May, 1689, as follows:

The Texas . . . are a very well governed (*política*) people, and plant large
quantities of maize, beans, calabashes, cantaloupes, and watermelons. They
say that they have nine settlements, I mean towns (*pueblos*), the largest one
being fifteen leagues long and eight or ten wide. It must contain eight hundred
heads of families (*vecinos*), each one having a large wooden house plastered
with clay and roofed with lime, a door attached to the house, and its crops. In
this way they follow one after another. . . . They are very familiar with the fact
that there is only one true God, that he is in Heaven, and that he was born of
the Holy Virgin. They perform many Christian rites, and the Indian governor
asked me for ministers to instruct them, [saying] that many years ago a woman
went inland to instruct them, but that she has not been there for a long time;

and certainly it is a pity that people so rational, who plant crops and know that there is a God should have no one to teach them the Gospel, especially when the province of Texas is so large and so fertile and has so fine a climate.

To this argument for occupying the Texas country, de León added the report of a rumor that there was another French settlement farther inland, in the region which he had not explored.

True to their promise, and with the cooperation of the government in Mexico, in the following year, 1690, de León and Massanet returned east with a party, reached the westernmost village of the Texas (Hasinai) confederacy, near the Neches River, and founded there the first establishments in Spanish Texas. This event, it is now plain, was not merely the result of the La Salle expedition, but was the logical culmination of the long series of expeditions made to the eastward from New Mexico and of the expansion of the Nuevo León-Coahuila frontier, and more especially of the quest, begun as far back as the time of Castillo and Martín, for the "great kingdom of the Texas." This is the principal explanation to be offered for the fact that the first Spanish outpost in eastern Texas was placed, not on the Bay of Espíritu Santo, where the French menace had occurred, but several hundred miles to the eastward. It was put among the Indians whom the Spaniards so long had hoped to reach.

San Juan Bautista:
Mother of Texas Missions

ROBERT S. WEDDLE*

In 1700 the Spaniards established a small mission on the Mexican side of the Rio Grande, thirty-five miles downriver from present-day Eagle Pass. This mission settlement, San Juan Bautista, played a significant role in the development of Spanish Texas and in the creation of other missions both in Texas and Coahuila. Through this small settlement came numerous individuals who figured prominently in southwestern history. The French adventurer Louis Juchereau de St. Denis; dedicated Catholic missionaries such as Antonio de San Buenaventura y Olivares, Félix de Espinosa, and Francisco Hidalgo; the founder of San Antonio don Martín de Alarcón; the American soldier-explorer Zebulon Pike; and the Mexican general Antonio López de Santa Anna on his way to the Alamo were among those who traveled through San Juan Bautista.

In this article, Robert S. Weddle, the leading contemporary historian of the Spanish mission period, describes the founding of San Juan Bautista and shows that most of the Spanish missions established in Texas owed their origin to this mission. Weddle's study is more than the history of one mission; it is a survey of Spanish missionary activities in

*Robert S. Weddle, "San Juan Bautista: Mother of Texas Missions," *Southwestern Historical Quarterly*, LXXI (April, 1968), 542–563.

eighteenth-century Texas. Weddle's books on early Texas history include THE SAN SABÁ MISSION: SPANISH PIVOT IN TEXAS *(Austin, 1964);* SAN JUAN BAUTISTA: GATEWAY TO SPANISH TEXAS *(Austin, 1968); and* WILDERNESS MANHUNT: THE SPANISH SEARCH FOR LA SALLE *(Austin, 1973).*

Tucked away out of the mainstream of the twentieth century, thirty-five miles down the Rio Grande from Eagle Pass, Texas, is the tiny village of Guerrero, Coahuila, where decaying buildings of stone and adobe testify to a colorful past. Almost forgotten, but for the old mission church still standing outside the village, is the vital role this community played in colonial history. Here was the mission settlement of San Juan Bautista del Río Grande, gateway to Spanish Texas and parent of missions, both in Texas and Coahuila.

From 1700 to 1716 San Juan Bautista was the most advanced outpost on the northeastern frontier of New Spain. From 1716 until the early part of the next century it served as the mother of missions—though the parent, in many instances, came to be outshone by its offspring. Encompassing both religious and military arms of the Spanish colonization effort—both missions and presidio—the settlement, after 1772, gave greater emphasis to the sword than to the cross. This change was brought about by the intractable nature of the advancing Plains Indians, the Apaches and the Comanches, and by the role of Presidio del Río Grande as a link in the chain of fortifications formed along the river under the king's New Regulation. Through all its various roles and many functions, the settlement was witness to the passing processions of history until the final closing of the gateway following the Mexican War. The way station at the gateway received travelers from both directions: bearers of sword and cross from the south; from the north the "pagan" souls who were curious about, if not actually thirsting for, the Christian religion.

Early travelers beyond the Rio Grande were attracted to the vicinity of San Juan Bautista by its two important river crossings: Paso de Francia and Paso Pacuache. These fords were key passages for Indians of the region long before the coming of the Spaniards; the Europeans were guided to them by the natives. It may be assumed, therefore, that at least one of the two fords was used by Spaniards several years before Alonso de León forded the Rio Grande on April 2, 1689, on his way to find La Salle's Fort St. Louis.

The two missions founded in 1690 on the Neches River by members of the de León-Damián Massanet expedition were the only ones in eastern Texas which antedated San Juan Bautista. The Spaniards, provoked by the French, had leaped prematurely into an area too far removed from supply bases. These missions were doomed to early failure; the mission builders were forced to withdraw, to lay the foundation anew in order to advance a step at a time. One of the vital steps which had been missed in the premature effort was San Juan Bautista.

To most of the missionaries who had taken part in the first Texas venture, the mere name "Tejas" was so odious that they cared not even to pronounce it. Father Massanet, invited by the viceroy to suggest other mission sites in Coahuila, spurned the offer. At this point he disappears from history. But one missionary in the group would have remained with the Tejas Indians, had the choice been his. From the hour of departure he planned to return to renew the interrupted missionary effort. The burden of laying the proper foundation, of advancing step by step, was to be borne upon the shoulders of this exceptional missionary—Father Francisco Hidalgo.

The first step was taken in 1698, when the guardian of the College of Querétaro sent Hidalgo and Father Diego de Salazar to the borders of Coahuila and Nuevo Reino de León to establish missions. After establishing the Mission Santa María de los Dolores de la Punta at Lampazos Naranjo, Nuevo León, the two missionaries moved the following year to the Río de Sabinas, ten leagues northward, to the place called "Camino de la Nueva Francia y de los Tejas." On June 24—the holy day of St. John the Baptist—the new mission of San Juan Bautista was dedicated, with 150 Indians of the Chaguanes, Pachales, Mescales, and Xarames nations present.

Hidalgo was left in charge of the new mission, soon to be joined by friars Marcos Guereña and Antonio de San Buenaventura y Olivares. Despite their early promises, however, the Indians soon fled, and the missionaries withdrew to the Mission Dolores. Father Olivares went to Monclova to negotiate with the governor of Coahuila, Francisco Cuerbo y Valdés, for military assistance which would enable them to continue their work among the uncivilized Indians. The governor responded by sending twenty men under the command of Major (*sargento mayor*) Diego Ramón to accompany the friars to the north and northeast, "where countless heathens live without knowledge of the light of the Gospel," to "ascertain whether there are some nations which wish to be settled in the society of our Holy Mother Church and to the obedience of His Majesty."

Father Félix de Espinosa, who later served many years at the relocated Mission San Juan Bautista, tells of the founding:

> They arrived at some marshes some two leagues from the Río del Norte on January 1, 1700, Day of the Circumcision of the Lord. They named this site the Valley of the Circumcision, and with more than five hundred Indians of the same nations which they had gathered on the Sabinas River, the first mission, San Juan Bautista, was planted, restoring the name which had been used previously.

The first buildings were made of straw, including the church and dwelling houses. For several months all three priests lived in one tiny grass hut, which Father Olivares viewed as being grossly inadequate, for it failed to turn the weather.

Not long after the new mission was planted, the priests received a traveler from the land of the Tejas. He was José de Urrutia, a Spanish soldier who had remained with the Indians when the missionaries withdrew from Mission San Francisco de los Tejas. Urrutia found Father Hidalgo most eager to hear news of his beloved Tejas, and Father Olivares ready to utilize his knowledge of the country beyond the Rio Grande. Olivares and Urrutia soon formed an expedition which penetrated the Texas Hill Country as far as the Frio River, where they found a multitude of friendly Indians of various Coahuiltecan nations. The natives expressed an interest in baptism and promised to settle themselves in a mission, if one were established close at hand. Reluctantly, Olivares left these willing Indians to return to San Juan Bautista, but a vision began to take shape in his mind. He envisioned San Juan Bautista as a base from which he and the other missionaries would carry the Gospel to the waiting hordes, beyond the mighty river in the "pagan land" of Texas.

To come first, however, were new missions adjacent to San Juan Bautista. On March 1, 1700, Major Diego Ramón reported the founding of Mission San Francisco Solano. Ramón, through his interpreter, informed the Coahuiltecans of the "Sarames, Papanac, Paiaguan, Ysiaguan" nations that,

His Majesty (God keep him) would favor, protect, and succor them only with the motive of converting them to the Catholic faith and to obedience to him, and for the usefulness which will follow the salvation of their souls so that, at the end of their days on earth, they may enjoy the benefits of eternal life.

The mission founded, Ramón took his twenty soldiers and returned to Santiago de la Monclova, leaving the three missionaries to their own devices. Untamed Indians from the wilds, principally the Tobosos, raided the mission's livestock, sought by intimidation to dissuade the more docile tribes from remaining in the settlements, and from time to time kidnapped women and children. Father Olivares urged Governor Cuerbo y Valdés to provide the missions with military protection, and the governor promptly relayed the plea to the viceroy, count of Moctezuma y Tula. Father Salazar, who remained at Mission Santa María de los Dolores, undertook the long journey to Mexico City in the summer of 1700 to confer with the viceroy on the needs of Dolores and the two Rio Grande missions under his jurisdiction, which now had more than nine hundred natives in their care. With him on this journey went two Tejas Indians to testify to French intrusion upon Spanish territory for the purpose of trading guns for horses. Strengthening the northern missions, Salazar suggested, would enable establishment of others "farther out on the Camino Real," the road which led to the Tejas nation and also to Espíritu Santo (Lavaca) Bay, which had in years past been populated by Frenchmen. In response to Father Salazar's plea for protection, José de Urrutia (who had come along as interpreter) was designated as protector of the Indians. It was a stopgap measure, however, and six months later, when the bishop of Guadalajara came to visit the northern missions and to consecrate the bells of San Juan Bautista, a conference was held to study the needs of the new foundations. As a result, Father Olivares was sent to the capital to request the viceroy to station a garrison of soldiers to help gather the natives and to defend the missionaries on the Rio Grande. Impressed by this priest's dramatic accounts of recent murders at the missions, the viceroy ordered that a "flying company" of thirty soldiers be established on the Rio Grande. The company was "not to stay permanently in one place but to go where it is needed ... in order to free the missionaries and inhabitants from the invasions of the barbarians. . . ." Placed in command of the company was Major Diego Ramón, who left Monclova toward the end of July, 1701, to employ the thirty soldiers in assisting the work of the missions.

Early in 1702 a third mission, San Bernardo, was placed "two musket shots" from the first. By May 20, four hundred Indians of the Ocanes, Pacuacian, and Pachales nations had gathered for instruction under direction of Father Alonso González. The following year, with San Buenaventura de Aguirre serving temporarily in the post of Diego Ramón, the flying company took the form of a presidio, acquiring for the first time an adequate *plaza de armas*, on which ten new flat-roofed houses were built.

With the presidio as the hub of the settlement and with the three missions clustered around it, there was a scarcity of water, pasture, and fields close at hand. The Indians of San Francisco Solano, because of the water shortage, fled back to the wilds. Father Olivares, soon joined by Father Francisco Hidalgo (just completing his term as guardian of the College of Querétaro), went after the natives and succeeded in settling a small band of Xarames at a new location, sixteen leagues to the west. At the new site, San Francisco Solano became known as Mission San Ildefonso. In 1708 the Indians fled again, this time to escape the ravages of the Tobosos. The church ornaments were returned to San Juan Bautista until the mission could be moved to the Rio Grande, three leagues north of the other missions, at a place called San José. Here it remained until 1718, when it was moved to the San Antonio River in Texas and became Mission San Antonio de Valero.

From San Juan Bautista, expeditions crossed to the east bank of the Rio Grande in order to become better acquainted with the region. In 1707 Martín de Alarcón, serving his first term as governor of Coahuila, proposed moving Mission San Bernardo to the Frio River. This stream could be reached from San Juan Bautista, he believed, by sailing a canoe down the Rio Grande to the mouth of the Nueces and ascending that river to its confluence with the Frio.

A short time later Alarcón ordered Diego Ramón, with thirty-two men from the presidios of San Juan Bautista and San Francisco de Coahuila, to cross the Rio Grande and seek out the nomadic tribes on the other side. Accompanying the *entrada* as chaplain was Father Isidro Félix de Espinosa, who heard confessions of all the soldiers before they departed. Ramón engaged the troublesome Pelones Indians, probably in the vicinity of present Coahuila, and returned to San Juan Bautista, after twenty-six days in the wilderness, with large numbers of Indians, including both mission prospects and prisoners of war.

The missionary fathers at San Juan Bautista continued to look beyond the Rio Grande. Father Hidalgo had not given up his plan to return to the Tejas, and Father Olivares still harbored the memory of his trip to the Frio about 1700. In 1709 Father Olivares, serving as guardian of the college at Querétaro, left his post to journey northward and join an expedition being readied at the Rio Grande settlement. Besides the guardian, the group consisted of fourteen soldiers under Pedro de Aguirre (who was serving as commandant of the presidio of San Juan Bautista in the absence of Diego Ramón) and Father Espinosa, who was to keep the diary. The expedition penetrated to the Colorado River to check on reports that the Tejas Indians, eager to renew their contact with the Spaniards, had moved westward to that river in order to be near them. The rumors proved false, and the voyagers accomplished nothing as far as reestablishment of the Tejas missions was concerned. Perhaps the most solid achievement of the journey was the reconnaissance of the upper San Antonio River. The picture of this location would remain vivid in the mind of Father Olivares—as the memory of his early work among the Tejas remained with Father Hidalgo—until at last he was able to return and plant a mission there.

Olivares subsequently went to Spain to plead the cause of the Tejas missions before the king. There was no immediate evidence that the voyage bore fruit. Discouraged, he returned to his mission of San Francisco Solano on the Rio Grande.

Father Hidalgo, with all resources apparently exhausted, decided upon a desperate plan for achieving his objectives. On January 27, 1711, he wrote to the governor of Louisiana, inquiring about the welfare of the Tejas and asking for French cooperation in establishing a mission for those Indians. In 1712 he left San Juan to retire to Querétaro, where two years later he learned the fate of his letter, almost four years after it was written.

The French governor of Louisiana, Antoine de la Mothe, Sieur Cadillac, had received the letter in 1713. Eager to establish the trade connections which the French colony required for survival, Cadillac saw in the message the opening he needed. He sent Louis Juchereau de St. Denis, commandant at Biloxi, laden with goods to trade, looking for Father Hidalgo. St. Denis, not finding Hidalgo among the Tejas, continued on to the Rio Grande. He and three companions came to the fort of Captain Diego Ramón on July 19, 1714, and were placed under house arrest until the captain could obtain instructions from the viceroy. While he waited, the wily Frenchman convinced Ramón of the advantages of contraband trade with the French and persuaded the commandant's granddaughter to become his wife. The pleasant interlude came to an end the following March, when an escort of soldiers sent by the viceroy took charge of the prisoner and conducted him southward to give an accounting to high government officials in Mexico City.

St. Denis returned in the autumn, bringing news of all that had occurred: he had been before the viceroy, the duke of Linares, and had made a written declaration, telling how he had come seeking the mission of Father Hidalgo. The viceroy's advisers had warned the viceroy of some of the implications of St. Denis's coming: the French had learned the route to the Rio Grande; they could with impunity introduce their merchandise into the northern provinces in violation of the orders of the Spanish king. The viceroy should move to reoccupy East Texas by establishing missions without delay.

A general junta approved the recommendations August 22, 1715, and the viceroy chose Domingo Ramón, son of San Juan Bautista's commandant, to lead the military phase of the expedition. St. Denis himself was appointed conductor of supplies at a salary equal to that of Domingo Ramón. The Frenchman had come back to claim the hand of Diego Ramón's granddaughter, Manuela, before going again into the Texas wilderness.

While the settlement was occupied with the festive wedding, the bride's uncle, Domingo Ramón, was leading his Texas-bound expedition slowly northward, the pace geared to that of the droves of livestock. It was April 18, 1716, when the caravan crossed the Arroyo de Castaño, two leagues from San Juan Bautista, to find the captain of the presidio, Diego Ramón, his officers and men riding out to meet it. After an exchange of salutes, the train passed near the *plaza de armas,* circled around, and made camp in a cornfield near one of the missions. Domingo Ramón spent the next day procuring provisions and making arrangements for departure. April 20 was spent in reaching the opposite bank of the Rio Grande at Paso de Francia. Domingo Ramón wrote in his diary, "I set up my camp on the other side of the river with extreme happiness." San Juan Bautista had launched its first full-scale founding expedition beyond the big river.

Ties with the parent settlement had yet to be broken. A soldier of the Presidio del Río Grande, José Galindo, went back to take a bride. While the wedding festival went on for two days, St. Denis resumed his own honeymoon. Father Espinosa, in order that he might go with the expedition, was busy turning over the presidency of the Rio Grande missions to Father Pedro Muñoz. Mass was celebrated at Mission San Bernardo and rogation prayers offered for the success of the coming journey. The sacred viaticum was administered to Father Antonio Margil de Jesús, and the other priests bade him a tearful farewell, not dreaming that he would rise from his bed and overtake them almost by the time they had reached East Texas. The march finally got underway April 27. Alongside Father Espinosa and the other priests went Father Francisco Hidalgo, who at last had brought about his return to the Tejas.

Absent from the group, however, was Father Olivares, despite the fact that he had been singled out along with Hidalgo to lead the missionary endeavor. He remained for the time being at his Mission San Francisco Solano at San José. He, like Hidalgo, had a plan, and he now saw the opportunity to put it into action. Before news came back from the East Texas missions, he was already headed south to tell his idea to the viceroy, the Marqués de Valero.

Olivares quickly won official approval for moving his mission from San José to the San Antonio River in Texas, where it would bear the name of Mission San Antonio de Valero. He started northward without waiting for the new governor of Coahuila y Texas, Martín de Alarcón, who was to lead the founding expedition. The priest reached San Juan Bautista on May 3, 1717. He presented to Captain Diego Ramón and retiring Governor Joseph de Eca y Múzquiz the viceroy's order for ten soldiers to serve as an escort for his train on the journey to the San Antonio River. The officials refused to furnish the soldiers. Impatiently, Olivares retired to his mission at San José to await the coming of Alarcón, who had not yet reached Saltillo.

In the meantime St. Denis had returned to San Juan Bautista with a mule train of contraband merchandise for trade with the Spaniards.

News of his movements had preceded him, and Diego Ramón felt compelled to seize at least a part of the goods. St. Denis again went to Mexico City to square himself. Governor Alarcón, arriving in Saltillo, received an upsetting letter from Olivares in which the friar complained of the negligence of Ramón, the haughtiness of the Indians, and the illicit trade being carried on by St. Denis, in league with all his in-laws, the Ramóns. The letter so aroused Alarcón that he immediately began an investigation of the French mercantile operation, causing months of delay in starting his journey toward the San Antonio River. Olivares was the first to resent this procrastination, and to question the governor's motives.

By the time Alarcón reached San Juan Bautista, his plans for entering Texas had become quite secondary. His primary objective was to get to the bottom of the illicit trade with the French; he suspected corruption in high places at Presidio del Río Grande. Although there were plenty of grounds for suspicion, however, Alarcón was unable to come up with the proof. Diego Ramón evidently had chosen well his cadre of followers, and Alarcón met with a solid wall of evasiveness. The governor was forced to end the investigation without achieving results. St. Denis, imprisoned in Mexico City for four months, at last won his release but was enjoined against leaving the city. When his arrest was ordered a second time, he fled northward, reaching Natchitoches on February 24, 1719, probably having stopped to visit his wife and child at San Juan Bautista on the way.

Alarcón's investigation prevented his departure from San Juan Bautista before winter began, in time to take needed supplies to the missionaries suffering privation in East Texas. At last, at the insistence of the president of the Rio Grande missions, Father Pedro Muñoz, Alarcón provided fifteen soldiers to go with Father Miguel Núñez de Haro and a mule train of supplies for the Tejas missions. Crossing the Rio Grande early in December, the caravan pushed on through severe weather until January 28, when it reached the Trinity River to find it at flood stage. Father Núñez, after sending eleven of the soldiers back, remained on the Trinity two months waiting for the waters to subside. He at last cached the supplies and began the return journey. The following July the supplies were found safe by a second expedition from San Juan Bautista and taken on to the eastern missions.

Meanwhile, Governor Alarcón had departed from San Juan Bautista for the San Antonio River on April 9. Father Olivares, moving his mission ornaments and supplies, left San José on April 18, to reach the San Antonio on May 1. He received possession of the site of San Antonio de Valero from Alarcón the same day.

Even after the mission and presidio were founded on the San Antonio River, San Juan Bautista continued to succor the far-flung settlements. The mother of Texas missions was obliged to perform many and varied services in fulfilling her role of parenthood. Frequently the assistance needed was material; from her storehouses she furnished what the Texas missions could not produce for themselves. At other times the need was spiritual, as when Father Olivares's horse fell with him and broke the priest's leg. Olivares sent to the Rio Grande for a confessor, and Father Pedro de Muñoz answered his call. When, in the summer of 1719, word came to San Juan Bautista that the East Texas missionaries were fleeing ahead of a French invasion, it was Father Muñoz again who sprang to action. By September he had succeeded in raising a small force which set out to give what aid it could. The meager band, carrying a message from Muñoz that no further help could be expected, met the retreating missionaries twenty leagues from the edge of the Tejas country. The two groups went together to San Antonio, where most of the missionaries from East Texas remained. Father Espinosa returned with the relief expedition to San Juan Bautista, hoping to find other aid.

The hoped-for aid was a year and a half in coming. Alarcón's successor as governor of Coahuila y Texas, Joseph de Azlor y Virto de Vera, Marqués de Aguayo, and his force of five hundred reached San Juan Bautista en route to Texas on December 20, 1720. The governor began crossing the Rio Grande the day after Christmas; the operation was not completed until March 23, 1721. Aguayo established a record by crossing the largest force the gateway had yet seen. And his expedition consumed more time in the crossing than any other.

On reaching East Texas, however, he confronted St. Denis, and the French force withdrew to Natchitoches. When Aguayo departed from Texas in May, 1722, he left ten missions where there had been seven prior to 1719, four presidios where there had been two.

In 1727 Father Miguel Sevillano de Paredes inspected the Rio

Grande missions. At San Juan Bautista he found 71 families of Mescales, Filijayes, and Pastalocos, a total of 240 Indians, of whom 210 were Christians. Since the mission had been established, 364 baptized Indians had died there. At Mission San Bernardo were 200 natives: 45 families of Pacuaches, Pastancoyas, Pastalocos, Pachales, and Pamasu. Of the 200 Indians, 165 were faithful Christians and 35 were being instructed in the catechism. Both missions had large herds of livestock and raised crops of beans, cotton, corn, and vegetables. Each had a beautiful church, properly adorned for worship.

Hardly was a settlement launched or a move made on the northern frontier of New Spain during the first half of the eighteenth century without the direct involvement of San Juan Bautista. Troops and auxiliaries from the Rio Grande community aided both José de Escandón in the settlement of Nuevo Santander and don Pedro de Rábago y Terán in his reconnaissance from Coahuila to La Junta de los Ríos. The Franciscan priests at San Antonio, meanwhile, pressed out upon new missionary frontiers to form a settlement of three missions on the San Xavier River (now known as the San Gabriel), near present-day Rockdale, for Indians of the Tonkawan, Attacapan, and Karankawan nations. The San Xavier missions were ill-starred from the beginning. They had demanded an increase in expenditures, taxing the royal treasury beyond its limits. Probably a result of these circumstances was a proposal to end the missionary effort on the Rio Grande, to divert its resources to other endeavors, such as converting the Apaches and giving increased support to the San Xavier project.

Father Alonso Giraldo de Terreros, returning to San Juan Bautista as president of the Rio Grande missions after having served as guardian of the College of Querétaro, authored such a proposal. Late in 1751 he was ordered by the college to send one thousand goats to the San Xavier missions, "in order that, with this subsidy, those new sons of the church may have the means with which to continue Christian and civilized life." Father Terreros was to use his own judgment as to other items from the older missions which could be used in the new ones. The following February, Father Miguel Pinilla, passing San Juan Bautista on his way to San Xavier, took charge of the goats. Further instructions were issued that each mission should send to San Xavier as many horses as might be spared. Only a sudden change of plans, attributable to the misfortunes of San Xavier, saved the Rio Grande missions. But the proposal to abolish the mother missions in order to provide succor for new settlements in Texas would be heard again.

At this stage the Apaches, constantly harassed by their enemies, the Comanches, had begun to see the advantages of an alliance with the Spaniards. Finding the missions at San Antonio not prepared to take them in, they turned to Father Terreros at San Juan Bautista. The priest, accompanied by the Coahuila lieutenant governor, Juan Antonio Bustillo y Ceballos, and Lieutenant Vicente Rodríguez from Presidio de San Juan Bautista, met with the Apache chiefs on December 13, 1754, in the vicinity of present-day Piedras Negras, Coahuila. A site eighteen leagues west of San Juan Bautista and two leagues from San Fernando de Austria, founded one year earlier, was agreed upon.

By the end of March, 1755, eighty-three Apaches were living there at the Mission San Lorenzo. All came from the other side of the Rio Grande. The buildings erected and the irrigation system constructed, Terreros went to Querétaro to seek support for the mission, leaving other priests in charge. By early autumn the Indians grew restless, and on October 4 they sacked the mission, set fire to the buildings, and fled. The mission would never rise again. Yet the experience at San Lorenzo strengthened, rather than weakened, the argument for placing missions in the Apaches' own country, farther north. The prime mover for the second Apache mission, as for the first, was Father Terreros, whose wealthy cousin, don Pedro Romero de Terreros, pledged a subsidy of four thousand pesos during the first year for each mission founded for the Apaches and other tribes north of San Juan Bautista.

Early in December, 1756, the founding expedition for the Mission Santa Cruz de San Sabá, headed by Father Terreros, stopped at San Juan Bautista. Close behind came Colonel Diego Ortiz Parrilla and twenty-seven soldiers whom he had recruited on the way north to serve in the protecting Presidio de San Luis de las Amarillas. The travelers spent a few days at the gateway before taking up the march anew for San Antonio, where they spent a winter of discord before proceeding to the San Saba River to found the new mission and presidio the following April 17.

First news of the disappointment that was being experienced at the new Mission San Sabá (at present-day Menard) came to San Juan Bautista in midsummer 1757. The Apaches had failed to congregate.

Then, on a chill March afternoon, 1758, a rider came hurrying in from the river crossing, bearing news to the gateway that left it in a state of shock; the Comanches and their allies, more than two thousand strong, had demolished the Mission Santa Cruz de San Sabá and murdered a number of its inhabitants. The news was carried south to the governor and to the viceroy, and Captain Manuel Rodríguez of Presidio de San Juan Bautista received orders to put his garrison in readiness and to commandeer the horses of the adjacent missions. But the officials had no real intention of sending help. They could scarcely help themselves.

The Mission San Sabá, like that of San Lorenzo, would never rise again. In August, 1759, Colonel Parrilla led an expedition aimed at punishing the northern tribes for their attack upon the Spanish settlement. San Juan Bautista furnished twelve soldiers, six militiamen, and twenty mission Indians, led by Captain Rodríguez, to the expedition. The Spanish force was turned back at a fortified Taovayas village on the Red River (present-day Spanish Fort), with nineteen killed, fourteen wounded, and nineteen missing. The Spaniards failed to demonstrate the superiority they had claimed. Thenceforth the forces of New Spain must tred lightly in dealing with the Comanches and their allies.

Colonel Parrilla journeyed to Mexico City to explain to the viceroy the new set of circumstances on the frontier. He was not allowed to return to the post, being replaced by Felipe de Rábago y Terán, deposed commander of the San Xavier garrison, which now formed a part of the garrison at San Sabá. It was Rábago who was partially responsible for involving San Juan Bautista once again in the founding of new Apache missions. Now serving as president of the Rio Grande missions was Rábago's only friend among the missionaries, Father Diego Jiménez. This priest, one of those who had abandoned the Apache mission on the San Saba River before it had a chance to succeed, now looked toward a new effort at a different location. Rábago, at the same time, was eager to make a new beginning in order to remove the blotch from his name which resulted from his misdeeds at San Xavier. Finding the Apaches near San Sabá favorably inclined toward missions, he wrote to Jiménez for help and advice. Jiménez immediately left San Juan Bautista for Rábago's post, a hundred leagues to the north. After talking with some of the chiefs, Father

Jiménez returned to his headquarters at Mission San Bernardo to write to officials at the College of Querétaro that he had never seen the Apaches "less opposed to being congregated than at present."

The Apaches, now on a buffalo hunt to provision themselves for the winter, had agreed to congregate on the upper Nueces River upon their return. Ministers had been appointed by the college for two new missions at that location. Jiménez suggested that the two missions on the Rio Grande might furnish corn and tobacco for the Apaches until the necessary supplies were sent by the commissary general. But the older missions themselves were operating with difficulty; if their small surplus were turned to the support of the Apaches without recompense, it would be impossible to maintain the missions in the future. As Father Jiménez pressed zealously forward, the mother missions once again were in danger of being bled to death by their offspring. The two new foundations (at present Camp Wood and Montell) were being placed contrary to the viceroy's wishes. But Father Jiménez had no time to wait; he must take the Apaches while they were willing to come. Thenceforth the Rio Grande missions would suffer from lack of care by the missionaries, who now directed their attention to the new conversions on the Nueces.

Jiménez, joined by friars Joaquín de Baños and Diego Martín García, reported under date of February 7, 1762, on the condition of the missions of the presidency of the Rio Grande. The Mission San Juan Bautista at that time had 1,434 baptisms to its credit since its beginning, though only 34 had been accomplished in the last eleven years. There had been 343 marriages in the church, and 1,066 persons had died with the sacraments. The mission at that time had 216 Indians, of whom 150 took communion and confessed.

San Bernardo Mission, since its founding in 1702, had recorded 1,618 baptisms, and 377 persons now lived in the missions. Since the founding there had been 388 marriages, and 1,079 persons had died after receiving the sacraments. The report continued:

> The ministers of San Bernardo presently are seeing after the conversion of the Apache Indians, which it appears will be attained through the efficiency and perseverence of Captain don Felipe de Rábago y Terán. . . . The other two missions of this presidency are those of Santa Cruz and Nuestra Señora de la Candelaria, which is just being founded . . . they remain in embryo until the approval of the Superior Government is obtained. . . .

Almost three years later Jiménez reported that San Juan Bautista's Indian population had been reduced by half, from 216 to 109, since the 1762 report. San Bernardo's had declined by a smaller percentage, from 377 to 325. On the other hand, the two new missions of San Lorenzo and Candelaria, fifty leagues to the north, each had more than 400 Lipan Apaches, though many of them were warlike and treacherous and none well taught, because the viceroy had not yet seen fit to provide a regular garrison to protect the missions. What protection the missions had was afforded by a contingent of soldiers provided by Captain Rábago of Presidio de San Sabá.

But the soldiers and the financial support so long hoped for by Father Jiménez never came. In 1767, when the king's inspector general, the Marqués de Rubí, passed by on his tour of frontier forts, he found the Candelaria Mission abandoned. San Lorenzo was in the care of two missionaries, who had no Indians to teach.

In June, 1768, the garrison from San Sabá was brought to San Lorenzo by Felipe de Rábago, who acted without authority. Here it remained most of the time until June, 1771, when the Spanish settlement on the upper Nueces River finally was abandoned.

The principal role of San Juan Bautista del Río Grande in succoring missions in Texas now was ended. The founding of Laredo in 1755 had opened a new gateway to Texas, and much of the traffic which formerly had passed near San Juan Bautista thereafter followed the lower road. After 1772, with the establishment of the new line of presidios along the Rio Grande, the sword took precedence over the cross in the Spaniards' dealings with the Indians, and the missions began to decline. On November 22, 1772, the missions of San Juan and San Bernardo were transferred from the College of Santa Cruz at Querétaro to the province of Jalisco.

When, in December, 1777, Father Juan Agustín Morfi visited the Rio Grande missions as chaplain of the Teodoro de Croix inspection expedition, he found little to praise about the accomplishments of the settlement. He noted the unfinished San Bernardo Church begun by Father Jiménez: "It is all of rock . . . and was up to the cornicing and near to being finished, but being so ill-suited to the place, with such expense required to finish it, there is not hope of doing so."

In another report Morfi noted the poor condition of the parish church of the presidio:

It is remarkable that in seventy-eight years so little effort has been given to the material improvement and adornment of the House of God. . . . the father chaplain is required to say mass in a little room which was meant for a sacristy, without doors, without whitewash, and without other adornment except the altar table and one loose Cross of wood leaned against the wall.

All in all, his eyes saw a dirty little village where people lived in needless squalor, a rich land which was going to waste because the inhabitants were too indolent to work it, scores of Indians who paid lip service to the religious dogma but had hardly any understanding of the sacred words they spoke in the ritual. Father Morfi remarked that

Progress of these Indians in Christianity is almost imperceptible. . . . They confess, they take the sacraments, they fast, they hear Mass, and attend prayer and explanations of the doctrine; but all this is as commanded and with a grade of piety so low as hardly to be recognizable as Christianity. It is not difficult to discover the cause of their failure. . . . These Indians will never be made Christians until they are first made men.

In 1781 Teodore de Croix arranged the transfer of the Coahuila missions from the Franciscans of the province of Jalisco to the religious of the Colegio de Propaganda Fide of Pachuca. In an inspection report signed February 15, 1790, don Juan Gutiérrez de la Cueva found that the friars of Pachuca had done well with the missions, and the mission churches were well maintained. San Bernardo, however, was using the first church built for that mission. Standing nearby was the huge stone church begun a quarter century earlier by Father Diego Jiménez but never finished. The baptistry dome and the vaulted roof of the sacristy were complete, but the rest of the structure was still uncovered. The present missionary, said the inspector, planned to finish it.

Such apparent optimism was belied, however, by the statistical part of the report. San Juan Bautista Mission now had only 63 Indians, and San Bernardo, 103—hardly enough to warrant the expenditure necessary for completing a church as grand as Father Jiménez's dream.

In 1797 the *vecinos* of Presidio del Río Grande, having long hungered for the expansive and fertile mission fields, petitioned for division of those lands. Nevertheless, almost three decades passed before such a petition was granted.

One year after Mexico had won her independence from Spain, in 1821, the first Coahuila delegate to the Mexican Congress, Antonio

Elosúa, asked the president to order that the lands of the four missions under the jurisdiction of Presidio del Río Grande be distributed among "the most worthy inhabitants of the frontier," in accord with the decree of the Spanish Cortes of September 30, 1813. The missions, said Elosúa, were a living anachronism. They had no neophytes and, for all practical purposes, they had ceased to function in 1810. In his opinion they should have been subjected to secularization, "with all its implications," but this had not been done because of the disrupting effects upon the missions of the first wave of insurgence.

In accordance with the deputy's petition, the distribution of the mission lands was ordered on July 13, 1823. Yet for some reason the order was not carried out until some years later. On March 16, 1826, the new governor, Victor Blanco, decreed the division of the lands and waters, and commissioned C. Nicolás Elizondo for the task. On January 22, 1829, Miguel de la Peña certified that distribution of the lands was complete.

By legislative decree of August 27, 1827, the village which had come into being around the mission settlement of San Juan Bautista del Río Grande was renamed Villa de Guerrero.

It would be many a day before the name Guerrero came into popular use. Much stirring history remained to be enacted at Guerrero—or Presidio del Río Grande, as it continued to be called. But the mission period now was at an end. San Juan Bautista had completed its role as mother of missions.

Stephen F. Austin

Eugene C. Barker*

Texas was under Spanish rule for three hundred years. Although the Spaniards explored the country, established missions, and introduced their language, laws, and customs to Texas, few permanent settlements were made. The population of Texas grew slowly until the government permitted colonization from the United States. The first Anglo-American to secure permission to bring settlers from the United States to Texas was Moses Austin, who had resided and prospered in Missouri when that territory had been a Spanish colonial possession. Moses Austin's death in 1821, however, placed responsibility for colonization in the hands of his son, Stephen.

Stephen F. Austin's role in colonizing Texas gained for him the title "the father of Texas." In this article, Eugene C. Barker (1874–1956), whose long career of distinguished service at the University of Texas earned him the title "father of Texas history," outlines the contributions that Austin made to the growth and development of Texas. Barker also describes some of the admirable personal qualities that Austin demonstrated in his long years of service to the people of Texas. Barker's 1925 book on Austin has been called a "classic in American biography."

*Eugene C. Barker, "Stephen F. Austin," *Southwestern Historical Quarterly*, XXII (July, 1918), 1–17.

Considering the difficulties of his task, the completeness of his responsibility for its accomplishment, and its far-reaching results, Stephen F. Austin has claims to being the greatest colonial proprietary in American history.

He was born in Wythe County, Virginia, November 3, 1793, moved to Missouri at the age of five, spent four years (1804–1808) at different Connecticut schools and two at Transylvania University, and then, at the age of seventeen, returned to Missouri, with schooling complete, to plunge into his father's complex business, a part of which he took over in 1817. In 1813 he was elected to the territorial legislature of Missouri, and by successive reelections served until 1819; in 1815 Governor William Clark gave him an adjutant's commission in the Missouri militia; in 1818 he became a director in the ill-fated Bank of St. Louis; two years later Governor John Miller appointed him judge of the federal circuit of Arkansas; and at the beginning of 1821 he was editing a newspaper at New Orleans. With training and experience of such breadth and versatility and with his intimate knowledge of frontier life, Austin at twenty-eight was well prepared to be the founder and patriarchal ruler of a wilderness commonwealth.

He embarked with his father somewhat dubiously upon the colonization of Texas, and it was partly in obedience to his father's dying wish that he determined to continue the undertaking alone. But having begun, he spent himself in singular devotion to the healthy growth of Texas and the welfare of the colonists whom his influence brought to the country and for whose prosperity he felt a personal responsibility. In moments of despondency, when particularly harassed by public duties and anxieties, he longed for "a small farm, a moderate independence, and a wife," but for the most part he had no time for thoughts of self. His conception of his task extended farther than the mere planting of a number of families in an uninhabited waste; it was to create there a high-toned, intelligent, prosperous, and happy society. "Such an enterprise as the one I undertook in settling an uninhabited country," he wrote in 1832,

must necessarily pass through three regular gradations. The first step was to overcome the roughness of the wilderness, and may be compared to the labor of the farmer on a piece of ground covered with woods, bushes, and brambles, which must be cut down and cleared away, and the roots grubbed out before it can be cultivated. The second step was to pave the way for civilization and lay the foundation for lasting productive advancement in wealth, morality, and happiness. This step might be compared to the ploughing, harrowing, and sowing the ground after it is cleared. The third and last and most important step is to give proper and healthy direction to public opinion, morality, and education . . . to give tone, character, and consistency to society, which, to continue the simile, is gathering in the harvest and applying it to the promotion of human happiness. In trying to lead the colony through these gradations my task has been one of continued hard labor. I have been clearing away brambles, laying foundations, sowing the seed. The genial influences of cultivated society will be like the sun shedding light, fragrance, and beauty.

Ten years of retrospect no doubt helped him to formulate this statement of his purpose, but it is perfectly clear that his aim was in mind from the beginning. To another correspondent he wrote:

My ambition has been to succeed in redeeming Texas from its wilderness state by means of the plough alone, in spreading over it North American population, enterprise and intelligence, in doing this I hoped to make the fortunes of thousands and my own amongst the rest. . . . I think I derived more satisfaction from the view of flourishing farms springing up in this wilderness than military or political chieftains do from the retrospect of their victorious campaigns. My object is to build up, for the present as well as for future generations. . . . I deemed the object laudable and honorable and worthy the attention of honorable men.

In some ways the time was ripe for his undertaking in 1821. The westward movement had crossed the Mississippi and reached the borders of Texas, and the panic of 1819 and the reorganization of the land system of the United States in 1820 cooperated to stimulate emigration to lands that combined the attractions of princely abundance, accessibility, fertility, and cheapness that amounted in effect to a free gift. Austin's greatness, therefore, consists not in having overcome difficulties of transportation and communication to induce reluctant colonists to reclaim a distant and inhospitable land, but in the tact with which, on the one hand, he governed his independent western frontiersmen, curbing their intolerance of the "foreigner" and their disgust at his political ineptitude, while, on the other, he won and held the confidence of Mexican statesmen, soothing their fear of the disloyalty of the colonists and the ultimate absorption of Texas by the United States. Austin stated his problem in a very few words in a letter of 1829:

I had an ignorant, whimsical, selfish and suspicious set of rulers over me to keep good natured, a perplexed, confused colonization law to execute, and an unruly set of North American frontier republicans to controul who felt that they were sovereigns, for they knew that they were beyond the arm of the Govt. or of law, unless it pleased them to be controuled.

Fortunately, though it seemed to him ruinously unfortunate at the time, the revolution and the political upheaval incident to the establishment of Mexican independence carried Austin to Mexico in the spring of 1822, after many of his colonists had already arrived, and kept him there for a year securing confirmation of his grant, which had been made by the Spanish regime. There during the brief space of eleven months he saw the executive government go through the stages of a regency, an empire, and a military triumvirate—Agustín de Iturbide elevating himself to the imperial throne by Napoleonic methods and being himself overthrown by Antonio López de Santa Anna, posing as a liberal—while the legislature traveled through a provisional *junta gubernativa,* a sovereign elected congress, a rump (the *junta nacional instituyente*), and back again, after the fall of Iturbide, to the congress. With little money, and reduced at last to the extremity of selling his watch, Austin possessed his soul in such patience as he could and gently nagged a national colonization law through Iturbide's rump parliament, only to have it annulled by the return of the legitimate congress and its sweeping decree repealing all acts of the empire. He had won his case, however, and congress instructed the executive to confirm his contract in the terms of the imperial law. Incidentally he had learned the language, gained the confidence and esteem of such men as Anastacio Bustamante, Lorenzo de Zavala, Ramos Arispe, and Lucas Alamán, and obtained an insight into Mexican personal and official character that was the key to his future success. For a foreigner he had exercised a remarkable influence upon the shifting committees of the various legislative bodies. He was largely responsible for the passage of the colonization law, tried his hand at drafting an imperial constitution which combined some of the features of the Constitution of the United States with the Spanish Constitution of 1812, and, on his departure, left with Ramos Arispe a document which probably in considerable degree shaped the *acta constitutiva,* the provisional constitution which bridged the transition from empire to federal republic.

Austin returned to Texas with extraordinary powers. The governor had already invested him with general authority to govern the colony until the regular state administration could be extended to it, and now, by decree of the national government, this power was more specifically defined and enlarged. He was supreme judge, save that in capital cases he must submit his decision to the commandant general of the Eastern Interior Provinces before execution; he could issue regulations for the government of the settlements when the national laws did not apply; he was commander of the militia, which it was his duty to keep in efficient state of organization, with the title of lieutenant colonel, and with authority to wage offensive and defensive war on the Indians; he had sole power to admit immigrants to or exclude them from his colony, which covered an area larger than Massachusetts; and, acting with a commissioner appointed by the governor, he could give title to married men for 4,600 acres of land, subject to improvement in two years, and could greatly augment that amount to men with large families, or who established gins, sawmills, or other public conveniences.

Most of this power Austin retained for seven years. The legislature, it is true, was organized in 1824, when Texas was united with Coahuila to the south, but, aside from passing the state colonization law, its attention until 1827 was centered on the formation of the constitution, so that there was very little legislation for Texas. A local ayuntamiento or municipal government was established in 1828, but for several years this took little of the burden of administration from Austin, because, though he steadily refused to accept office in the ayuntamiento, the members of that body looked to him for guidance and both state and federal authorities showed a disposition to hold him responsible for the smooth working of the local government, while of the land system he retained direction throughout the colonial period. From inclination as well as from necessity, he followed democratic methods of administration, dividing the colony into districts and allowing the inhabitants to elect alcaldes, or justices of the peace, and militia officers, himself hearing appeals from the former and directing the latter. But in the matter of legislation he acted alone, promulgating, with the approval of the political chief at San Antonio, a brief civil and criminal code which was in operation for five years. In his management of the lands of the colony he followed from the beginning the practice of issuing titles only on official surveys and of recording in permanent form all papers connected with the title, including the surveyor's plat of the land. The government made no allowance for the expenses of administration, and in the early days taxation was impossible, so that, except for fees of alcaldes and constables, the cost of government fell heavily upon Austin. This was particularly true of his management of the land business, while he was at constant expense also in entertaining travelers and prospectors, sending expresses, giving presents to Indians, and often furnishing munitions and supplies for Indian campaigns.

Anticipating some of these expenses, and wishing also, naturally, compensation for his industry and enterprise, Austin had, before planting a single colonist, arranged, with the knowledge of Governor Antonio de Martínez, to collect 12½ cents an acre for the land in his grant, assuming himself the cost of surveying land and of issuing and recording titles. He advertised this in plain and unambiguous terms, and the original settlers accepted it gladly, because elsewhere in Texas they had no right to settle or acquire land at all. The imperial colonization law of 1823, in accordance with whose terms, after its repeal, Austin's grant was confirmed, greatly enlarged the headrights which he had planned to allow settlers and provided that he himself should receive as compensation for his labors some 65,000 acres for each two hundred families that he introduced. Whether this was intended to annul the 12½ cent agreement is open to question. Austin thought not, and so explained on his return from Mexico in the summer of 1823. Where each settler could have 4,600 acres for the asking, the empresario's 65,000 acres were not likely to yield much ready money for current expenses. Nevertheless, some of the colonists now objected to the payment and carried their complaint to the political chief, who had replaced the governor at San Antonio, and he ruled against Austin's right to charge for the lands. Instead, he fixed a scale of fees for the surveyor, the land commissioner, and the state, which Austin thought had no warrant in law. He contented himself, however, with making a straightforward defense of his reasons for charging the fee, pointing out the risks, hardships, sacrifices, and expenses he had suffered, and asking plainly if he had not given in labor and responsibility the equivalent of the 12½ cents an acre which the colonists had agreed to pay him, or whether they could or would have obtained anything, except through his exertions. Many considered themselves in equity bound by their contracts, one declaring that no candid man in the colony denied the obligation, but Austin relinquished them all and made an arrangement with Felipe Enrique Neri de Bastrop for a division of the fee which the political chief had prescribed for the latter as commissioner. It yielded much less than his contracts with the colonists would have done, but it avoided friction between them and the political chief. The colonization law which the legislature passed in 1825 recognized the justice of Austin's position and authorized empresarios to collect a fee from their settlers in addition to the generous premium of land allowed by the state.

A few of the colonists were already grumbling because they saw Austin granting three, four, and five leagues to some while he allowed them only a paltry 4,600 acres. They were ignorant of Spanish and knew nothing of his powers except what he or his secretary and the commissioner Bastrop told them. Might he not be imposing upon them and exploiting them for his own advantage? Had he any authority either to grant land or govern the colony? The political chief's interference in the matter of the fees helped to strengthen their suspicion, and uneasy whispers increased to a respectable rumble of discontent. The political chief assured them that Austin's authority was ample in every respect, but the excitement subsided slowly and did not disappear until Austin convinced the leaders of his power by arresting them and threatening to send them to San Antonio for trial. The threat and a heart to heart talk were sufficient, and they soon became his staunch supporters. Austin ascribed much of his trouble to the colonists' ignorance of the language, their exercise of the sacred American right to abuse a public official, and the absence of definite laws.

You know [he wrote in 1825] that it is innate in an American to suspect and abuse a public officer whether he deserves it or not. I have a mixed multitude to deal with, collected from all quarters, strangers to each other, to me, and to the laws and language of the country. They came here with all the ideas of Americans and expect to see and understand the laws they are governed by. . . . Could I have shown them a law defining positively the quantity of land they were to get and no more and a code of laws by which they were to be governed I should have had no difficulty—but they saw at once that my powers were discretionary, and that a very great augmentation to their grants could be made, and thus the colonization law itself and the authority vested in me under that law holds me up as a public mark to be shot at.

With the readiness of the colonists to "growl" and "grumble" and "mutter," "without knowing why, or without being able to explain why," he was not, however, disposed to quarrel.

It arose [he said] from a principle which is common to all North Americans, a feeling which is the natural offspring of the unbounded republican liberty enjoyed by all classes in the United States; . . . jealousy of those in office, jealousy of undue encroachments on personal rights, and a general repugnance to everything that wore the semblance of a stretch of power.

Another duty that brought Austin some enemies and much annoyance was that of keeping criminals and men of bad character out of the colony. He required certificates of character from all who obtained land, and though, in the nature of things, these certificates could be hardly more than formal statements of "parties unknown," he made remarkably few mistakes. He banished several from the colony in 1823 and 1824 under threat of severe corporal punishment, and in one case applied the lash. Some of the exiles took refuge in the neighboring colony of the Mexican empresario Martín de León and avenged themselves by making false reports about Austin to the government, and others settled in the no-man's-land on the borders of Louisiana and Arkansas and deterred honest emigrants from proceeding to Texas by tales of violence and anarchy. To an enquirer alarmed by such stories in 1829 Austin wrote, "in proportion to our numbers, we are as enlightened, as moral, as good, and as 'law abiding' men, as can be found in any part of the United States, and greatly more so than ever settled a frontier—an opinion whose substantial accuracy the historian must confirm. For, besides the supervision of immigrants which good policy as well as law required, the great majority, especially of the earlier colonists, were men of family, seeking homes, not speculators or adventurers. The state colonization law of 1825 put a premium on marriage by allowing married men four times as much land as unmarried men, while Austin had previously required ten single men to unite into a "family" to obtain a league, the headright of a married man.

It would be impossible to exaggerate Austin's labors in the early years of the colony. A letter to the political chief in 1826 gives a clue to their character and variety. He had left San Felipe on April 4 to point out some land recently conceded to one of the state officials and had been detained by excessive rains and swollen streams until the 29th. On May 1 he had begun the trial of an important case that had lasted seven days; at the same time he had had to entertain a delegation of the Tonkawa Indians, and make preparations for a campaign against another tribe; to talk to and answer questions of many "foreigners" who had come to look at the country, explaining and translating the federal constitution and some of the laws for them; to receive and pass upon applications for land, hear reports and issue instructions to surveyors; and to correspond with superior civil and military officers. This, the 8th, his first free day since returning, was mail day, and he had received two communications and dispatched five. Too much of his time, he once complained, was consumed in settling "neighborhood disputes about cows and calves," but it was the patience with which he devoted himself to the minutiae of the colony as well as his intelligence and ability in more important things that accounts for his success. During these years he gathered by painstaking surveys and personal observations data for a map of Texas, published by Henry S. Tanner in 1829; charted Galveston Bay and the several harbors and navigable rivers of the state; promoted trade with the United States and kept a stream of immigrants flowing into the colony; encouraged the erection of gins and sawmills and the establishment of schools; and exercised throughout a most remarkable influence over the legislature at Saltillo in matters affecting the interest of the colony. To mention but a few instances of this, he was responsible in considerable degree for the liberal terms of the colonization law; his arguments prevented the constitutional abolition of slavery in 1827 and secured the labor law of the next year, permitting the continued introduction of slaves in the form of indentured servants; and in 1829 his desire to protect the colonists against suit for debts contracted before coming to the country found expression in what we should now consider a sweeping homestead law. He himself was a member of the legislature in 1831–1832, and was reelected in 1834 but was prevented from serving by his detention in Mexico.

Burdened as he was with the affairs of his own colony, he found time to answer the calls of others. He repeatedly exerted himself to obtain titles for families who had drifted in and settled on the eastern border of the province before the passage of the colonization law; and he was always ready to give other empresarios the benefit of his knowledge and experience. Green C. DeWitt was deeply indebted to him for such success as he enjoyed; David G. Burnet drew heavily upon him; and Haden Edwards received advice that ought to have saved him from the folly of the Fredonian Rebellion. He perceived very clearly the mutual interest of all in the peaceful and rapid development of Texas, and, with the field so vast and the laborers so few, he welcomed every additional effort in the promotion of that end. Some of his fellow empresarios, however, without his vision and interest in the permanent growth of the country, doubted his sincerity and blamed him for embarrassments and failures due to their own impatience, greed, and unwillingness to adapt themselves to Mexican racial characteristics and sensibilities. What was needed in Texas, he said, was

men, . . . not open mouthed politicians, nor selfish visionary speculators, nor jealous ambitious declamitory demagogues who will irritate the public mind by inflamitory criticisms about temporary evils and by indulging in vague surmises. We need men of enlightened judgement, disinterested prudence, and reflection, with a great stock of patience, unshaken perseverance and integrity of purpose. Men who will calmly put their shoulders to the wheel and toil for the good of others as well as for their own, and who will be contented to rise with the country without [trying] to force it forward prematurely to overtop the genl. level of prosperity by undue individual advancement. A band of *such* men firmly linked together by the bonds of mutual confidence and unity of purpose and action could and would make Texas the garden of North America.

He did not of course, as we have seen, escape misconstruction by his own colonists, but this he philosophically recognized as inevitable—and even necessary, in a way—to the success of the colony.

To have been universally popular amongst the settlers for the first two or three years [he said] would have endangered all, for it would have excited vague jealousies in the [fear?] alone that I was conciliating popular favor in order to wield it in a particular way. To have been universally unpopular endangered all in another way, for it would have totally destroyed that degree of popular confidence and character abroad which was necessary to draw emigration and it would also have deprived me of the power of controuling the settlers sufficiently to have prevented them from destroying themselves. . . . The reflecting and worthy part of the settlers have always adhered to me firmly throughout. [The other class] abused me over their grog and at times have had weight enough to require humoring and management to keep within bounds, but they effectually removed all suspicion that I was courting the favor of a rabble for the purpose of wielding it, and in this way they did me and the colony a service, though without knowing or intending it, and I used their abuse of me to advance the public good and establish myself more firmly in the confidence of my rulers.

He was conservative in declaring that the "reflecting and worthy part of the settlers" adhered to him, and they were always a vast majority. They brought him their personal troubles and perplexities, and surrendered completely to his guidance in every crisis through which the colony passed. This was true in 1826, when he led them against Edwards's rebellious "frontier republicans" at Nacogdoches; in 1829, when he obtained the exemption of Texas from President Vicente Guerrero's emancipation decree; in 1830, when he reconciled them to the federal decree limiting immigration from the United States, while taking steps to secure its suspension; in 1832, when, after the expulsion of Bustamante's garrisons from Texas during his absence, he convinced Colonel José Antonio Mexía of the colonists' loyalty to the liberal party of Santa Anna; in 1833, when colonists petitioned for the separation of Texas from Coahuila and sent him to Mexico to urge its approval; and, finally, in 1835, when the settlers resisted Santa Anna's encroachments on republican government, for without his advice and organizing influence very few would have been ready then to take up arms. The revolution once begun, he was called to the command of the army—much as George Washington went to Cambridge—to quiet the claims of rival aspirants, and, when order was established and the campaign under way, they sent him to the United States to find money and munitions to maintain it.

His control of the settlers in every essential movement as they increased from a few hundred in 1821 to many thousand in 1835 proves him a great leader. The confidence of Mexican officials, despite their innate fear of Anglo-American expansion—which was constantly stimulated by the efforts of the United States to acquire Texas—proves him a diplomat of no mean ability. With both groups his success was due to his absolute honesty and fearless candor.

His one purpose was the advancement of Texas. "I feel," he said only a few months before his death,

a more lively interest for its welfare than can be expressed—one that is greatly superior to all pecuniary or personal views of any kind. The prosperity of Texas has been the object of my labors, the idol of my existence—it has assumed the character of a *religion* for the guidance of my thoughts and actions for fifteen years.

He sincerely believed until the beginning of 1836 that the best interest of Texas lay in its loyalty to Mexico, that the colonists and the government had, therefore, a common interest in its development, and he was the efficient apostle of that faith. He felt some fear of the outcome of republican government in Mexico; he knew that the people were not fitted for it, but hoped they might stumble along until education and experience prepared them for it. At the same time, as a prudent man would in his position, he sometimes contemplated a condition of anarchy or oppression that would render continued loyalty impossible. In such a contingency, though he shrank from it, he favored independence; never, until shortly before his death, annexation to the United States. As an "independent speck in the galaxy of nations," he wrote in 1829,

Europe will gladly receive our cotton and sugar, etc., on advantageous terms in exchange for "untariffed" manufactured articles. We should be too contemptible to excite the jealousy of the Northern Mammoth, and policy and interest would induce Europe to let us alone. I deem it more than probable that the great powers would all unite in guaranteeing the Independence of little Texas. There are many powerful reasons why it should be to their interest to do it.

On his attitude toward annexation there is an abundance of material from 1830 to 1835, and there can be no doubt of his sincerity. This conclusion does not rest alone on an interpretation of Austin's own statements, for in 1834 Anthony Butler attributed to him his failure to buy Texas. Two reasons for opposing annexation Austin gives, the land system of the United States and slavery.

If that Govt. should get hold of us and introduce its *land* system, thousands who are now on the move and who have not yet secured their titles would be totally ruined. The greatest misfortune that could befall Texas at this moment would be a sudden change by which any of the emigrants would be thrown upon the liberality of the Congress of the United States of the North.

This he wrote to his brother-in-law in 1830. A few months later he wrote that he should "oppose a union with the United States without some *guarantees*, amongst them I should insist on the perpetual exclusion of slavery from this country." No doubt the tariff figured in his consideration, and it is evident, too, that he believed that a strong population in Texas would ultimately wield such an influence with the government as to be freer under Mexico than under the United States.

Austin's views on slavery, despite the quotation just read, and a number of other expressions equally unequivocal, require explanation. He successfully opposed constitutional emancipation in 1827, urged in vain at the same time that immigrants be permitted to continue bringing slaves from the United States, obtained the withdrawal of Guerrero's emancipation decree in 1829, and declared in 1835 that Texas must be a slave state. The contradiction is more apparent than real, but when all is said some inconsistency remains. The truth seems to be that he did deplore slavery, but that he recognized its economic necessity in the development of Texas. Most of his colonists were naturally to be expected from the neighboring slave states, but slave owners would not come if forbidden to bring their slaves, and others who did come would be greatly hampered by the lack of free labor. About the time of this letter he seems to have felt that a satisfactory compromise might be reached by the labor law of 1828, which, in effect, established the peonage system of Mexico. He wrote in 1831,

Negroes can be brought here under indentures, as servants, but *not as slaves*. This question of slavery is a difficult one to get on with. It will ultimately be admitted, or the free negroes will be formed by law into a separate and distinct class—*the laboring class*. Color forms a line of demarkation between them and the whites. The law must assign their station, fix their rights and their disabilities and obligations—something between slavery and freedom, but neither the one nor the other. Either this or slavery in full must take place. Which is best? Quien sabe? It is a difficult and dark question.

In 1832 the labor law was modified, limiting contracts thereafter to ten years; hence, perhaps, his declaration for slavery in 1835. His defense of existing slavery in 1826–1827, it should be added, was based on what he considered guaranteed vested right, his original contract with the Spanish government, under which his first families were introduced, having recognized slavery by augmenting a settler's headright in proportion to the number of slaves he owned.

I have tried to present in this short paper something of the personality of Austin as he revealed himself in his work. He was a grave, gentle, kindly man, charitable, tolerant, affectionate and loyal, naturally impulsive but restrained by habit, sensitive, lonely, and given too much, perhaps, to introspection. He enjoyed social companionship, but his position set him apart from the colonists and made close friendships with them difficult and rare. He smoked, danced now and then, loved music (he played the flute in his younger days), and his bills show occasional charges for whiskey, brandy, and wine. He was well educated, widely read for his opportunities, and a clear thinker. His letters in their straightforward precision and naturalness remind one of Franklin. He worked incessantly, unselfishly, and generally most patiently. In short, he appears to me a lovable human character, with many charming qualities.

On returning from his mission to the United States in the summer of 1836 he was persuaded to be a candidate for the presidency. He consented with indifference and took his defeat by Sam Houston with equanimity. He had been absent from the country for the better part of three years on public business, part of the time in a Mexican prison; his personal affairs were greatly neglected, and he welcomed the prospect of leisure to put them in order. However, when his victorious rival asked him to be secretary of state, he consented, in the belief that he could be useful in bringing the infant republic to the favorable notice of older governments. As usual, he immersed himself in public duties to the utter neglect of self. He died from overwork and exposure on December 27, 1836. For fifteen years he had held the destiny of Texas in the hollow of his hand, and characteristically his last conscious thought was of its welfare. He waked from a dream thinking that the United States had recognized its independence, and died in that belief. His death thus, at the age of only forty-three, on the eve of the fruition of all his labors, with the country redeemed from the wilderness and others assuming the burden of responsibility that had deprived him of home, wife, and family, was one of fate's grim ironies—a distressing personal tragedy.

The Signing of Texas's Declaration of Independence: Myth and Record

R. Henderson Shuffler[*]

Various episodes in Texas history are surrounded by myths and misconceptions. This is particularly true of the signing of Texas's declaration of independence from Mexico. The late R. Henderson Shuffler, director of the Institute of Texan Cultures, pointed out that there has been confusion concerning the exact date the declaration was signed, the building in which the convention took place, the exact site of the building, and even the name of the town in which the convention met.

Shuffler's article answers many of the questions surrounding the drafting and signing of the Texas Declaration of Independence. It also affords an excellent example of the methods used by historians in separating historical fact from fiction. The illustrations of Independence Hall, mentioned in the text of the article, are not included in this edition. As Shuffler notes, no photograph of the original building has been positively identified. The shrine to Texas liberty at Washington State Park—mentioned in the closing paragraph of Shuffler's article—has been constructed and is open to visitors.

°R. Henderson Shuffler, "The Signing of Texas's Declaration of Independence: Myth and Record," *Southwestern Historical Quarterly*, LXV (January, 1962), 310–332.

Each March 2, Texans celebrate the anniversary of Texas's declaration of independence. The height of emotion with which this anniversary is observed is matched only by the depth of ignorance about the original event and about the surroundings in which it occurred.

The principal observance is customarily held at Washington State Park, in the village that was, on March 2, 1836, the birthplace of Texas independence. A group of devoted patriots gather in the little rock auditorium on the park grounds to hear a program sponsored by the Texas Independence Day Organization. Later they visit the small white frame building nearby, which is called a "replica" of Texas's original Independence Hall. There they view a weird assortment of pictures, clippings, and artifacts in battered display cases, including a badly corroded steel blade which bears a crudely lettered tag with the completely inaccurate legend, "This knife made in this blacksmith shop before the Declaration was signed."

In front of the hall they see the statue of George Campbell Childress, "author of the Declaration," two other monuments, and the gilded upper half of an old "Washington hand press." Later, many file through the restored home of Anson Jones, last president of the Texas Republic. The house has been moved to the park from its original setting on the nearby Jones plantation, Barrington.

On the campus of the University of Texas, a group of students fire a pair of cannon and someone makes a speech. Throughout the country, alumni of the university hold their annual Independence Day meetings, devoted primarily to discussions of prospects in football and appropriations and a report on current academic progress at their alma mater.

It is customary, when the legislature is in session, for a stirring speech to be made in each house on the glories of Texas independence. In hundreds of Texas schoolrooms, where March 2 is a holiday only when it happens to fall on a Saturday or Sunday, history teachers remind their pupils that "on this day, in 1836, the Declaration of Independence was signed at Washington-on-the-Brazos." The teachers may be forgiven the inaccuracy of this statement; they probably took it directly from the Texas history text used, with state approval, in their school. Or, if they have visited the shrine of Texas liberty, they may have acquired a part of their misinformation from the official road marker erected by the State Highway Department at the point where the road to the town of Washington turns off the Navasota-Brenham highway. The sign reads:

WASHINGTON STATE PARK
SITE OF THE SIGNING OF THE
TEXAS DECLARATION OF INDEPENDENCE
March 2, 1836

Less easily forgiven is the fact that most teachers, many speakers at the annual Washington State Park ceremonies, legislators, and even some who speak at the university celebrations, continue to repeat the most inaccurate and most popular fiction concerning the happenings at Washington in March of 1836. This is the story that the founding fathers of the Republic of Texas met in a blacksmith shop, furnished without charge for the occasion by a devout old patriot, Elder Noah T. Byars. There, the story goes, on March 2, amid anvils, plowshares, and discarded farm equipment, they signed the Texas Declaration of Independence.

There is conclusive evidence that the Texas Declaration of Independence was not signed on March 2, that the building in which the convention met was not a blacksmith shop (nor, as some say, a gunsmith shop), and that it was not supplied, rent-free, for this purpose by Noah T. Byars. Nor was the village in which the convention met then known as Washington-on-the-Brazos; it was simply called the "Town of Washington," to distinguish it from the capital of the United States, customarily referred to at that time as "Washington City." For some unaccountable reason, the building in which the Convention of 1836 met has been one of the least-known structures in Texas history. There is an amazing confusion of opinion concerning its size, shape, and exact location, and an equally amazing lack of documentary evidence concerning these matters.

The late Louis Wiltz Kemp, in his *Signers of the Texas Declaration of Independence,* proved quite conclusively that the declaration was first signed on March 3, with additional signatures added later as delegates straggled in from remote areas. He also disposed of the myth of the rent-free blacksmith shop, by publishing a copy of the original agreement in which eleven business and professional men of the town of Washington agreed to pay to Messrs Byers & Mercer, the sum of One Hundred and Seventy Dollars, being in consideration of the rent of the house owned by them, on Main Street, for the term of 3 months to commence on the 1st day of March next—Said Byers & Mercer are to have the house in complete order & repair for the use of the members of the convention to meet in March next—for which purpose Said building is rented by us.

To this may be added the evidence of Byars's petition to the Third Legislature on December 20, 1849, in which the old gentleman recounted his efforts to collect the rent, first, by petition, from the Republic of Texas, then, by suit, from the individuals who had rented the building. On January 23, 1850, the Committee of Claims and Accounts reported no evidence could be found to substantiate his claim, and on February 6 the committee report was adopted by the legislature and the matter tabled. It was more than a century before anyone would assume responsibility for paying this irregular claim.

There is no documented explanation of why Byars alone attempted to collect the rent. The firm of "Byers & Mercer," listed in the rental agreement, was more correctly styled "Byars & Mercer, merchants and partners, trading in the Town of Washington." The partners were Noah T. Byars, gunsmith, and Peter M. Mercer, real-estate speculator. The deed records of Washington County show that Byars & Mercer bought and sold much land and town real estate in and around Washington during the boom period of 1835 and 1836, and again for several years after the revolution.

The commonly accepted story that Noah Byars moved out of his blacksmith or gunsmith shop to make room for the convention appears to be pure myth. The statement in the rental agreement that the owners agreed to "have the house in complete order & repair" by March 1 could be interpreted as referring to an old building, already in use. William Fairfax Gray, in his diary under date of March 1, however, recorded that the convention met "in an unfinished house, without doors or windows." William P. Zuber, who attended the convention as a spectator on March 10, said of the building, "It was new, having been built very recently for a commercial house, but its first use was by the Convention."

There is also evidence that Noah Byars operated his gunsmith shop in Washington at another location before and during the time of the convention. He was paid for repairing arms for the First Company of

Texas Volunteers from New Orleans on November 20, 1835, and for the "Louisville Co. of Volunteers" on December 20. In his petition to the Congress of the Republic in December, 1837, and in a petition to the legislature of the state on December 17, 1849, Byars stated that he was operating a gunsmith shop in the town of Washington in February of 1836, "during the session of the Provisional Government at that place." The provisional government first convened at Washington on February 22, 1836. Byars stated in his petitions that he was appointed armorer to the Texas forces by the provisional government at Washington, and left immediately for the field, "with his Sadlebags full of Tools on his Shoulder, and served faithfully for the term of one Month as Armorer," before being given leave because of illness. He stated that his shop was kept in operation during his absence by a journeyman and an apprentice, and that upon his return from the army, he continued its operation until he had repaired "the rise of 500 stand of Arms." This activity leaves little time for moving the gunsmith shop, and Byars made no mention, either in the petition dealing with his gunsmith work or in the petition concerning rental of his building, of any connection between the two.

No known memoir of a resident of Washington during the time the old Independence Hall was standing mentions the use of the building as a smithy. Dr. John Washington Lockhart, who came to Washington in 1839 at the age of sixteen and lived there many years, said the building was used as a town hall and courthouse in the early 1840s, was occupied for a time by the Flora & Ackerman dry-goods store, and was later the site for balls and parties as well as protracted meetings. A number of authorities report that during the period from 1842 to 1845, when Washington was the capital of Texas, the house of representatives met in old Independence Hall. Frank Brown, who also moved to Washington in 1839 and lived there several years, stated "the building was in after years utilized for business purposes," and mentions its use by Francis Dieterich, from 1842 to 1844, as a combination store and dwelling.

There is a genuine mystery surrounding the building which was unquestionably one of the most important historic landmarks of the Republic of Texas. Although it stood for at least a quarter of a century and was widely known and used, it was not depicted with other historic buildings in any known early Texas history. No detailed description of the building has been found in any publication outside of a few memoirs, and the testimony of eyewitnesses in these memoirs is conflicting.

William Fairfax Gray, who gave much excellent detail in other descriptions, confined his comments on the convention hall to "an unfinished house, without doors or windows." W. P. Zuber, who also attended the convention but did not set down his impressions until years later, gave more complete, though possibly less reliable, detail. He said, that

The house in which they sat was a two-story frame; but they occupied only the 1st floor. It fronted on the south side of Main Street, about twenty feet, and extended south about forty feet. It had two doors; one in the middle of the front end; the other in the east side, near the southeast corner; the latter being closed.

On another occasion, Zuber wrote:

Its weather boarding was split clapboards four feet long, which were dressed with the drawing knife, and the roof was of oak boards two feet long. It was not ceiled or carpeted. Its staircase was on the outside; I think on the west side. . . . no painting about it, it was new having been built very recently for a commercial house but its first use was by the Convention.

Lockhart described the building as

a one-story house with the gable toward the street, and situated immediately on the street with a double door in the center of the end opening on the street with one or two steps leading into it; there was one window on the left of the door in front; on the north side were some four or five small windows; none of the windows had glass in them, but were closed by wooden shutters; on the end, or back, of the house was a single door, with perhaps one window. I do not recollect exactly with regard to this or the south side, but if I do remember aright, it had no openings. The house was about 25 feet in width by 50 feet in length, was an ordinary frame, weather boarded with common clap boards split with a froe and smoothed with a drawing knife. The boards were common oak boards about four feet long and made from trees which grew in the Brazos bottom. It was not ceiled, but was what we commonly call a shell, and was covered with two foot roof boards. There were a few large post oak trees growing around it.

Frank Brown said the hall was still standing in 1861 when he last visited it. "It was one-storied, built of pine boards, about 35 x 25 feet floor space. It stood on a corner fronting Main street, perhaps 400 yards south from the river."

From these conflicting reports a few reasonable deductions are possible. Independence Hall was a crude building, actually not completed at the time it was used by the convention. It was a frame structure with clapboard siding and an oak roof. The room in which the delegates sat was not ceiled, but since Zuber added "or carpeted," it obviously was floored. The building was twenty to twenty-five feet wide and thirty-five to fifty feet long.

Since both Lockhart and Brown described the building as one-story, while Zuber said it was two-story, it is probable that it was a high-gabled building of the type commonly referred to as a story-and-a-half. It does not seem likely that the loft was ever finished for occupancy, since the merchant Dieterich is reported to have partitioned off a portion of the lower floor for living quarters, using the rest for his store. If the building had had an upper story, or a usable loft, he probably would have used it. This combination of circumstances throws considerable question on Zuber's mention of an outside stairway, which not only was not mentioned by other witnesses, but was precluded by their description of the building as one-story.

Only Zuber described the scene inside the hall during the convention. He reported that

a long improvised table, covered with writing and stationery, extended north and south, upon nearly the whole length of the floor, the delegates sat around it on chairs; The chairman occupying a seat at the south end. There were no seats for visitors and no bar around this table to prevent intrusions upon their deliberations. . . . Spectators entered the chamber at will, but they walked gently, so as not to annoy the delegates.

The problem of determining the exact site of the original building is even more difficult. The rental agreement, Byars's petition, and the memoirs of Lockhart, Zuber, and Brown all place it as fronting on Main Street, some 400 to 500 yards south of the bluff of the Brazos. Zuber and Brown state that it was situated on a corner lot. Kemp, after a study of old deed records, concluded that it must have been located at the corner of Main and Ferry streets, on lot 7, block 12, owned by Byars & Mercer.

The Galveston *News*, April 23, 1900, reporting dedication of the monument erected on July 4, 1899, "on the spot where the Declaration of Independence was signed," said, however, that the monument was located "at the corner of Brazos and Ferry Streets, on the northwest corner of the plot on which the house stood in which the declaration of independence was adopted."

Zuber placed the building as facing north; in Lockhart's description it faced west. Brown said only that it faced Main Street. The fact that most of the original streets of the town of Washington have been closed and erased by time and that the names of the remaining streets are unknown to the present residents makes is impossible to check the location on the ground today. The lack of an authentic plat of the town as it was in 1836, or at any other time, for that matter, further complicates the problem.

The only known plat of the town, "Washington-on-the-Brazos, Texas, in the time of Jim Johnson now fmn. [freedman], then a slave, who lived there before the war," shows a well-laid-out town, with numerous intersecting streets and avenues, none of which, unfortunately, are labelled "Main," "Brazos," or "Ferry." This plat does offer a few possible clues, however. It shows the roads from the two ferries coming together at the top of the bluff, to feed into what is now the main north-south street of the town, running directly in front of the present Washington State Park. The second east-west street intersecting this thoroughfare, south of its beginning at the juncture of the ferry roads, is much wider than most other streets of the town, and in the center of this street, near the heart of the town, is a blocked-off area marked "City Market." It is quite logical to assume that the street beginning at the juncture of the ferry roads would be called "Ferry Street" and also logical to assume that the wide intersecting street, with the City Market in its center, would be "Main Street."

One other clue is offered by this plat. On the east side of the street which may have been Ferry Street, about half a block south of its intersection with what may have been Main Street, is a property marked with the name of "Lott." The location of the site of the three-story brick Austin House, built in Washington in 1854 by Jessie and Robert Lott, is known. It adjoins the Washington State Park on the south and lies approximately the correct distance from the 1899 monument to allow for a site—of the size required for Independence Hall—to have occupied the northwest corner of the block, with the monument marking the northwest corner of the corner lot.

On this basis, it is indicated that the true site of the original Independence Hall lies in what is now the southwest corner of that portion of Washington State Park which lies between the stores of Washington and the Brazos River. The building would parallel what is now the principal street of the town and face north into the park.

While none of the early histories of Texas carried pictures of Independence Hall, later historians have shown an amazing lack of reticence and a startling inconsistency on this score. Illustrations accompanying this article will prove this point. Most of them are sketches, because no photograph of the original building has been positively identified. This is strange in itself, since the structure was of sufficient significance to have attracted photographers and is known to have been standing a number of years after photography became reasonably common in Texas.

The illustrations generally fall into two distinct patterns, following either the school of thought established by the late N. M. Wilcox of Austin and fostered by the Reverend J. B. Blackwell of San Antonio, or being patterned after an old photograph of uncertain origin which is believed to be a likeness of the original building. The Wilcox-Blackwell conception pictures the building as having a two-story front section, with a one-story projection at the rear, and normally shows an outside stairway leading to the upper story at the front. The other pattern, into which the "replica" on the park grounds falls, depicts a one-story building with a high-pitched roof on one side, tapering to a low shedlike projection on the other. Neither exactly fits the descriptions left by eyewitnesses, even on the points on which these witnesses seem to agree.

The Wilcox-Blackwell version, with its two-story front, is based upon Zuber's description, given in a letter to N. M. Wilcox, January 27, 1908. An unidentified artist made a sketch based upon this letter, and many persons have accepted the sketch as authentic and accurate. The Reverend J. B. Blackwell states that a number of years ago, after several trips to Austin and a search of the material in the state archives, he employed an artist to paint a picture based principally upon the Zuber letter to Wilcox. Later, Blackwell constructed a balsa-wood model of the building as depicted in the painting. This model was displayed at the Big Foot Wallace Museum in Big Foot, Texas, and later at the Daughters of the Republic Museum in Austin. Numerous photographs of this model, or drawings made from it, have been published in recent histories as representing Texas's Independence

Hall. "I could not claim without a doubt that mine is a true replica," Blackwell writes, "neither have I at any time made such a claim."

The first published copy of the photograph on which the opposing school of thought in this matter is based appeared in 1925. The cutlines to the picture read:

> The gunsmith shop of N. T. Byars at Washington, Texas. In this building the Convention assembled, signed the Texas Declaration of Independence, adopted the Constitution, and issued orders. This building was the first capitol of the Republic of Texas. (Office of Texas Sec. of State, Div. C., File box 6, No. 96, Letter B., 12-20-1849.)

If the reference given could be proven to apply to the photograph as well as to the letter identified, it would clear up completely the mystery concerning Independence Hall. The document marked "No. 96, Box 6, B," and dated December 20, 1849, was recently located in the Memorials and Petitions File of the Secretary of State for 1849 at the archives of the Texas State Library. It is a petition from N. T. Byars to the legislature for payment of his claim for rent on "a House," for the use of the convention in 1836.

The Byars petition, however, makes no reference to an accompanying photograph, and nothing else has been found in this file to indicate that such a photograph was submitted.

The photograph, which appears to be heavily retouched and is blurred in reproduction, was republished in 1935 in a Texas history text, identified only as the "Old Capitol at Washington."

A biography of Francis Dieterich, published in 1958, carries a clear, apparently unretouched photograph of the same building, which is identified as coming from Ellison Photo Company, Austin. The author, Dora D. Bonham, has stated that she has no authentication for the identification of this portrait beyond the information in Ellison's files. Ellison Photo Company has an album of old prints in which a copy of this clear photograph appears, identified as "N. T. Byars' blacksmith shop, in which the Texas Declaration of Independence was signed." The Ellison shop also has two excellent negatives of this picture, enlargements from a small picture originally acquired from an unknown source. Alfred Ellison, owner of the shop, says he does not know when, or from whom, the original photograph was secured.

If this photograph is authentic, and the descriptions given in memoirs now available are even reasonably accurate, the building must have been remodeled between the time it was seen by the writers of the memoirs and the time at which the photograph was taken. Quite obviously, neither of the narrow gabled ends of the building in the photograph was suited for its front; instead, the long side exposed to view, with its two double doors, appears to be the main facade. Also, the clothes of the men in this picture indicate that it was taken some time in the 1880s or 1890s, rather than in the 1860s. The changes in the building and the possibility of its having been standing in the 1890s are within the realm of probability. There is, however, no concrete evidence to sustain such assumptions.

Regardless of the exact architectural style involved, it is safe to say that in early February, 1836, Byars & Mercer had under construction, on a corner of Main Street in the town of Washington, a crude frame building, approximately 25 by 50 feet in dimension. It was one of the largest buildings in town; one of only two or three frame buildings in a village composed largely of log huts. At the time, Washington appeared to be on the verge of a boom, and a building of this type for sale or rent was apparently a sound investment.

The settlement, which had grown up on the south bank of the Brazos just below its juncture with the Navasota River, at the point where Andrew Robinson had operated a ferry since 1822, had been laid out as a town in the spring of 1835. The townsite company, headed by Robinson's son-in-law, John W. Hall, had conducted its first auction of town lots on January 8, 1836.

The new town boasted a number of advantages. Andrew Robinson's ferry served the traffic of one of the oldest and most-traveled roads in the settled portion of Texas, the La Bahia road. The Brazos was navigable by steamboat from the coast to Washington, but Hidalgo Falls, an obstruction in the river just above the town, prevented the boats from going farther except in seasons when the river was unusually high. The location of the town, high on a bluff, was advertised as being extremely healthful, in contrast with the miasmic bottomlands of the lower river country.

Throughout the latter part of 1835, the new town of Washington had been challenging the position of its older downriver neighbor, San Felipe, as the center of political activity in Texas. Both San Felipe and Washington had been suggested as the meeting place for the Consultation of 1835. On October 17, 1835, some of the delegates to the Consultation had met at Washington, some at San Felipe. Both groups had adjourned until November 1, because of the threat of war at Gonzales. By November, Stephen F. Austin, commander at Gonzales, had influenced the delegates in favor of his old colonial capital of San Felipe.

When the Consultation opened in San Felipe on November 1, a few diehards still held out at Washington. On November 3, Robert M. ("Three-Legged Willie") Williamson, delegate from Mina (Bastrop), had moved adjournment to Washington, but had been voted down, forty to one, and the group from Washington had reluctantly joined the rest at San Felipe two days later. On November 17, General Sam Houston had made a similar motion, which carried, only to be vetoed by Governor Henry Smith on the grounds that Washington had no press and had not provided suitable conveniences for the seat of government.

On December 13, however, when the Consultation called for a convention to meet in March to consider the question of independence, it named Washington as the meeting place. On February 16, after bitter quarrels had torn the provisional government to shreds, the General Council voted to move to Washington also, in order to lay its quarrels before the new convention.

This civic victory imposed its own problems. The town of Washington was small and primitive. Having once been denied the seat of government because of a failure to provide proper facilities, the business and professional leaders of the town did not intend to allow this to happen again. Eleven of them banded together to rent the building being constructed by Byars & Mercer and to offer it for the use of the convention. What provisions they made, if any, for the discredited provisional government, are unknown.

Washington had other visitors to provide for at the same time. In his diary under date of February 10, Colonel Gray reported meeting "a Mr. Whitely, who is going to Washington to attend the court, which is set to meet there on the 15th." Gray also reported that Captain Sidney Sherman's company of Kentucky Volunteers was at Washington from February 13 until around the 27th. Later, as many as 200 volunteers were reported hanging around the town, along with visitors, gamblers, and other hangers-on attracted by the convention.

A less hardy village might have been overwhelmed by this influx of visitors and combination of historic events. The people of Washington, apparently, were unabashed. Gray recorded that when he first approached the town on the road from Nacogdoches he was greeted by a curious sight.

Arriving at the ferry, we saw Capt. Sherman's company on the opposite bank, drawn up in order, and a crowd of citizens, drawn up to receive them in *military style*, resembling in a striking degree Falstaff's famous corps.

A couple of days later Gray was "glad to get out of so disgusting a place." He wrote that

It is laid out in the woods, about a dozen wretched cabins or shanties constitute the city; not one decent house in it, and only one well-defined street, which consists of an opening cut out of the woods. The stumps still standing. A rare place to hold a national convention in. They will have to leave it promptly to avoid starvation.

The food was particularly unpalatable to the visitor from Virginia. His first meal, he recorded, was a supper which "consisted of fried pork and coarse corn bread and miserable coffee." Breakfast the next morning was "of the same coarse and dirty materials that we had last night." This was at John Lott's place, which some called a hotel. Later, Gray moved his boarding place to the widow Pamela Mann's house, where General Houston was staying, and reported a slightly better fare.

Rooming accommodations were even worse than the food. Many of the visitors slept under the trees, Gray reported, in spite of the inclement weather. He stayed first at John Lott's,

a house, called a tavern . . . which was the only place in the city at which we could get fodder for our horses. [The tavern consisted] of only one room, about forty by twenty feet, with a large fire place at each end, a shed at the back, in which the table was spread. It was a frame house, covered with clapboards, a wretchedly made establishment. . . . The host's wife and children, and about thirty lodgers, all slept in the same apartment, some on beds, some on cots, but the greater part on the floor.

Gray considered himself lucky to share a cot with "a decent Tennesseean."

By the time the convention was under way, Gray teamed up with the patrician Lorenzo de Zavala and three delegates from San Antonio to rent a carpenter's shop for private sleeping quarters.

Robert M. Coleman, who attended the convention as a delegate from Mina, wrote in 1837 that Washington, during the convention, boasted a large number of grog shops which did a thriving business. He also mentioned "the gamblers and dissipated multitude which the session of the convention had collected at that place."

All was not roistering and celebration at Washington, however, in the days just before the opening of the convention. Gray reported that on the night of February 27, "I found considerable excitement prevailing at Washington, owing to the news from Bexar." A messenger had brought from Gonzales a copy of the letter from Colonel William Barret Travis to "Andrew Ponton, Judge, and the Citizens of Gonzales," dated February 23, 3:00 P.M. It announced that "The enemy in large force is in sight," and asked for men and provisions. Gray said that on Sunday, the 28th, he contributed one dollar to a collection raised by the citizens of Washington to send an express eastward with the news.

On Sunday, the 28th, Gray also recorded the arrival of a second message from Travis, dated February 24, stating that Antonio López de Santa Anna and his army were in Béxar and had bombarded the Alamo for twenty-four hours. That same evening he noted the arrival of a number of delegates to the convention, including Lorenzo de Zavala, whom he described as "the most interesting man in Texas."

The arrival of Sam Houston, delegate from Refugio, on the afternoon of Monday, the 29th, Gray said,

has created more sensation than that of any other man. He is evidently the people's man, and seems to take pains to ingratiate himself with everybody. He is much broken in appearance, but has still a fine person and courtly manners.

Monday was a warm day, threatening rain from the south, Gray noted. In the night, a genuine Texas norther, accompanied by rain, hail, and thunder, struck. By morning, the thermometer had dropped to 33° and everybody at Washington was shivering and exclaiming against the cold.

Notwithstanding the cold [Gray wrote], the members of the Convention . . . met in an unfinished house, without doors or windows. In lieu of glass, cotton cloth was stretched across the windows, which partially excluded the cold wind.

The Convention of 1836 opened at 9:00 o'clock, Tuesday morning, March 1, with forty-four members present. According to Gray, George Campbell Childress, thirty-two-year-old delegate from the municipality of Milam, called the opening session to order. Childress was a man of presence, trained and experienced as both lawyer and editor, and carried with him a considerable "prestige item," in the form of a $5,000 fund for the cause of Texas independence. He had visited Texas in 1832 or 1834 at the invitation of his uncle Sterling C. Robertson, agent of the Nashville Company in colonizing the area which had become the municipality of Milam. There is evidence that Childress had returned to Texas in 1835 with the purpose of procuring lands for one of the several Texas land companies promoted by Samuel Swartwout of New York. He had arrived at the Red River on December 13, 1835, and had reached Robertson's headquarters at Sarahville de Viesca, just above the falls of the Brazos, on January 9, 1836.

It is clear that Childress made himself felt in the opening session of the convention. He was one of three members of the first committee named that morning to examine the credentials of delegates-elect. That afternoon he made the motion that the president appoint a committee of five to draft a declaration of independence, and he was named chairman of that committee.

The story has been told that Childress drafted the Texas Declaration of Independence in Tennessee, before he left for Texas, and brought it in his pocket to the convention. Elisha M. Pease, who was in Washington during the convention, serving as secretary to the provisional government, has been quoted as saying, "It is generally understood that Mr. Childress brought the draft of the declaration with him to the convention." W. P. Zuber referred to Childress as the author of the document.

In the Declaration of Independence File at the archives of the Texas State Library, there is a statement quoting the late state archivist Harriet Smither as saying that Childress's original draft of the declaration, with corrections, was in the files of the archives of the Texas State Library. An unsigned typescript in the same file, apparently by Miss Smither, carries the statement: "The first draft of the declaration is, I think, unmistakably in Childress' hand."

Actually, there are two handwritten copies of the declaration in the state archives; one is the well-known signed "original," a photographic copy of which has long been displayed in the Capitol of Texas. The other, an unsigned copy of unknown origin, was examined by the best handwriting experts available and compared with letters in the Archives and at the University of Texas which are known to be in Childress's handwriting. This study established that both the draft and the signed copy now in the state archives are in Childress's handwriting. When, at around 9:30 on the morning of Wednesday, March 2, George C. Childress "reported a Declaration of Independence, which he read in his place," he apparently read from a document written in his own hand. The declaration was adopted, without amendment, except for the addition of a caption, "in less than one hour from its first and only reading," according to Gray.

Minutes of the convention show that a motion by Houston to have the declaration reported by the Committee of the Whole and engrossed and signed by the delegates, carried unanimously. This was followed by a motion by Benjamin Briggs Goodrich that five copies be prepared for immediate distribution to Béxar, Goliad, Nacogdoches, Brazoria, and San Felipe. Printer Gail Borden was to be requested to print 1,000 copies in handbill form, from the San Felipe copy, for wider distribution.

It would have taken some time for the five additional handwritten copies to be produced. Gray said, later the same day,

A copy of the Declaration having been made in a fair hand, an attempt was made to read it, preparatory to signing it, but it was found so full of errors that it was recommitted to the committee that reported it for correction and engrossment.

Under date of March 3, Gray reported that in the morning session "The engrossed Declaration was read and signed by all the members present. . . . It was forthwith dispatched by express in various directions." It may be assumed that the engrossed copy and all five of the copies for distribution were signed. This is at least indicated by the fact that Borden's handbill copies included signatures, although he inadvertently left off two—those of George C. Childress and his uncle, Sterling C. Robertson.

What happened to the handwritten copies is to this day a mystery. Texas was in turmoil from then until April 21 and all of the copies disappeared. Childress's engrossed copy was apparently deposited with the United States Department of State in Washington, D.C., by William H. Wharton. It was discovered in May, 1896, and returned to Texas through the good offices of Seth Shepard, a native Texan then serving as associate justice of the Court of Appeals for the District of Columbia. On the back of this document, someone had written, "Left at the Department of State May 28, 1836, by Mr. Wharton. The original." This is the signed copy now held by the state archives, a photographic copy of which is enshrined in a niche at the state Capitol.

There is no record of when the original Independence Hall disappeared, except that it was after 1861 and probably before 1899. Frank Brown stated that he visited the building in 1861. If any remnant of the structure had remained in 1899, when the first monument was erected on its supposed site, some mention of the ruins would certainly have been made in the newspaper accounts of the ceremonies. The only physical relic of the landmark in existence today is a battered chest, approximately fourteen inches wide, twenty-two inches long, and ten inches deep, made from planks of the old building. This relic is at the state archives. Known as "The Ark of the Covenant of the Texas Declaration of Independence," it was built by John M. Gould for Dr. Richard Rodgers Peebles, one of the group which rented the building from Byars & Mercer for use of the convention.

The first movement to establish a shrine to Texas independence around the site of its declaration originated with E. W. Tarrant, superintendent of Brenham public schools before the turn of the century. He interested his school children, who, over a period of several years, raised funds for erection of a marker at the site of Independence Hall. In 1899, citizens of Brenham became interested and formed the Texas Independence Monument Association, for completion of the monument fund and arrangement of suitable unveiling ceremonies.

Originally set for March 2, 1899, the unveiling ceremonies were postponed because the monument was not completed. The date of July 4, 1899, was next announced, but heavy floods along the Brazos in June made it impracticable for visitors to reach the scene. The unveiling was finally held on April 21, 1900. In the spring of 1915, Governor James E. Ferguson signed a bill, introduced in the legislature by Representative Sam D. W. Low of Washington County, establishing Washington State Park. The fifty-acre plot, between the town of Washington and the Brazos River, included the site on which the original Independence Hall was believed to have stood. A granite monument near the park entrance commemorates this event. In 1936 the Texas Centennial Commission added 450 acres and numerous other improvements to the park.

The small white frame building, which is called a "replica" of Independence Hall, was built in 1926 and dedicated at Washington State Park on June 3, 1926, in ceremonies sponsored by the Washington Park Commission and the Brenham and Navasota chambers of commerce. Senator Joseph Weldon Bailey was the principal speaker. Originally set for March 2, and then for April 21 but delayed both times by heavy rains, the ceremony was held on Jefferson Davis's birthday. The building was patterned after an early copy of the Ellison photograph.

Recently plans have been discussed for "raising a million dollars" to create a shrine to Texas liberty at Washington State Park. It might be well to spend the first few hundred on research.

Section II.

REPUBLIC, STATEHOOD, AND CIVIL WAR

Mirabeau B. Lamar and Texas Nationalism

DORMAN H. WINFREY*

The convention that adopted the Texas Declaration of Independence also drafted the Constitution of 1836, which established an
independent republic with a form of government much like that of the
United States. Sam Houston, the hero of the Texas military victory at
San Jacinto, was elected first president of the Republic. His
administration was devoted to organizing the new government and
gaining recognition from the United States.

Houston's successor as president was his political rival, Mirabeau B.
Lamar. Dorman H. Winfrey, former president of the Texas State
Historical Association and long-time state librarian of Texas, points out
that Lamar entered office imbued with an enthusiasm for developing
Texas into a republic whose power and influence would make her a
leader among nations. Soldier, poet, statesman, and visionary, Lamar
was a major proponent of Texas nationalism. Clear manifestations of
Lamar's nationalism appeared in various policies that he espoused as
president. As Winfrey observes in the following article, some of these
nationalistic policies were successfully implemented while others were
not. Even so, Lamar's lofty goals for Texas led the editor of the early
TEXAS ALMANAC to characterize him as one of "the purest patriots of the
age."

*Dorman H. Winfrey, "Mirabeau B. Lamar and Texas Nationalism," Southwestern Historical
Quarterly, LIX (October, 1955), 184–205.

For more on Lamar see Herbert P. Gambrell, MIRABEAU
BUONAPARTE LAMAR: TROUBADOUR AND CRUSADER *(Dallas, 1934), and
Stanley Siegel,* THE POET PRESIDENT OF TEXAS: THE LIFE OF
MIRABEAU B. LAMAR, PRESIDENT OF THE REPUBLIC OF TEXAS *(Austin,
1977).*

Nationalism has been described as a concept so complex and
changing that it defies a short, logical definition. Boyd C. Shafer, who
has written on the subject in his *Nationalism: Myth and Realty,*
observes that nationalism of the past two centuries may mean "(1) the
love of a common soil, race, language, or historical culture, (2) a desire
for the political independence, security, and prestige of the nation, (3)
a mystical devotion to a vague, sometimes even supernatural, social
organism which, known as the nation or *Volk,* is more than the sum of
its parts, (4) the dogma that the individual lives exclusively for the
nation with the corollary that the nation is an end in itself, or (5) the
doctrine that the nation (the nationalist's own) is or should be
dominant if not supreme among other nations and should take
aggressive action to this end." Critics of nationalism characterize it as
a curse on the human race responsible for intolerance, uniformity,
militarism, and international wars. Advocates of nationalism, on the
other hand, see its blessings in the forms of stability, economic order,
progress, and the spiritual and intellectual improvement of the
country. Most persons do agree that nationalism as the group symbol
during the present stage of civilization has been the prime characteristic of modern history.

The 1830s and 1840s were decades in which the full impact of
nationalism had important results on the European continent.
Simultaneously, during these decades, a nationalism not unlike that in
Europe was responsible for changes taking place in Texas. Before
Texas revolted against Mexico in 1836, Texan nationalists were
undecided toward which of three directions they should incline. One
Texas group favored loyalty to and development under Mexico;
another expressed a desire to be annexed by the United States; and a
third found the idea of an independent republic appealing. As the
revolution progressed, those who advocated a separate existence for

Texas gradually obtained the upper hand in administrative circles, so that on successfully completing the military revolution Texans made the idea of an independent republic become a reality.

The first president of the new republic was Sam Houston, Texas's military commander at the decisive battle of San Jacinto. To Houston fell the problem of initiating and consolidating the "upstart" nation—a task which left him scant time for promoting nationalistic designs. At the conclusion of his two-year term, however, his successor, Mirabeau B. Lamar, entered office imbued with an enthusiasm, not for just holding on, but for seeking the development and aggrandizement of the young republic into an empire that could one day be termed great. In the fashion of later German patriots, Lamar wanted this infant to emerge from the shadows and to seek and to find its place in the sun. To carry out such a program for Texas and Texans, Lamar became the first major proponent of nationalism in the young republic.

Mirabeau B. Lamar was born in Georgia on August 16, 1798. He had a desultory schooling but was an omnivorous reader. As a boy he became an expert horseman and an accomplished fencer, began writing verse, and painted in oils. Lamar became secretary to Governor George M. Troup of Georgia in 1823, was married in 1829, purchased a newspaper at Columbus, Georgia, during the same year, and in 1835 journeyed to Texas to collect historical data for a projected book. After reaching Texas, Lamar decided to settle in the Mexican province. Characteristically, he immediately declared for Texas independence and joined the Texas army as a private. As the battle of San Jacinto was about to start, Lamar was verbally commissioned a colonel and assigned to command the cavalry. In the first national election held in September, 1836, Sam Houston was elected president of the new republic and Lamar, vice-president. By constitutional provision Houston was not permitted to hold office for a second term, and in the presidential campaign of 1838, after the two other presidential candidates committed suicide before election day, Lamar was elected chief executive by an almost unanimous vote.

Lamar was completely devoted to the welfare of Texas, and he has been characterized as among "the purest patriots of the age." He was ambitious, had a dynamic personality, and took full advantage of the potential nationalism to carry out his desires for a greater Texas.

Lamar's term of office began with Texas in a precarious situation. Only the United States had recognized its independence; the new nation had no commercial treaties; Mexico was threatening invasion; the Indians were menacing; the treasury was empty; currency was depreciated.

It was characteristic of Lamar to divert the thoughts of his constituents from the harassments of the moment toward laying the foundation of a great empire. Particularly strong evidences of nationalism appear in the attitudes expressed by Lamar concerning one's devotion to and the supremacy of the state, the question of annexation, races and nationalities, military policies, a national bank, and national education.

Beginning with his inaugural address, Lamar used the theme of nationalism to keep the Texans contented, to create a pride in the individual and the state, and to make the population conscious of the potential greatness of the Republic. His policy was to promote the "true basis of all national strength and glory" and to "awaken into vigorous activity, the wealth, talent, and enterprise of the country." By being strong and united, Texas, Lamar reasoned, was far ahead of most frontier countries, and "under the most trying circumstances, from the dawn of the revolution up to the present period she has maintained a dignity, sobriety, and harmony which might stand as an example to older and longer established governments." He told the Texans that actually there were few dangers to be faced and that Texans were in possession of a larger share of the world's blessings "than almost any other people on the Globe." If there were difficulties at times, the people "should remember that they are evils of a temporary nature which time and patriotism will remove." Lamar reminded the Texans of the unprecedented success of the recent revolution; he pointed out that the high and honorable station that Texas had attained among the nations so suddenly "must be a source of pride and gratulation to every individual."

Lamar's eyes were "exclusively directed to the glory of the nation," and he became a strong advocate for supreme loyalty to the state. In his first speech to Congress on December 21, 1838, he urged that the citizens of Texas "faithfully observe all national obligations." In order for Texans

to realize the high aspirations of patriotism; to raise our country to that proud eminence and distinction which she is capable of attaining, it is only necessary that we lay aside all selfishness in our legislations, and direct our views to the general rather than to individual interests.

Lamar told the Texans that their republic, based as it was on "chivalry and heroism," was something new and powerful; he commented on the "enviable power which Providence has given to us." Then he suggested that the populace "duly appreciate the privileges of our peculiar position." In the future it was recommended that Texans look "with a single eye to her [Texas's] glory and greatness and sacrifice all narrow-minded selfishness upon the hallowed altar of patriotism."

In any state, Lamar felt, the national character of the people had to be preserved. He reminded his audience of the character of the Athenians and the Romans and suggested to Texans:

Let it be our study then, to preserve our national consistency by showing to the world, that the people who could practice the most exalted clemency and all the high principles of humanity in war, are equally capable of pursuing the path of wisdom, justice, and moderation in the administration of their civil affairs.

To promote a feeling of national character, Lamar constantly used the term "Texian." The word, generally applied to Anglo-American citizens of colonial and revolutionary Texas, gave this group special status when rapid colonization took place. To God's chosen Texians there was a trust to be discharged; it was to "elevate our young Republic into that proud rank which her unrivalled beauty and unbounded wealth entitle her to take among the nations of the earth." Texian Lamar did everything he could to play well the role that God had given to him.

Lamar demonstrated a strong nationalistic feeling in his references to the subject of the annexation of Texas to the United States. Although the people of Texas had strongly favored annexation to the United States on September 5, 1836, the election of Lamar to the presidency brought a changed attitude. Lamar conceded that after the battle of San Jacinto the situation in Texas was unstable and there could have been justified desires for annexation. At that time Texas was without credit, war still threatened, and many localities had been destroyed. But in November, 1838, Lamar observed that conditions in Texas were excellent, that the people worked in peace and safety, and that the Texans were a powerful and prosperous people. Lamar suggested that the decision favoring annexation be reversed because "we have risen from our prostration with redoubled energies. And shall we now in the midst of glorious hopes and increasing vigor, persevere in a suicidal policy, originally founded in necessity rather than in choice?"

Although many persons had with justification favored early annexation, Lamar made it clear that he had never favored such a move at any time. In his inaugural address in December, 1838, Lamar said:

> Notwithstanding the almost undivided voice of my fellow-citizens at one time in favor of the [annexation] measure, . . . I have never been able myself to perceive the policy of the desired connection, or discover in it any advantage, either civil, political, or commercial which could possibly result to Texas. But, on the contrary, a long train of consequences of the most appalling character and magnitude have never failed to present themselves whenever I have entertained the subject, and forced upon my mind the unwelcome conviction that the step once taken would produce a lasting regret, and ultimately prove as disastrous to our liberty and hopes as the triumphant sword of the enemy. And I say this from no irreverence to the character and institutions of my native country, whose welfare I have ever desired, and do still desire above my individual happiness, but a deep and abiding gratitude to the people of Texas, as well as a fervent devotion to those sacred principles of government whose defence invited me to this country, compel me to say that, however strong be my attachment to the parent land, the land of my adoption must claim my highest allegiance and affection.

Lamar warned that, if annexation should come it would mean that Texas would yield the rights of declaring war or making peace, of controlling the Indian tribes within her borders, of regulating her own commerce, and of forming her own alliances and treaties. He looked upon annexation as the end and not the beginning of a new era, saying:

> When I reflect upon these vast and momentous consequences, so fatal to liberty on the one hand, and so fraught with happiness and glory on the other, I cannot regard the annexation of Texas to the American Union in any other light than as the grave of all her hopes of happiness and greatness; and if, contrary to the present aspect of affairs, the amalgamation shall ever hereafter take place, I shall feel that the blood of our martyred heroes had been shed in vain—that we had riven the chains of Mexican despotism only to fetter our country with indissoluble bonds, and that a young Republic just rising into high distinction among the nations of the earth had been swallowed up and lost, like a proud bark in a devouring vortex.

A strong warning was sounded by Lamar that when annexation came to Texas, slavery, "upon which our character, prosperity, and happiness as a free people must necessarily depend," would be abolished. Other dreadful things awaited Texas when annexation took place. The nation would be divided into territorial districts, it would be ruled by alien governors and judges, and laws would be administered which Texans had no part in enacting. As a part of the United States, the sovereign Republic of Texas would be "reduced to the level of an unfelt fraction of a giant power" and would become a mere tributary vassal "pouring her abundant treasures into the lap of another people than her own." Texas, "the cornucopia of the world," would carry into the United States wealth far surpassing the influence that it would be able to exert as a state. There was no need to give Texas wealth to the people of the United States when, by remaining sovereign and exercising proper management, it would be possible to carry "to the door of every citizen of the Republic, peace, plenty, and protection."

To help in his arguments against annexation, Lamar pointed out that while the annexation question was being considered, the national pride of Texas had been often insulted by the United States. He reviewed the attitude which many persons in the United States government circles had toward Texas. Many of these officials hurled insults at Texas and looked upon Texans as a "band of desperadoes." Lamar conjectured that "there are species of national indignities which a proud and spirited people may not bear, and which a patriot, jealous of his Country's as his own honor, should feel bound to resent." Texas had waited long enough for the United States to approve annexation, and Lamar felt that "we can not, with any show of national pride or dignity of character, renew the negotiation." Lamar put the annexation question to the people by asking:

And shall we blindly & madly precipitate ourselves into the deadly and destroying embraces of such a baleful people. Are we prepared to receive our laws from their hands and to hold our rights and our institutions by the tenure of their clemency & justice, whilst we can enjoy tranquility and safety under a better government of our own creation? We have been told by them distinctly that they will not receive us as brethren—that our country is but the home of the wicked and the worthless, where vice is pestilential and virtue laughed to scorn; and yet like the spaniel that licks the hand that assails him, we continue knocking for admission at the door from which we are abruptly ordered with indignity and insult.

Lamar made such a strong appeal to Texas nationalism for a separate existence that in 1838 public opinion veered in the opposite direction to what it had been in 1836. The desire among Texans for a separate nationality was relatively strong while Lamar was in office, but by 1845 the population was anxious to identify itself with the United States.

Lamar, like many nationalists in need of a scapegoat, found it advantageous to turn to minority groups. He became race conscious, and there are strong evidences of nationalism in what he had to say about race and nationality. He liked the French; they had been champions of freedom and had, like the Texans, fought a glorious revolution. The Spaniards, on the other hand, were an inferior people and could not be trusted. On one occasion Lamar remarked, concerning the president of Costa Rica, that "it must be borne in mind that he is a Spanish American; and my long acquaintance with that race will not allow me to vouch for their sincerity and good-faith in any case whatever." The "free and independent" Anglo-Saxons, with "the ties of a common language and a common ancestry," had made many contributions to mankind; Lamar felt that Texans could profit by adopting what this "genius" race had to offer. In his opinion, Spanish civil law was inferior to English common law, and he said,

We [Texans] shall exercise the exalted privilege of appropriating and enjoying the benefits of a liberal jurisprudence originated by the wisdom, and for centuries defended by the valor of the Anglo-Saxon race.

Slavery was championed by Lamar because of his belief that Negroes were an inferior race. He maintained that the system of slavery in operation at that time was the best relation which had ever been established between the laboring and governing portions of mankind. He reasoned that

there is an unintectual [*sic*] toil to be performed, and menial services to be rendered; and it is infinitely better (whenever it is practicable) to assign those duties to that class of our species whom Providence has so signally fitted for the task, than to impose them upon our own brethren, who are our equals in every respect, except in the gifts of fortune.

Lamar maintained that in society such a division as master and servant was a law of God, because "He has clearly indicated the line of distinction between them by colour and character." It was Lamar's feeling that the system of slavery in the South "seems to be established by God for the amelioration of the black man, and for the relief of the white man; and one which, as far as my observation and experience enable me to judge, is productive of the greatest advantage to both races."

The strongest evidence of Lamar's nationalistic feelings regarding race, however, were displayed in his attitudes towards Indians in Texas. Lamar announced in his first inaugural address that his policy toward the Indians would be directly opposite to that of his predecessor, Sam Houston, who was held to have been too lenient. The hostile Indians on the frontier were a constant danger to the new republic, and Lamar's references to "barbarious, impudent, and hostile Cherokees," "wild Comanches," and "skulking Kikapoos," contributed to arousing Anglo-American fear and hostility.

According to Lamar, the Indians as a race were "insensible to all moral obligations." He felt that there was no way for Indians and American settlers to live side by side on friendly terms; he invited an observation of the failure of the United States Indian policy to support his belief.

> The white man and the red man cannot dwell in harmony together. Nature forbids it. They are separated by the strongest possible antipathies, by colour, by habits, by modes of thinking, and indeed by all the causes which engender hatred, and render strife the inevitable consequence of juxtaposition.

Lamar favored a policy of removal or extermination for the Indian tribes in Texas. "I experience," he said, "no difficulty in deciding on a proper policy to be pursued towards them. It is to push a vigorous war against them ... without mitigation or compassion." In a speech to both houses of the Texas Congress on December 21, 1838, Lamar devoted much time to the Indian situation. He said that the frontier settlements had to be given adequate protection against the Indians and that "honor, humanity, and patriotism, conspire to enjoin this duty." Lamar forecasted the possibility of an Indian war, but said

> I am by no means desirous of aggrevating the ordinary and inevitable calamities of war, by inculcating the harsh doctrine of the lex talionis toward the debased and ignorant savages ... when it [war] cannot be avoided it ought to be so met and pursued as will best secure a speedy and lasting peace. If that better mode consists in severity to the enemy, then severity to him, becomes clemency to all.

Moderation toward the Indians, Lamar contended, had proved worthless in the past. The Indian was cruel to all persons under any circumstances, and Lamar could not understand why the Indian was so insensible to the dictates of justice and humanity when the "white man for centuries furnished him examples of clemency and kindness." The Indians had been shown kindness, mercy, and consideration, but Lamar felt that these benevolences on the part of the Anglo-Americans had been mistakes. He advised that a new policy be pursued. His harangue against the Indians in Texas is not too different from utterances made by nationalists against minority groups in other localities.

As long as we continue to exhibit our mercy without showing our strength so long will the Indian continue to bloody the edge of the tomahawk, and move onward in the work of rapacity and slaughter. And how long shall this cruel humanity, this murderous sensibility for the sanguinary savage be practised? Until other oceans of blood; the blood of our wives and children, shall glut their voracious appetite? I would answer no. If the wild cannibals of the woods will not desist from their massacres; if they will continue to war upon us with the ferocity of Tigers and Hyenas, it is time we should retaliate their warfare, not in the murder of their women and children, but in the prosecution of an exterminating war upon their warriors, which will admit of no compromise and have no termination except in their total extinction or total expulsion.

A good example of the rhetoric which Lamar used to stir the emotions of the settlers and thus help him to carry out his Indian policy is found in an address which he made on February 28, 1839, calling for volunteers for the protection of the frontier. Lamar said that he was requesting aid to combat the "fierce and perfidious savages" who were attacking the helpless, exposed, and defenseless inhabitants on the frontier. He pictured a breakdown in the entire frontier defense unless aid came at once from the interior regions. Lamar tested the patriotism of the fortunate interior settlers by asking:

Are you, citizen soldiers, willing to repose quietly at home while your countrymen and brethren are bleeding under the tomahawk and their families are the unresisting victims of the scalping knife? Can you sleep upon your pillow, with the voice of lamentation in your ears? Are you insensible to noble deeds—dead to the love of fame; too frigid for and too timid for danger? No. Such is not the character of Texans.

Lamar said he knew that Texans had chivalry and virtue and that the Indian challenge would be met. The times were precarious, and he suggested that the "chivalry of Texas show itself." To protect the frontier areas men were wanted who were ready to fight and suffer privations, but of equal importance were those "whose energy and public devotion will supply the deficiencies resulting from the present conditions of our public finances."

A prime example of Lamar's Indian policy in operation is found in the expulsion and extermination of the Cherokee Indians in East Texas in 1839. Lamar pictured the Anglo-Americans in Texas situated between two great enemies: The Cherokee Indians, on one side, and the Mexicans, on the other. If the two forces ever made contact, then the Texans were doomed. In a message to Congress on November 12, 1839, Lamar, with some good evidence to back his claims, accused the Cherokees of having been in secret negotiations with the Mexicans. Then there were other reasons for getting rid of the Cherokees: "They were of all the Indian tribes the most enlightened; and at the same time, our most inveterate and wily foes." Among the Indian tribes the Cherokees were believed to have "superior intelligence," a factor which caused them to be feared by the settlers. Also, the whites were unable to trust the "Punic faith" of the Indians. A main reason, however, why the Cherokee Indians had to be removed from East Texas was that there was not enough land for the Indians and the growing white population. Lamar said that some persons had called to his attention that white settlers were encroaching upon the Indian land, but that he could not agree with this claim.

I am not aware of the fact myself. If the spirit of speculative enterprise has been pushed by any of our citizens beyond the boundaries of prudence; and has awakened the savages to a war upon our whole community, it is certainly a matter to be much regretted; but being involved, it becomes the nation to meet the exigencies with promptitude and energy.

The Cherokee Indians were accused of entering East Texas as intruders (non-nationalists) without a valid claim to any land. Lamar cautioned that the Texas government simply could not afford to let the Indians remain "situated in the very centre of its empire." It was not possible to admit the Indian claims to any land because that "would be parcelling out our territory to strangers and intruders." Such a concession to the Indians would mean that "an alien, independent and innately hostile people" would be situated "within an organized, enlightened and sovereign government." The Texas government would not permit such a thing to take place, and Lamar made this position clear when he said, "It is the settled policy and determination of the Government to remove beyond our territorial limits, every Indian tribe that has no rightful claim to reside in Texas."

In April, 1839, both Indians and Texans were mobilized for war in East Texas. Lamar wrote to the Cherokee Indian chief, The Bowl, that Texas would not permit his tribe to exercise a sovereignty that conflicted with that of Texas.

The people of Texas have acquired their sovereignty by many rightful and glorious achievements, and they will exercise it without division or community with any other People. They can recognize no alien political power within their borders, and you and your tribe, having no legitimate rights of soil or sovereignty in this country, can never be permitted to exercise a conflicting authority.

Lamar offered to remove the Indians at government expense and to make payments for improvements that had been made on the land. The Cherokees did not accept this offer. Lamar then issued an ultimatum and cautioned The Bowl to "listen to the voice of reason and of power."

The principal battle in the war between the Cherokees and the Texans was fought on July 15 and 16, 1839, in present-day Henderson and Van Zandt counties. The Cherokees were defeated and driven out of Texas. Lamar's plan had worked well, and he was by 1840 in a position to deal with the remaining Indian tribes. He said,

When the emigrant tribes shall have been removed, the few which claim the right to remain, will not have the means of giving us annoyance, and should they attempt it, there will be no difficulty in punishing them as badly as they deserve.

The greatest manifestation of nationalism, as conceived by Lamar, was his dream of an empire. He visualized a Republic of Texas that would extend from the Sabine River and Gulf of Mexico westward to the Pacific Ocean. A part of this vision existed in legal theory, if not in fact, for the First Congress of the Republic of Texas had on December 19, 1836, declared the southern and western boundary of Texas to be the Rio Grande from its mouth to its source and then a line due north to the forty-second parallel. Santa Fe was in the area held to be Texas territory, although nothing had been done prior to 1841 to implement this vast claim. Lamar's first step toward the realization of the "great empire" dream was to try to gain control of Santa Fe. Such a westward extension of Texas power would aid in pushing the Republic's boundary to the Pacific. Other than a desire for additional territory, Lamar felt that the acquisition of Santa Fe would increase trade and commerce. He also had an honest but mistaken belief that the people of Santa Fe desired to live under Texas sovereignty.

There are evidences of nationalism in the methods that Lamar used in trying to get the territory and people of Santa Fe to come under Texas jurisdiction. On April 14, 1840, Lamar addressed a letter to the people of Santa Fe. In it he gave a short history of what the Anglo-Americans had done in Texas, reviewed the efforts Texans had made to work peaceably with the Mexicans, and explained how finally, after Texas had been subjected to a Mexican military despotism, freedom had been achieved. Then Lamar pointed out the prosperity Texas had enjoyed since the Mexican yoke had been thrown off, the recognition given by European powers, the development of natural resources, the growth of population, and "commerce extending with a power and celerity seldom equalled in the history of nations." After painting a glowing picture of the prosperous Texas position, Lamar, playing the role of a humanitarian nationalist, made his point.

Under these auspicious circumstances we tender to you a full participation in all our blessings. The great River of the North, which you inhabit, is the natural and convenient boundary of our territory, and we shall take great pleasure in hailing you as fellow citizens, members of our young Republic, and co-aspirants with us for all the glory of establishing a new happy and free nation.

Some commissioners, accompanying the expedition, would be sent to Santa Fe to explain to the citizens there the many things the two localities had in common "which so emphatically recommend and ought perpetually to cement the perfect union and identity of Santa Fe and Texas."

The 321-man expedition, although never expressly approved by Congress, left Brushy Creek, east of Round Rock, in southern Williamson County, about June 19, 1841, for Santa Fe. That Lamar did take into account the likelihood of nationalism in the Santa Fe locality is shown in his address entitled, "An Address to the Citizens of Santa Fe," taken by members of the expedition. In it Lamar pointed out to the people of Santa Fe that he felt it was his obligation to assert jurisdiction over the territory that had been acquired by Texas in the recent revolution. He felt that the population of Santa Fe had suffered from Mexican rule as Texas had. Lamar made it clear that Texas claimed the Santa Fe territory and that the position of the Santa Fe government was

temporary only and will have to give way to a more enlarged and liberal policy—Although residing within our established limits you are at present paying tribute to our enemies, professing allegiance to them and receiving Laws from their hands a state of things utterly incompatible with our right of sovereignty, and which certainly cannot be permitted of long continuance.

Texas must assert her claim because it was inconceivable for the people of Santa Fe to pay taxes to, and be governed by, an alien power. While Lamar said in one breath that he had no desire to extend Texas jurisdiction if it was not wanted, he warned in the next sentence that the people and territory of Santa Fe were a part of Texas and as such could not exist as a separate and independent locality. He made it clear that Santa Fe would eventually be compelled to unite with Texas.

That which you will have to do *ultimately*, we invite you to do *now*, not from any desire to promote our own interest at the sacrifice of yours, but for the exalted purpose of diffusing the blessings of our institutions and of giving to all who reside within our territory the freedom we enjoy.

The offer Lamar was making to the people of Santa Fe was not intended to come in the voice of "artillery but in the language of affections." Nevertheless, some statements Lamar made appear to contain both artillery and affection, and at times the citizens of Santa Fe might have had difficulty in knowing which would be fired in the next paragraph. There was little doubt what Lamar had in mind when he stated, "Our purpose is simply to place before you the rights which we claim, and to admonish you of the change in your condition which the force of circumstances will inevitably bring about at no distant period, either with or without your consent."

Lamar listed at great length all the evils of the Mexican government and the advantages to be enjoyed under Texas control. With reference to the national banners of the two countries, he asked:

Which of the two will you select? Will you shelter yourselves under the broad banner of the Single Star, which sheds luster wherever it floats, and lights the brave to victory and glory; or will you prefer still to cling to the unsightly *Cactus* which gives you no sustenance but thorns you as you embrace it. If you choose the latter, then is your deplorable condition too justly represented in your National emblem; for what can we esteem you but the unfortunate reptile that writhes in the beak of your voracious bird?

Lamar told the people that it was the policy of Mexico "to destroy your manly energies and degrade you in your own estimation; to keep you *blind* that you might not assert your *rights*, and weak that you might not resist your wrongs." The people were mere slaves under Mexican jurisdiction, Lamar declared, and conditions would never improve under Mexico because she was "an unnatural parent, a monstrous mother—who turns with a phrenzied appetite to prey upon her offspring!"

It was evident, Lamar pointed out, that the Texans had a high regard for the people of Santa Fe by the fact that Texans were willing to share their blessings with them. The pride of the inhabitants of Santa Fe was played up to when Lamar complimented them with the following:

> We have been told by those who have long resided among you, that you are a brave and industrious and an honest people—simple in your manners, generous in temper, and inflexible in your principles; and it is precisely on this opinion of your worth that we predicate our friendship for you and are ready to receive you in a common government. A proposition which we could certainly never think of making to a people whose integrity and chivalry we had any reason to suspect.

Lamar knew that the population of Santa Fe was predominately Catholic, and he promised that there would be no change in the religious establishment. He was also aware that the population was mostly Mexican and took great pains to explain that the North Americans were not prejudiced against the Mexican people but against the Mexican government.

The Texan Santa Fe expedition, harassed by Indians and suffering because of insufficient provisions and scarcity of water, for approximately three months made its way to the northwest. By October 5 the entire expedition had passed into the hands of New Mexican troops under Governor Manuel Armijo. Not a single shot had been fired; the adversities and limitations of the Great Plains environment had defeated the Texans and Lamar's nationalistic dreams of westward expansion.

Lamar realized that the military forces could be used as a strong stimulus to promote nationalism, and he wished to create a strong army and navy. One of his first addresses to Congress outlined the combined Indian and Mexican threats and warned that an established military force "could not, compatible with safety, be either small or inactive." A strong army would deter Indian depredations, inspire a confidence which would lead to a rapid settlement of the frontier, and "at the same time form a nucleus around which the chivalric yeomanry of the land would rally in the event of another invasion from our national foe." Lamar admitted that it would cost money to support an army but reasoned that, even so, "a people who value their liberty and safety above all price, will consider every burthen light which is necessary to the maintenance of their national character and independence." It was his conviction that "a well regulated militia is the strongest and surest bulwark of liberty."

Fidelity to the country was the soldier's first duty, and Lamar said to carry out his program to build a strong army one purpose would be "to foster a spirit of military pride and emulation among the people." Under no circumstances was there to be a failure "to maintain order and subordination *within* and to repel all aggressions from *without.*"

The trained militia might be ample to meet the threats which Texas faced, but Lamar expressed his faith in the volunteer soldier, for he said, "I would still prefer, in the hour which tries men's souls, to rest the nation's defence, upon the zeal, the valor, and the patriotism of the citizen soldier."

Along with a strong army, Lamar felt that it was necessary that Texas maintain a strong navy. He warned members of Congress on December 21, 1838, that the Texas navy was prostrate, while Mexico was increasing her strength. It was necessary that Texas, with such a long maritime frontier, have a strong navy for protection; Texas commerce had to be protected "from insult and depredation on the high seas."

Frequently Lamar increased the personnel and ships of the Texas navy by executive fiat. Without congressional approval, he ordered the Texas navy into the service of the rebellious Mexican state of Yucatán. Lamar was always able to justify his unauthorized actions by charging that an imminent Mexican invasion was near or that it was necessary to make a demonstration of naval power. It was not possible for a navy to operate like an army because navy officers had to be trained. Lamar told the Congress that it was utterly impossible to "disband the accomplished and gallant officers who have embarked in our naval service." The navy had been an expense, but not to have operated the navy "might have involved the country in great disaster and an irreparable loss of reputation."

To nationalist Lamar, as to nationalist Alexander Hamilton of an earlier period, reputation and honor were to be saved and even augmented not alone through military policy. To stabilize the country's economy, Lamar even advocated a Bank of Texas. He went further than Hamilton; the Bank of Texas should be a truly national bank operated solely by the state. He called attention to the success that the national bank of Alabama had enjoyed. No part of the profits of this bank went to shareholders, but all went to the government, which, in turn, gave support to building canals, roads, bridges, and other objects of public improvement. Lamar stressed that

there is an obvious distinction between a *national bank*—this is a Bank instituted for the benefit of *the nation* (which is another name for *the People;*) whose stock shall belong exclusively to the nation; and whose business shall be regulated by the *agents* of this nation, made subject to the same responsibilities as those of its *representatives in Congress*—there is a marked difference, I say, between a Bank of *such* character, and one in which half, or more, of the stock is owned and administered by individuals, independently of the supervision of the People.

While the Bank of the United States bore the name of a national bank, Lamar pointed out that four-fifths of its stock—and in that proportion a preponderance in its control—was vested in individuals. Such a bank as this, Lamar said, certainly was not a national bank. The Alabama bank, however, was a true national bank because "its stock is the property of the state exclusively, and subject alone to the control of the government, through its *agents,* who are vigilantly kept to a strict responsibility to the *sovereignty of the state.*" A national bank, Lamar felt, would work better in Texas than in the United States because the Texas "government is one, and integral; and admits of no exciting conflicts of state rights and federal powers." In Texas the national bank would be the exclusive property of the Republic and under the complete control of its fiscal agency. All classes in Texas would benefit from the national bank.

The planter, the mechanic and the laborer, are as much entitled to the immunities and privileges of the government, as the speculator, or the money dealer. Let all trades be free. Let all rights be equal. The constitution has so ordained it, and so let us carry it into practice. The fostering hand of legislation should be extended to all classes of society. Each individual of a patriotic people cherishes, supports, and defends the government; and none have a peculiar and exclusive claim to rewards or privileges in the exercise of their industry.

Once the people understood how such a bank was to function, how sound such a system was, and how rewarding the system would be, it could not fail "to enlist the national pride of a large majority of our fellow citizens."

Texans were aware, however, of Andrew Jackson's opposition to a national bank and this, combined with a shortage of cash in the Texas treasury, contributed to the failure of Lamar's efforts.

By contrast, however, Lamar's advocacy of a system of state education met with approval in Texas. A proper state-controlled education, based on the Lamar plan, included such nationalistic beliefs as instilling in the youth the love of the country, a sense of public duty, and devotion to the state. Lamar approved the educational methods the Greeks had used because "the Knowledge diffused among the people there comprised the duties of religion, obedience to the laws, inflexible honor, contempt of danger and Superior to all; the love of country." To emphasize youth's obligation to the Republic, Lamar again referred to the Greeks and advocated, "Cultivate those principles of public duty their fidelity to which won for the Spartans at Thermopylae the noble inscription of the Grecian port, that those who fell there died in obedience to the Laws of their Country—."

In a speech Lamar made to Congress on December 21, 1838, a speech which University of Texas president William L. Prather once called "a trumpet call to duty," Lamar gave his ideas for the educational need.

Our Young Republic has been formed by a Spartan Spirit—let it progress and ripen into Roman firmness and Athenian gracefulness and wisdom. Let those names which have been inscribed on the standard of her martial glory, be found also on the page of her history, associated with that profound and enlightened link in the chain of free States, which will some day encircle, and unite in harmony the whole American Continent. Thus, and thus only, will true glory be perfected; and our nation which has sprung from the harsh trump of war, be matured into the refinements, and the tranquil happiness of peace.

Lamar told the same Congress that for a republican government to be a success a sound system of education must be established. "It is admitted by all, that cultivated mind is the guardian genius of Democracy, and while guided and controlled by virtue, the noblest attribute of man."

At times, Lamar appears to have had in mind the benefits the state would have enjoyed from the establishment of an educational system. In case of a war, he predicted, an educated population would prove a great asset; otherwise, "war would be conducted without the science necessary to secure success."

Lamar, however, wanted young Texans to be educated only in certain fields. He felt that it was dangerous for students to go abroad and study because they might become contaminated with "ideas that were adverse to the true policy of the nation." He stressed that it was essential that "our youths should not only be educated at home, but that their education should be a *national one.*" Texans either favored or were converted to Lamar's educational ideas, and the Congress did approve adequate measures for the establishment of a system of state education. Thus nationalism played a part in earning for Lamar the title "father of education in Texas."

It would be impossible to determine the full impact that nationalism, as used by Lamar, had upon events in Texas history during and following his administration. A few facts, however, do appear evident. Negatively, Texas nationalism was not strong enough to acquire Santa Fe, nor was a national bank ever established in Texas. In some ventures, however, Lamar's appeals to nationalism may have been successful; the Indian policy, although costly in lives and money, was considered a success. Lamar's use of nationalism may be credited with the building up of the military forces and to some extent with the establishment of a system of education. It is debatable whether Texas's annexation to the United States was delayed or hastened by Lamar's attitudes. Regardless of the influence Lamar's use of nationalism may have had upon Texas history, one thing does appear certain. Had he ignored nationalism he most probably would never have been characterized and numbered among "the purest patriots of the age."

A Glimpse of Life on Antebellum Slave Plantations in Texas

ABIGAIL CURLEE HOLBROOK[*]

Although slavery had existed during the Spanish period, the number of slaves in Texas prior to the 1820s had been small. The institution grew rapidly with the coming of Anglo-American planters and farmers from the Old South. At the time of the Texas Revolution there were only 5,000 slaves in Texas; on the eve of the American Civil War twenty-five years later there were over 180,000 slaves in the state.

Abigail Curlee Holbrook has devoted many years to the study of the Texas plantation system. She believes that Texas slaves were generally better treated than their brothers and sisters in other slave states but admits that even in Texas cruelty and injustice existed in the master-slave relationship. In the present article, Mrs. Holbrook describes the housing, food, clothing, health care, amusements, and religion of slaves on the principal Texas plantations. She concludes that kindly feelings existed between the two races on most Texas plantations. In this respect, Mrs. Holbrook follows the lead of early twentieth-century southern historian Ulrich B. Phillips, whose books

Abigail Curlee Holbrook, "A Glimpse of Life on Antebellum Slave Plantations in Texas," Southwestern Historical Quarterly, LXXVI (April, 1973), 361–383.

AMERICAN NEGRO SLAVERY . . . *(New York, 1918) and* LIFE AND LABOR
IN THE OLD SOUTH *(Boston, 1929) were pioneer works on the subject.
For more critical views of the institution of slavery readers should see
recent works by Kenneth M. Stampp, John W. Blassingame, and
Eugene D. Genovese.*

Slaves made an invaluable contribution toward the development of
antebellum Texas. Without their labor the clearing of land for
settlement would have been materially reduced or delayed and the
cultivation and production of Texas cotton, corn, sugar, and other
crops would have been but an asterisk on the pages of history. The
existence of slaves and the availability of their labor provided a
measurable quantity and quality of food and fiber for the record of the
world, not to mention producing a cultural impact on Texas which
cannot be ignored.

The life of a Texas slave was usually somewhat easier than that of a
brother in the other southern states. The fertility of the soil helped to
make it so; the salubrious climate lifted all spirits, even those of slaves.
However, the white settlers were stimulated by the physical and
emotional freedom evoked by the satisfaction of a fresh start. For the
blacks this stimulation was lacking. Although the lives of both blacks
and whites were as varied as the individuals themselves, and although
their housing, food, clothing, health, recreation, education, religion,
and attitudes differed from plantation to plantation and from one area
of Texas to another, discernible patterns evolved and definite trends
can be delineated.

Of prime consideration to any settler—white pioneer or Negro
slave—was housing. For a home site most settlers chose a tree-covered
rise or hill, with a spring or stream nearby. They needed both the wood
and the water to make life bearable for themselves and their servants.
Shelter from the weather was the next imperative. Normally the
settlers used the materials at hand; and, although there were
exceptions, the slaves were housed in much the same manner as their
masters. The early houses of both were of logs, those of the masters
being more commodious than those for the slaves. Usually the cabin
for a slave family was a one-room building, about 20′ × 20′, with a

fireplace for cooking and heating. A loft, reached by a ladder built against a wall, was the sleeping room for the boys if the family was a large one.

As the planter prospered, his own log house was expanded either with additional rooms or wings constructed of logs or with a frame addition. Other planters replaced the log house with a new frame or brick building. With the growing sophistication of the establishment, servants might be moved in to occupy a wing of the "big house" or might have cabins in the yard. But field hands usually remained in cabins at least a quarter of a mile from the main house. On large plantations the hands might be divided into two or more groups and the houses for different families be located near the lands which they cultivated.

The evolution of the slave quarters often followed the same course of development as the big house, with log structures being replaced by frame or even brick buildings. Log buildings were difficult to maintain, for they dried out and had to be rechinked and pointed up frequently, diverting many man-hours of labor from more profitable duties. Also, the women found them difficult to keep clean, and most planters early recognized the correlation between cleanliness and healthy productivity. At first, the floors of the slave cabins were of dirt, swept to the hard pan. Skins of bear, deer, and other animals frequently covered their surface. Later, puncheon or board floors were added, as planters learned that wooden floors seemed to promote better health than dusty ones. Each cabin had one or more doors, and some had one or more windows cut through the logs, with shutters of wood to keep out the cold and rain. A cabin might have a front porch or "gallery," and occasionally an additional lean-to. Such dwellings have been described as warm and comfortable, but certainly not all were so, by any means.

The furnishings of these slave homes were simple and plain, usually made on the place and in place. Many had "Georgia Hoss" beds; that is, beds constructed with a post approximately four or five feet from one wall and five or six feed from the adjoining wall. Poles or planks extended from the post to the walls, thereby making a frame for the bed; rope or rawhide was then stretched across the frame to support the mattress. Mattresses were stuffed with hay, straw, corn shucks, moss, or cotton. A few lucky slaves even enjoyed the warmth of feather beds. Wooden chests, boxes or sometimes trunks protected the slaves' Sunday clothing, while "de rest hund on de peg." Completing the household effects were stools, homemade chairs with cowhide or splint bottoms, and perhaps a table. A shelf, resting on two pegs driven into the wall, usually held a tin bucket and a gourd dipper. A few former slaves remembered the chinches (a type of bedbug) that might infest the cabins, along with spiders and other unwelcome guests, but masters and overseers fought these disturbers of sleep. Because of the insects and for other sanitary reasons, slaveowners usually insisted that slave houses be scalded or scrubbed often and that bedding be aired. Regular cleaning of the cabins was the rule, not the exception, on Texas plantations.

The layouts of various plantations illustrate habits and customs relating to housing. The dependencies (such as slave quarters and other outbuildings) of Willis Whitaker of Cass County in Northeast Texas were of brick and faced a regular street. Evidence of one of Whitaker's methods of maintaining discipline among his 140 or so slaves also faced on the street—the jail, a structure divided by a solid wall into a room for the men and another for the women. Not too far away, east of Marshall in Harrison County, William T. Scott's slaves lived in 20' × 20' cabins built about a hollow square where all the merrymaking took place.

In the "Red Lands" of Rusk County, about ninety miles west of Shreveport, was Monte Verdi, the home of Julien Sidney Devereux. The Negro cabins here were built fairly close to the spring, while the cabins for the Devereux family were a few hundred yards away. In 1846, under the supervision of Julien's father, John William Devereux, the men built the cabins while the women grubbed and burned brush. John Devereux recorded in his "Memorandum and Common Place Book" that the construction, from stump to smokehouse, took three days. The mansion at Monte Verdi, still a well-known landmark, was begun on a beautiful nearby hill in 1855. Julien Devereux wanted to get his wife and small children out of their log house, which was "too open and cold." The slaves did not construct this home, which was a long time abuilding, being still unfinished when Devereux died in May, 1856. Whether the slave cabins, which must also have been "open and cold," received improvements at this time is not known.

Slightly east and south of Monte Verdi was "Blount's Free Negro

Quarters," as his neighbors dubbed Stephen W. Blount's plantation near San Augustine. Here the slave quarters consisted of eight frame cabins, 20' × 20', each with a brick chimney. In front of each fireplace was a hole where fifteen or so bushels of sweet potatoes were stored, to be used for roasting and for flanking 'possums. The homes of master and slaves were both constructed of pine.

In Central Texas in 1850, Churchill Jones acquired about 28,000 acres on both sides of the river at the falls of the Brazos, to establish an integrated operation of growing, milling, and selling cotton. He sent his son James ahead from Alabama with overseers and a hundred bondsmen to open up the operation. They were to build cabins in the bottom land for the slaves, with those for the family on higher ground. Jones wanted everything to be in first-class order for his family's arrival. Since at first little furniture would be brought, he directed that scantlings be cut to make the beds for his family's home. He also commended one of the young overseers for making "the negroes keep themselves and houses and beds fixed up."

Not too far away, in Salado, the Elijah Sterling Clack Robertson family lived in log cabins until they build their mansion in 1852. The mansion included the twenty-two rooms of the main house, made of cypress lumber, and a service area of stone, with stone servants' quarters adjacent to the big house. Some of the slave houses adjoined each other. This well-maintained property is one of the few complete displays remaining today of the Texas antebellum plantation.

Over on the Brazos, Jared E. Groce, the earliest large owner of slaves in Texas, had built on his plantation, Bernardo, a 55-foot long house of cottonwood logs, hewed and counterhewed as smooth as glass. It was two stories, with many refinements. In the backyard, he had a 30' × 30' "Bachelors' Hall" for guests, along with a cabin for the doctor, plus the usual dependencies. Groce built quarters for his hundred or so slaves about three-quarters of a mile from the big house. These cabins, made of logs, faced one side of a large lake and stood close to the overseer's house, a large kitchen, a dining hall, and a day nursery to care for the children while their mothers worked.

In Brazoria County was Ellersly, the mansion of John Greenville McNeel, with an overseer's house and a street of brick houses for the slaves leading off from the main road. In 1935, when the author visited the plantation, the mansion was no longer there, having been destroyed by a fire that started in the hay stored in its once-elegant rooms. The slave quarters were in ruins, with roofs off and the bricks tumbled about; but the overseer's house, which was also of brick, was still inhabited. During the heyday of life at Ellersly some of the house servants occupied a wing of the main house. John McNeel's brother Leander H. McNeel owned Pleasant Grove, described by many as more elegant than Ellersly, but not even traces of the slave quarters and other buildings of that establishment remained in 1935. There too some of the house servants were always available in a wing of the main house.

Waldeck, about three or four miles from Columbia, was a two-story home with black marble fireplaces, built by Colonel Morgan L. Smith. Some Waldeck slave quarters were of logs, but most were of brick made on the place. In November, 1859, Smith sold the plantation to Hamblin Bass, formerly of Georgia and Alabama. Bass was a builder and a real farmer. He had his servants improve the grounds by paving the stream and establishing a reservoir for water and for fish. With the help of three of Bass's slaves, a contractor built at Waldeck a 30' × 30' brick smokehouse, 20 feet high, on a line with the servants' rooms and kitchen in the backyard of the big house. The servants burned the lime for the bricks used in the large smokehouse from rock, and then made the bricks. The contractor charged $125 in gold for his services. In 1864 Bass built a new brick cabin for some slaves and he planned to put up five more. The war did not prevent his making improvements and taking care of his servants.

For a year after moving to Texas, Bass's daughter, Rebecca Adams (Ann Rebecca Pattillo Bass Adams), and her family lived at Waldeck, but the Brazoria County area was too low and damp for the health of Mrs. Adams. Consequently, Dr. Robert Adams moved his family to the Huckaby place, about three or four miles from Fairfield in Freestone County. The family itself moved in carriages while the forty or fifty Negroes traveled along in wagons. Each night the slaves set up a tent for the family and laid a carpet before they made the beds. When they saw the log house on their newly purchased plantation, the Adams children burst into tears. They had just left Waldeck, one of the great mansions of Texas. The children had never lived in a log house; and they did not want to. At first they preferred to stay in the tent, but in time they came to enjoy their log home.

Log cabins, whether occupied by the planter or by his slaves, needed constant care; however, the amount of attention that the Negroes gave their cabins depended upon the standards of the masters and the overseers. Thomas E. Blackshear, who lived near Navasota, noted in his diary that he had given his more than one hundred slaves half a day off to scald their cabins and mend their clothes. In his "Plantation Rules," Dr. Charles William Tait of Columbus required "every negro cabin to be inspected every Sunday morning, to see that it is kept clean." Much of the lime on the planters' bills was used to whitewash Negro homes and other outbuildings.

Food was also the planter's ever present and, at times, pressing problem. The most usual foods in the house and in the cabin were bacon, corn bread, milk, and coffee, with whatever additions the season and circumstances would permit. During the first years of settlement the failure of the mast crop could cut the supply of bacon, and in the spring after a large immigration or a short crop, corn was often scarce, causing some distress for man and beast. From Cole's settlement in 1834, Dr. Asa Hoxey, who had come to Texas the year before with money and servants, wrote that all the corn had been consumed at least two months before and that his Negroes were living exclusively on beef, consuming about a hundred pounds daily at two cents a pound. In 1843 and 1848 Ashbel Smith's slaves suffered for lack of corn for bread.

Thomas J. Coffee wrote to his wife in Galveston in 1846 that he was sending her some butter and cornmeal from their plantation on Oyster Creek. He and the servants (Coffee listed sixty-eight slaves in 1850) were living on squirrel and venison, melons, peaches, and fowl. Polly, who was in charge of the poultry, had a good variety. Coffee himself had to remain at the plantation to care for some fifteen or twenty of the slaves who were "lying up" (ill) and required attention.

Not far away, Hamblin Bass was complaining about the poor way he was living. In 1862 Bass had had two plantings of vegetables die for lack of water. He had plenty of the "solids, such as bacon, beef, pigs, chickens, lard, flour, milk and butter," but still missed the vegetables. Sweet potatoes of his last year's crop were a staple, too. Bass was giving his Negroes a varied diet, however. All that year he had been feeding them pickled beef, which had been made the fall before from seventy-five beeves. Not a piece had been lost, he commented, it was still sweet and good. From a Mexican he had bought five hundred goats and two hundred mutton sheep. "I have just began [sic] to feed the negroes upon the goats. I kill six every morning and the negroes like them, as they are very fat." Bass reported 223 Negroes in the census for 1860. His daughter Rebecca Adams was saving garden seeds for her father, and Bass had remarkable success with the seeds she sent him. He had more peas than he had ever raised and as fine beets and beans. One more rain that year would give him corn enough for three years, he reported. Bass was a superior planter and a generous provided for his own table and for that of his slaves.

Meanwhile, to her husband, now in the service, Mrs. Adams wrote that they had killed hogs in the coldest weather. She commended the slaves upon the way in which they had managed the chore. She now had 9,219 pounds of pork and 100 gallons of lard on hand, and inquired how much of this meat and other produce of the plantation should go to the Confederate government. George, one of the slaves, was to haul the corn, potatoes, and cotton, each of which went to a different government representative.

The manner of serving the food varied slightly from plantation to plantation. "Come and get your meat" was the summons on Sunday morning on the Scott plantation, which brought the slaves to receive meal, flour, tobacco, syrup, and at times sugar, fresh beef, and fresh pork. On this plantation the cooks prepared a special diet for the children, "pot liker" and corn bread being the usual food.

In his "Plantation Rules," Tait provided that the overseer should serve out to every working hand once a week 2½ to 3½ pounds of bacon, according to circumstances. If milk and butter were plentiful, less meat was given; if molasses was included, a quart was allowed instead of a pound of meat. When dried beef was used, 5 or 6 pounds was the weekly allowance. Each slave received a peck of meal, unless potatoes were issued. "Lying-in" women were allowed a quart of coffee and 2 quarts of sugar, and they were fed from the overseer's kitchen for two weeks. Tait also provided that the Negroes were to be allowed to commence using the potatoes and the sugarcane on October 1.

By 1856, for a number of reasons, the serving of uncooked food to the Negroes and leaving them to do their own cooking had become unpopular in Texas. The Negroes frequently ate a week's supply in two or three days; or the food was poorly prepared because of careless or untrained cooks. Much waste resulted. Furthermore, it seemed unjust to require the working hands to come home after their labors and spend their evenings preparing food.

Under the system of a common kitchen, the overseer issued the supplies for the day in about the same measure as Tait provided. The breakfast might consist of bread and molasses and coffee, or sometimes pickled herring or mackerel. The midday meal included bread and boiled meat with one or more vegetables in season, made into soup or stew. When vegetables were scarce, dumplings of meal were made and boiled with the meat. During half the year the Negroes had baked sweet potatoes for supper; or they could have hominy, or bread and milk or clabber. Sometimes they saved some of their meat and molasses from dinner for the night meal. The overseer had to see that the food was well cooked, prepared on time, and apportioned fairly according to the needs of strong men, women, and children. With the supper on Saturday night, the overseer distributed the supplies for Sunday according to the number in the family. During the week the woman in charge of the nursery cooked the food for the children, with the exception of bread, hominy, and soup, which she usually obtained from the slave kitchen. Some thought that the diet of the children should include buttermilk or clabber, but not sweet milk and very little molasses. Masters in the South believed that their servants wasted less and enjoyed a more wholesome diet under this system.

At Stephen S. Perry's Peach Point plantation a common kitchen served all the field hands, but the Negroes had free access to other foods. In addition, they frequently supplemented their meals with eggs from their own flocks and with other delicacies. On sugar plantations the slaves had all the sugar and molasses they wished. Their cooking was done over fireplaces.

Mrs. Rosa Groce Bertlet described the magnitude of the food preparation at Groce's Bernardo plantation, with its hundred or so bondsmen. In order to have the workers in the fields by daylight, the call to arise came about 4 A.M. While the men were feeding the mules, the cooks were brewing pots of strong coffee. When the bell sounded at daylight, all the hands came to the dining hall for their "eye-opener"—a cup of steaming coffee. All then went to the fields, the men to the plows and the women to the hoes. At 7 A.M. the breakfast, consisting of ham or bacon, hot biscuits or corn bread, and fresh steak or chicken, was packed in tin buckets and sent to the fields in carts for distribution to the workers. Dinner was cooked and served at 12 o'clock in the same manner. At 6 P.M. or sundown all gathered together at the hall for a hot meal.

Less expensive and less bothersome than supplying the slaves with food was clothing the whole plantation. But clothing was regarded as highly important. In fact, when times were hard and a planter had not the resources to cover all his financial obligations, he would insist that he had to use his funds to feed and clothe his servants. During hard times the whites as well as the blacks wore buckskin and homespun materials. Easier times meant a return to bought fabrics. Planters calculated that the labor of a woman in the field could buy many more yards of cloth than she could spin and weave in the same time. By the bolt, planters bought osnaburg, jeans, kersey, lowells, and linsey-woolsey. Different weights of materials were used for the various garments. Lowell for summer was eight-ounce cotton material similar to brown domestic.

The materials that G. G. Williams was ordering of John Adriance of Columbia in 1849 differed little from those which Colonel John Hill (who listed 153 slaves on his state and county tax) was buying in 1857. From Ferguson and Brothers of Waverly, Hill purchased twenty-seven pairs of boys' Russetts (shoes) at $.95 each; four pairs of men's Russetts at $5.00; three pieces of Sandfords white jeans; six pieces of Kendell kersey; three pieces of Georgia Gray kersey; four pieces of Rocky Brook kersey—in all, 534¼ yards at a cost of $114.83 for the cloth and $35.25 for the shoes.

In October, among other expensive items, Hill was buying 120 pairs of men's Russetts for $174.80. He also bought a bale of blankets, 50 pairs at $3.75 for each pair. With the wrapper and Ferguson and Brother's costs, the blankets came to $160.38. Hill evidently had an interest in the firm because they charged him a base price and added only a 15 percent markup and the cost of cooperage and carriage. The next year Hill bought from the state penitentiary five bales (or 2,992 yards) of osnaburg and one bale (or 648.1 yards) of jeans, for a total cost of $402.32. From Ball, Hutchings and Company he bought five pieces (or 150 yards) of Georgia Plain and four pieces (or 160 yards) of Southern kersey. The total cost was $59.97. On June 24 he was back at the penitentiary for 1,849.2 yards of osnaburg and 551 yards of cotton jeans, costing $260.18. In April, 1859, he bought 619 yards of ¾ osnaburg for $61.75. In 1860 Hill listed 170 slaves on his tax list, and in March of that year he laid in a good supply of cloth: 4,158½ yards of ⅞ osnaburg, 536¾ yards of ⅞ cotton jeans, and 134 yards of other material. The total cost was $544.67, less credit for 192 pounds of wood, a ½ cent discount on 4,829 yards, and 5 percent for cash. His adjusted cost, therefore, was $471.68.

Other planters also bought from the penitentiary. Dr. Pleasant W. Kittrell was buying cloth and selling cotton there from 1856 on. His sister Mrs. Sarah Goree did so also in 1861. Most planters, however, obtained these materials from merchants who bought them from English or New England factories. A few planters had their cloth manufactured to order. Stephen W. Blount customarily sent a bale of wool to Georgia, his former home, and had jeans of half wool and half cotton made for winter clothing for his servants.

Some local manufacturing of Negro cloth developed in the 1850s in addition to that of the penitentiary. About 1858, H. Ware of Glade Springs in Harrison County began, with his slaves, a factory whose output included linsey, jeans, tweed, cassimere, Negro blankets, stocking yarns, and Russet shoes.

When war forced the women to return to the spinning wheels and looms, a number of Negro women were familiar with the whir of the wheel. Each November, for instance, Dr. Tait's female slaves had been testing their skill at night by spinning threads for plow-lines. However, the art of spinning was not a common one. It was hard work and supplies were scarce and expensive. In 1862 Mrs. Sarah Goree paid twenty-five dollars for a pair of cards, according to her brother.

In October, 1863, Rebecca Adams wrote her army husband that she was as busy as she could be trying to "get the negroes some clothes made before the cold weather." She expected to get 40 yards out of the loom on that day, making a total of 80 yards since he left home. By late January, 1864, she had turned out 250 yards.

Of necessity, her father, Hamblin Bass, with his large contingent of slaves, worked on a more extensive scale. On June 13, 1864, he wrote his daughter that he was going to Hempstead the next day to pick up two dozen wheels and four looms that he had bought the month before. He expected to have about fifty women at work. "I expect to have a time of it, but there is no other way to clothe the negroes but to make the cloth at home." By December Bass had about 600 yards of cloth off the loom. His best weaver made about 8 yards a day. The loom had been set up in the house formerly used by an overseer, but Bass expected to finish a special building to house it (at this time he mentions only one loom despite his earlier expectation that he would have four in operation). He had bought from a blockade runner that had run into Matagorda Bay 120 pairs of blankets for the Negroes, at $7 a pair. He paid for them in 10½ cent cotton, delivered to Columbia.

According to custom on most plantations, twice a year each slave received two new suits of clothes, plantation made. The mistress, the wife of the overseer, or one of the slaves, trained by the mistress, cut out the various garments. They were sewed by hand either by a Negro seamstress or by the owner's family, or by both. John Hill was most progressive when he bought a Singer sewing machine in 1860, at a cost of $110.70 delivered. Of these coarse garments each man was issued in the spring two pairs of pants, two shirts, and a straw hat; in the fall, two more pairs of pants (usually of a heavier material), two shirts, a coat, and a woolen hat. Twice a year, also, the women donned new dresses and "linins." According to Tait's records, this did not mean that on one day each spring and one day each fall every slave issued forth from his cabin resplendent from crown to toe in new raiment. Much time was required for the seamstresses to make four or five garments apiece for more than sixty slaves. In the spring of 1861, nearly a month—April 6 to May 3—elapsed between the times the first and last man received pantaloons. Issuing the shirts required an even longer time—from May 12 to June 19. For the men and boys June 1 was straw-hat day. The fall sewing interval was longer still, the first coat being issued on September 12 and the last one on November 19. Shoes were issued throughout the year as the individual slaves required footwear.

On Peach Point, Ellersly, Waldeck, and other large plantations a seamstress and her assistants were always busy in the sewing room, cutting and making garments. Occasionally some planters bought their Negro garments ready-made. In 1861, for instance, Mrs. Preston R. Rose purchased eleven kersey jackets for $22.38.

Such garments were designed for utility, not style. According to Wharton Collins, born in 1852 on the plantation of Leonard Waller Groce, he was just coming out of the "shirttail stage" when the war was over. Boys stayed in their shirttails until they were twelve or more years old, "really until they were ready to take up the field work." In his eyes the effect was picturesque when the wind was blowing and the young bondsmen were hoeing: they looked like a flock of white cranes with their wings flapping. "It was a pretty sight."

Others, however, saw nothing attractive about these garments. General James Hamilton was shocked at the scanty clothing furnished the hired slaves on the Retrieve plantation in Brazoria County by Major Abner Jackson. "In this dreadful cold weather, they have received a flimsy negro cloth & a scanty pattern at that." Four days later the general was modifying his several charges against Jackson. By then he understood that the Negroes "were about as well clothed as the average of Plantations in the Country were." The clothing did not compare with that worn by slaves in South Carolina and Mississippi with which Hamilton was familiar. He planned to give the Negroes a suit around before he left.

The town slaves from Galveston whom William Pitt Ballinger and Thomas M. Jack had placed in the care of Aaron Coffee of Halcyon during the war gave Coffee many worries. Three slaves, Dave, Tucker, and Alleck, had been impressed by the army for work at Fort Bates. Dave was caught stealing and was whipped by the soldiers, and he and his companions departed the fort. All but naked, they went home to Ballinger, who wrote Coffee to learn the reason for their condition. Coffee replied,

Tucker took all his pants & shirts & sold them for a mere trifle to [Negroes on] Mrs. Kyles place & one of my boys bought a part—Tucker remarking 'he *did not care a dam for such corn field-nigger clothing,*' as Master William and Master Tom Jack will give him city clothing.

As to Alleck, he took the same course except that he gave his garments to Agnus who put them in a tub and let them rot. Dave had disposed of his wardrobe in an equally effective manner. Coffee was indignant, for he was having a difficult time obtaining clothing.

It does not seem possible that four or even six ensembles could stand the wear and tear of a year's use, and yet they did. Mrs. W. B. Hanson said that Morgan L. Smith gave his Negroes Saturday afternoon off from their work to do their mending, washing, and bathing, so that they would be clean and tidy for Sunday. One of the duties of Tait's overseer was to see that every Negro appeared in the field on Monday morning in clean clothes. They did not get half of Saturday off, of course, when the crops needed attention or when sugar was being boiled. Sugar making was a round-the-clock procedure. Indolent servants might try to evade the rules about clean clothes, but lye soap was plentiful and was much used, though needles and thread were treasures.

Not all country slaves contented themselves with mere work clothes. Those on the Perry plantation used the proceeds of their own crops, eggs, and Sunday work to buy buckets, tobacco, net and cambric for mosquito bars, combs, stockings, flannel, five-dollar dress patterns, domestic, and straw hats, not to mention "sundries." They also bought extra shoes for themselves and their wives. The slaves of John Hill made so much money from their extra activities that Hill carried their earnings and expenditures in a double-entry record. They bought many extras for themselves and their homes. Planters of Texas tended to use such incentives more than the lash to maintain order and good behavior on their places. They encouraged the Negroes to have their own patches of land and to find other ways of making extra spending money. Some slaves thought that their masters should buy their private crops of cotton, corn, or potatoes, and their other products, such as baskets and nuts, and pay them premium prices at that. There is no evidence that their funds were used for anything other than satisfaction of their own desires.

Just as most letters mentioned the state of the crops and the weather, so did each carry comment on the health of the family and the neighborhood. Illness entailed suffering, irritability, expense, and a depleted labor force, all of which problems death intensified. What a train of ills beset the plantations: chills and fever, boils, mumps, measles, flux, rheumatism, cramp colic, choking quinsey, venereal disease, cholera, yellow fever, consumption, and unnamed infections. The Negroes seemed to be peculiarly susceptible to pneumonia. Remedies were herbs, teas, brews, quinine, calomel, blue mass, epsom salts, mustard, castor oil, aloes, and cupping. Many planters had their own treatments for minor ailments, but a serious illness called for a doctor. Of all diseases, the planters dreaded most yellow fever and cholera. During epidemics slaves who worked in the field one day could be dead the next morning. In 1833 cholera hit the area between the Brazos and Colorado rivers with dreadful results. Again in 1847 cholera struck, and the planters scattered their hands in the woods and suspended all work. E. D. Nash reported to John Adriance that a Mr. Gass had lost sixteen hands; Robert Townes and Abner Jackson lost nine; W. W. Williams lost one; and Thomas J. Coffee lost thirty-three—a severe financial blow since he had come to Texas only four years before and was burdened with security debts. Four years later cholera struck about Huntsville, and Colonel John Hume lost his seven-year-old son and thirteen of his Negroes. The epidemic spread to Indianola and Wharton County. On a Mr. Bolton's plantation there had been thirty-three cases with eight fatalities—among them the overseer and his son.

The servants on Perry's Peach Point plantation seem to have been fairly healthy. Days were missed from work, but not until the late 1850s did many deaths occur. Of the sixty-seven children born to Perry's slaves, seventeen died before reaching the age of five years, from "hooping cough," "fever and worms," and unnamed causes. Thomas E. Blackshear recorded several deaths in 1859, among them his "good negro man Edmund," upon whom he had leaned. Thomas Affleck, another newcomer to Texas, had reported few cases of sickness on his plantation, Glenblythe, near Brenham.

The mistress of the plantation apparently bore a large share of the burden of caring for the sick, if the actions of Mrs. Beverly LaFayette Holcomb, Mrs. Rebecca Adams, and Mrs. James F. Perry were typical. Of Mrs. Perry's ministrations to the slaves on Peach Point, her son's college classmate Rutherford B. Hayes wrote:

Mrs. Perry, for example, instead of having the care of one family, is the nurse, physician, and spiritual adviser of a whole settlement of careless slaves. She feels it her duty to see to their comfort when sick or hurt, and among so many there is always some little brat with a scalded foot or a hand half cut off, and "Missus" must always see to it or there is sure to be a whining time of it in the whole camp. Besides, to have anything done requires all time. It may be I am mistaken, but I don't think Job was ever "tried" by a gang of genuine "Sambo's!"

Once or maybe twice a year the planter paid his physician for medical services. During one year Julien S. Devereux paid $224.50 for doctors' visits to the house and to the quarters, prescriptions and medicine for his 70 Negroes, bandaging and splinting a broken bone, and attendance through the night and delivering in a difficult labor. In 1857 John Hill paid $353.00 to three doctors, Samuel P. Spiller, W. A. Rawlings, and K. W. Skinner; Hill had 157 slaves. His account included visits and medication in the office of the doctor, night visits to his three plantations, the cupping of Partha and placing of "blisters" behind her ear, and the cupping of another Negro woman. Mrs. Hill was attended at least twenty times. Slave Bob was seen frequently by the doctor, including one period when the doctor visited morning and night for three days and three times a day for three days. At one point Dr. Rawlings and Dr. Skinner held a consultation about one of the illnesses. Hill had an ever larger bill in 1858. Dr. Spiller charged him $521.60, but they settled for $500.00. Hill, who had 160 slaves on January 1, 1859, looked carefully to the welfare of his people, both white and black.

Naturally, work engaged most of the working hours of the slave, but he could take it lightly unless there was pressure to complete a particular task. Moreover, he could take a stolen vacation in the woods if the burden became too great, particularly when berries, corn, grapes, nuts, or sweet potatoes were plentiful. The Negro was a wise worker, for much of his work with hoe, saw, ax, or the sugar dipper was done to the rhythm of his songs and chants. Furthermore, on most plantations he knew that his nights were his own. Laughter, chatter, music, and dancing could be heard from the quarters until the overseer's curfew sounded. Sunday was a day of rest, infringement of which during emergencies moved the humane planter to apologize and to pay the slave for extra work.

Normally, the slave could count on at least three holiday periods: one at the "laying by" of the crops; one at the end of harvest; and one at Christmas. On many plantations a half holiday on Saturday was traditional. Then the bondsmen could work their own crops, tidy their houses, wash and mend their clothes, fish and hunt, and enjoy themselves in their chosen ways. Annually, provided the crops had been well cultivated, the Blount slaves were hosts to the Negroes in the neighborhood on the Fourth of July. On the night of the third, pits were prepared for barbecuing sheep, shoats, and beef. From the storeroom the cooks obtained sugar and flour which they transformed into cakes and pies. "A respectable repast" and many speeches prolonged the celebration late into the night. A second day off from work was given for recuperation.

When the cotton was gathered or the sugar made, the slaves on many plantations enjoyed a day of similar festivities. When no holiday was allowed, the slaves expressed themselves in their own fashion:

... they finished picking cotton today and came out of the field shouting and blowing their hornes like there had been a democratic victory. They came up this evening and extended the fence around the new house and helped clean up the yard. It improves the appearance of things very much.

From two days to a week was the usual Christmas holiday season. On some plantations the length of the vacation was determined by the time that the backlog burned at the big house. Much ingenuity was used in selecting and in prolonging the life of the "back-stick." During this season the Negro indulged his propensities for sociability, dancing, noise-making, and eating. If all the whites had responded to the call for "Christmas Gift!" he was tired and ready to return to work by the end of the holiday.

Religious life among the Negroes depended to a large degree upon the attitude of the master. Some owners encouraged church affiliations; others were indifferent; and a third group actively discouraged church membership of any kind. One reason for this last attitude was the fear that night meetings, religious or otherwise, were the precursors of runaways. Ashbel Smith had this reaction in 1843 to his slave Robert's traveling about to night meetings. Nevertheless, Smith's slaves were allowed to attend church and quarterly meetings.

Mrs. Holcomb of Wyalucing and Mrs. Perry of Peach Point conducted Sunday school classes for their slaves, as did many other families. The Perry slaves and those of their neighbors, the M. S. Munsons, had a church congregation of their own. At their services, uninhibited by the presence of the whites, emotionalism was unrestrained. Old Annaca, one of the Perry Slaves, refused to attend these services and returned to the Presbyterian church, saying, "They gus and disguss me."

Many servants were members of the congregations of their white folk. At Waldeck, however, the opposite was sometimes the case. The finest church building in Brazoria County was said to be the brick church building on Waldeck plantation. Over its door were inscribed the words, "Ethiopian Baptist Church—erected 1856." Morgan L. Smith had the white minister come out from Columbia to preach in this church on Sunday afternoon to his slaves, who were required to be "nicely fixed" for the occasion. White worshippers often came along with the preacher. Hamblin Bass continued this custom. In June, 1864, Bass wrote to his daughter, "The Reverend Jessie Boring spent about ten days with me about the first of the month. He preached in Columbia several times, and also for the negroes at Waldeck." Though emotionalism might often characterize their religion, worship was the greatest opportunity that the slave had for self-expression.

Bible study and special training for the occupations on the plantation normally constituted the only formal training that most of the Negroes received. Of more than 250 advertisements for runaway slaves, only 5 described the Negro as being able to read or figure. A sprightly house servant might learn from the master of mistress or the children at the big house how to read and write or how to distinguish among different papers in order to bring the master the desired one. A Negro foreman might absorb enough mathematics to keep a simple daily record of work done by the various slaves or of products ready for or sent to market. Some Negro children absorbed this in childhood from their white playmates. Often on leaving the classroom, the white children held play school and taught their lessons to the Negro children.

Doubtless some other masters acted as did Dr. Pleasant W. Kittrell, who encouraged carpenter Jordan Goree, slave of Dr. James L. Goree, in his work. Kittrell kept Jordan's books and aided him in his affairs. Consequently, Jordan built dwellings, gin houses, and gin screws in the vicinity of Huntsville and was able to earn and save considerable money. He lacked about a hundred dollars of having enough to buy his freedom from Dr. Goree when the war came. Kittrell apprenticed his own slave Billy to Jordan, and Billy made about thirty-five or forty dollars a month for his master, as Jordan had been doing for his master for some years. Kittrell also apprenticed his boy Fletcher to work in Dr. G. M. Baker's shop at Huntsville under Mrs. Probusco's George, a blacksmith. In 1861, R. Phillips, the tinsmith, hired Kittrell's boy Bob as an apprentice at sixty dollars a year. The Perry family boasted that two of their slaves sawed as much plank in a day without supervision as they did with oversight.

Similar conditions did not exist on every plantation. Too many masters were not willing to forego the labor of a slave while he received the necessary training; and a trainer was not always available. Many slaves did have their talents developed as farmers, gardeners, stockmen, brickmakers, brickmasons, carpenters, blacksmiths, tinsmiths, wagoners, saw mill workers, sugarmakers or helpers, gin operators, cooks, houseboys, maids, seamstresses, laundresses, nurses, preachers, and similar occupations. Too many, unfortunately, entered freedom with an inadequate education. Although their labor had advanced immeasurably the opening, development, and growth of Texas under the leadership of the white man, the vast number of Negroes were inadequately prepared for the role of citizen. Time would be required before the freedman realized that freedom meant more than owning a good horse, saddled and hitched at the rack; eating all the sardines and crackers he desired at the country store, or wandering into town without purpose.

The emotional relationships involving the Negroes on the plantations were as varied as their personalities and as changing as the circumstances of the moment. Much affection and loyalty toward each other characterized some, while others felt no ties. Some couples lived together because they were told to or directed by the overseer or master to consider themselves married. Others chose one mate and lived together all their lives. Still others felt free to roam and to change partners at will. Sometimes the broomstick ceremony (in which the couple stepped across a broomstick laid on the floor to symbolize their union) was used to join a male and female slave. The pleasure of others was to be married at the big house by the master or someone in authority. No legal ties were involved.

If slaves from different plantations married, the children were the property of the mother's master. One of Perry's slaves, Clarrissey, had a neighbor's servant for a husband for a time, and their three children belonged to Perry. On the other hand, Robert, a Perry slave, married a Munson woman, and their three or four children belonged to M. S. Munson. However, this type of marriage was discouraged because it could lead to truancy and to grief and sundered families should one of the partners be sold or should the owner move from the neighborhood.

The relationships between master and slaves were also as varied as the personalities concerned and the times and the occasions evoked. Concubinage did exist. How much was not and is not measurable. That sort of connection has always been difficult to prove; and death, murder, and shame sometimes grew out of such illicit relationships.

Old gossip about planting families has existed into the twentieth century and its supposed truth would depend upon the interpretation of known events or the attitudes of the storytellers. For example, take two points of view of the same event—an old settler died in a Negro cabin on the banks of the Brazos River. To one neighbor the event was a disgraceful example of miscegenation; another neighbor saw a man, broken in wealth and health, being nursed loyally by a former family slave until his death. Again, after attending the funeral of the scion of an "Old Three Hundred" settler, an oldtimer remarked to his companion, "Well, he was the only one of the boys to have white children."

Cruelty and injustice certainly existed in the master-slave relationship, but it was not the dominating characteristic. When cases of mistreatment came into court, the judges were usually fair in their interpretations and decisions. If the general public had not agreed with the judges the rulings of the courts would no doubt have reflected this attitude. Mistreatment did occur, of course, and more than one slave has charged that a master or mistress was cruel. Frances Spriggs (born in 1855), for instance, was given by Leonard Groce to his son Fulton as a wedding gift when he married Acenath Jackson. According to Frances,

Miss Cennie whipped me hard. She had nothing else to do. She whipped me when I stopped rocking Miss Courtney, and she beat me when I did not come running when she called me. She had the worst temper. She used to yell and scream at Mr. Fulton but he paid her no mind.

Here Wharton Collins, husband of Frances Spriggs Collins, took up the tale, "We were both born on the Leonard Groce plantation and Frances fell to Mr. Fulton when he married. 'Deed, Frances had it rough with Miss Cennie."

Nevertheless, Wharton and Frances Collins spoke with affection of the rest of the Groce family. Other ex-slaves remembered their former white families with affection. Old men and old women when they were in trouble turned to their former white folk and taught their children to do likewise.

Archival materials, newspapers, and interviews with many people reveal that, on the whole, kindly feelings existed between the two races. The plantations of Texas were not so large that personal relationships were limited to work and to reaping the benefits of the harvest. Slaves were known by name not only to the immediate family circle but to distant relatives and friends. They were individuals to the planters and their families, and they reacted toward their owners as individuals. Of course, the slave could not know the nature of his master's financial worries. Few, if any, had ever heard of mortgages and deeds of trust to cover the lands and even the slaves of a planter. However, they could recognize that the state of the weather and the crops affected affairs on the plantation, and they could share their master's concern about such conditions, even if they did not realize the seriousness of his worry.

The Civil War, with the Confederate government's cotton policies, the conscription of planters and overseers, the impressment of the finest men among the slaves, the taking of the best mules and horses for the army, and the general confusion, left agriculture in a disorganized condition. Plantations at the war's end were run-down, their resources depleted not only by enforced neglect but also by the loss of at least a third of their capital. Many of the planters were old if not dead, and the young men returning from the war were crippled, ill, malnourished, and confused—a defeated people unready to take on at once the tremendous task of rebuilding the economy and life in general.

On the other hand, the Negro left slavery possessing little more than his clothing (most of which had seen hard wear and few replacements), his iron skillet, his pots, and his tin buckets. Many stayed on the plantation for a time; but others left immediately. After all, they had been told they were free to go, and they went. Without shelter, food, clothing, and medical care, the Negro was to suffer before he learned to use his new freedom. His transition to freedom was an expanding and stimulating experience for all of Texas, but it was abrupt and explosive, and ripped apart the structure of one familiar, if unadmirable, way of life for the Negroes without providing any immediately workable replacement. Texas, and the South in general, has spent more than a century building a new and still imperfect structure of society to take its place.

The Texan of 1860

LLERENA B. FRIEND*

The fifteen years between annexation to the Union and the outbreak of the Civil War witnessed a tremendous increase not only in the number of slaves but also in the overall population of Texas. Attracted by fertile lands and generous land policies, settlers from other states and foreign nations migrated to the new state in ever increasing numbers. Formation of political parties, the war with Mexico, settlement of the New Mexico boundary dispute, payment of the public debt, and exploration of the western part of the state were all major developments of the period.

Llerena B. Friend, the biographer of Sam Houston and a careful student of the early statehood period, points out that by 1860 a distinctive Texas character had emerged. A tradition of "local loyalty, rugged individualism, pride in size, a history of independence, and a fearless fighting spirit" were all a part of the Texas tradition. In the following article Dr. Friend provides an interesting composite picture of the Texan of 1860 based largely upon census returns, travel accounts, diaries, and private journals.

*Llerena B. Friend, "The Texan of 1860," *Southwestern Historical Quarterly*, LXII (July, 1958), 1–17.

The Texan of 1860 was already regarded as a man somewhat apart and was considered, like Rudyard Kipling's Fuzzy-Wuzzy, as "a first class fighting man." One contemporary critic said that Texans had "little of union sentiment in their biographies" and "more of separateness in their geography, commerce, and history" than had the citizens of other states. This sense of separateness derived both from colonial experiences on a border between antagonistic races and from the ten years of national independence, but it rubbed off on men who came to the area after 1836 and again after 1845. The brevity of the war for Texas independence and its spectacular climax at San Jacinto, plus the reports of United States regulars as to the prowess, attire, and uncouthness of the Texans who participated in the Mexican War, tended to characterize the Texan as a fighter. It was no wonder that an East Tennessee farmer in 1861 encountered some Texas troops en route to Virginia and hailed his family: "Say, old woman, and you gals, all of you come out here, these are Texicans." A Texas soldier whose way east led through Alabama was amused at the "terror and apprehension" felt by the citizens of Tuscaloosa when they learned that a brigade of Texans had arrived in town. Events of 1860 to 1865 did nothing to diminish this military reputation. John H. Reagan once wrote that he would rather have been a worthy member of Hood's Texas Brigade than have all the honors that came to him, and those same Hood Texans were said to have had a place in the heart of Robert E. Lee that no other command ever won.

As Cassius pondered about Caesar, so might one conjecture: "Upon what meat did this our Texan feed that he was grown so great?" Is he to be explained in terms of his ancestry, his history, or his environment? The history is too long for telling here; the environment is intangible; the ancestry mixed. In this Sputnik day, televised meetings of historical associations could have animated cartoons to depict the prodigious growth of the Texan between 1850 and 1860, or a color chart could divide the subject into anatomical sections to show in which veins flowed Caucasian or Negroid blood. There might be a trace of green for Irish immigrants and a bit of royal blue to indicate descendants of the "first families of Virginia." In this less colorful and less animated situation, the more prosaic approach of the small print in the report of the United States census will have to suffice. A statistical approach can show something of where the Texan came from, what he did for a living, to which organizations he belonged, and where he worshipped. Almanacs and lists of imprints can fill in the details of his schooling, his travel facilities, and his reading habits. One may also check what his contemporaries said of him.

The first United States census was taken in Texas in 1850. A decade later the Eighth Census stated: "The vast region of Texas ten years since was comparatively a wilderness. It now has a population of over 600,000 [604,215], and the rate of its increase is given as 184 per cent." Many of these migrants had come to Texas to join their relatives, and most of the many were from the South, where ties of blood were strong and cousins several degrees removed were still considered "kissing kin." Their objective was to better themselves, whether to establish homes, escape punishment, or gamble on the rising value of land in an area "where mistakes were forgotten and dreams could come true." According to a Union soldier stationed in Texas in 1860,

within her limits are citizens from every State in the Union, as well as large numbers from foreign countries. They bring with them the habits and sentiments peculiar to their homes, and thus, unitedly form the basis of a hardy, vigorous, intelligent population.

Internal migration in the United States was responsible for most of the new residents of Texas. States which had been receiving immigrants before 1850 were sometimes losing citizens by 1860. Arkansas and Mississippi sent most of their émigrés to Texas, which was expanding its cotton frontier and following the natural geographic pattern to the West. From the North, Illinois, Indiana, and New York were the chief potential Texans, with Ohio and Pennsylvania next in line. The settlers brought their slaves with them. The ratio of colored population to the total in Texas was 27.5 percent in 1850; by 1860 Negroes were 30.2 percent of the whole.

Total foreign population grew from 16,744 in 1850 to 43,422 by 1860, with Germany, Mexico, and the British Isles the three chief sources. Almost half—20,553—of the foreign population was German. Coming on individual enterprise and initiative, immigrants from Germany, Prussia, and Austria, between 1831 and 1861, became assimilated in the economic and political life of Austin, Colorado, Fayette, Washington, DeWitt, and Victoria counties. In western Texas most of the Germans had been brought in by the Society for the

Protection of German Immigrants in Texas. Gillespie County, for instance, had a population of 2,736, of which 1,363 were foreign in birth. Comal County had a foreign population of 2,186 out of 3,837.

The French had increased over 300 percent in a ten-year period, to a total of 1,883. Frenchmen and Alsatians under Henri Castro settled the Castroville area; Victor Considérant led other French to the La Réunion, or Dallas, area. Norwegians settled in Bosque and Henderson counties; there were some two hundred Swedes in the state, and Karnes County had the first Polish colony.

Platted on a map, the 1860 population statistics reveal that the frontier line had practically reached the edge of the Great Plains. The more thickly populated counties lay on the main highways into the state: the route across Red River from Arkansas, the road from Shreveport to Marshall and Jefferson, and the Brazos River bottom with rail access by Harrisburg and Houston from Galveston Bay. Bexar and Cameron counties, lying off the well-traveled entrance ways, had large Mexican populations, and Brownsville also had a port with active trade up the Rio Grande dating from the Mexican War period. Islands of population scattered along the Rio Grande marked the important river crossings and the locations of Federal army posts. Most of the slave population was found in counties of relatively dense population, with Bexar and Cameron counties providing the exceptions. Bexar had less than two thousand slaves, and Cameron, because of its proximity to Mexico, had less than one hundred.

In terms of density of population, Texas's 237,321 square miles (approximately her present area as arrived at after the Compromise of 1850) had 0.98 persons to the square mile in 1850 and 2.55 in 1860. These people possessed 27,988 dwellings in 1850, or 5.22 persons to the house. In 1860 the number of dwellings—varying from an adobe hacienda to a board and batten cabin to an Abner Cook designed mansion in Austin, had increased to 77,428, and the average number of occupants was 5.45.

Washington County, in the heart of the cotton-growing area, had the highest average valuation per acre—$8.44 in 1859—while Starr County's average valuation per acre in 1858 was sixteen cents. Wichita County, not yet organized, had a land value of $1.62 per acre. The presence of railroads worked both ways; lines were built to tap the cotton area, and where the rails were laid, the land value increased. To

October, 1859, eight lines, the Galveston, Houston, and Henderson; the Buffalo Bayou, Brazos, and Colorado; the Houston Tap and Brazoria; the Houston and Texas Central; the Washington County Line; the San Antonio and Mexican Gulf; the Southern Pacific; and the New Orleans and Texas, had a total of 272½ miles of track completed, over 130 miles graded, and 85 or more miles under contract. The San Antonio and Mexican Gulf had only 5 miles in operation; the Houston and Texas Central could take the Texan farthest—75 miles. If he really wanted to traverse his state, he rode horseback or took the stage. Sawyer and Risher served most of the stage routes with either four-horse coaches or two-horse hacks, but there were also individual lines, such as that of Joseph Baker at San Augustine or Levi Hontz at LaGrange. Should the Texan prefer travel by sea, he took the Southern Steamship from Galveston or Indianola for New Orleans. Steamboats ran daily between Galveston and Houston, "leaving Galveston on the arrival of the New Orleans steamers, and Houston on the arrival of trains from the interior." Travel by rail or coach was not exactly luxurious. Mrs. Eliza Ripley, a refugee to Texas after the war broke out, said that she could not remember the timetable for the railroad between Houston and Beaumont, but recalled:

a dim idea [dawned] that it was intended to make a round trip daily, *Deo volente,* which implied "weather permitting"; but when rain soaked the wood piled by the road-side so that it would not make steam, or when sleet made the rails slippery, travel was entirely suspended. As both these contingencies existed the week we were in Beaumont, of course no travel could be thought of.

When the group finally departed, the woman pictures the trip:

After a long day's snail-like progress, the train stopping every few miles to take a load of wet and soggy wood, and every few minutes to get up steam, slipping, sliding, and sometimes refusing point-blank to budge until all the men got out in the mud and slush to "giv her a shove," we reached Houston after midnight, tired, cold, hungry, and cross, to find no conveyance at the muddy, inhospitable shed of a depot to carry us to a hotel.

In Houston, Mrs. Ripley might have stayed at the Kelly House, which carried an advertisement in the *Almanac for 1860,* as did the Washington Hotel at Galveston. It is unlikely that the *Almanac* had an ad for the hotel at which she stayed in Beaumont.

The only tavern at that picturesquely located town was less adapted to the accommodation of man than of beast. There was but one guest-chamber, and its only entrance was through a combination of office, bar, smoking, and lounging room, presided over by the landlord, a kindly, hunchbacked dwarf, whose wife, a comely intelligent woman, by the way, was the first "dipper" I ever saw.

Frederick Law Olmsted had, in 1857, reported meeting "some cultivated, agreeable and talented persons" in Austin, but his remembrance of his hotel there was not equally pleasant.

We arrived in a norther, and were shown, at the hotel to which we had been recommended, into an exceedingly dirty room, in which two of us slept with another gentleman, who informed us that it was the best room in the house. The outside door, opening upon the ground, had no latch, and during the night it was blown open by the norther, and after we had made two ineffectual attempts to barricade it, was kept open till morning. . . . When the breakfast-bell rang, we all turned out in haste, though our boots were gone and there was no water.

In 1850 the greatest number of Texans, 40,107 belonged in the age bracket of twenty to thirty years, with 186,797 under forty years of age and only 54,697 over forty. White males of military age, eighteen to forty-five, numbered 92,145. As to sex, even the most unprepossessing unmarried girl scarcely stood a chance to remain an old maid, with an excess of 15,704 males in 1850 and 36,000 in 1860. As Betty Paschal O'Connor expressed it: "There were more men than women in Texas; every woman, pretty or ugly, could marry some sort of man; therefore morality was demanded of her, and after marriage her flirtations were at an end."

Farming or planting was of course the chief industry. Improved farmland totaled 2,650,781 acres. In 1850 some 25,299 men were engaged in agriculture as compared with 7,327 in commerce, trade, and mechanics. The state reported 983 manufacturing establishments employing 3,449 persons in 1860, when the census broke its report on occupations into 187 classes. Only 265 men were classed as planters, but their plantations required 1,254 overseers. There were 51,469 farmers and 6,537 farm laborers. Teachers and music teachers to the number of 1,552 belonged to what the 1850 census had described as "pursuits requiring education." The fine arts were represented with three actors, six dancing masters, forty-five artists, and eight architects. All of the usual occupations were listed, along with four toymen and four catchers of wild horses. While no figures were given for domestic service in 1850, a decade later 3,541 servants were listed.

It should be interesting to compare size of families in 1960 as against those of 1860—perhaps the sizes may be somewhat similar. In 1860 there were 14,359 babies under one year of age. Population was growing, but death certainly came earlier than in this generation, filled with discussions of geriatrics. Barnes F. Lathrop, in his study *Migration into East Texas, 1835–1860*, comments on the near worthlessness of the mortality schedules of 1860 as a basis for vital statistics. It may be a reflection on the scarcity of doctors (1,471 physicians and five surgeons were enumerated) and the general state of medical knowledge, as well as the frontier environment, that "unknown" disease was responsible for 1,212 of a total of 9,377 deaths. Violent death brought an end to 680, of whom 29 were suicides and 121 were the victims of murder or homicide. The chief cause of accidental death was burns or scalds. Next to mysterious "unknown," pneumonia was the grim reaper for 964; typhoid fever took 702, and yellow fever claimed 430. Infantile illnesses were listed for 115, and teething was given as the cause of death of 199. Texas might be hell on women and horses, but the female of the species was hardier than the male, with a death total of 4,265 against 5,122 for the men. Of course there were more men than women. Ten deaths were attributed to insanity. The population schedule listed a total of 125 insane and 201 idiots. Sixty of the insane were recent residents of the State Hospital in Austin, established in 1860. Other eleemosynary institutions were the School for the Deaf, with its 27 pupils out of a total of 121 deaf persons, and the School for the Blind, with 12 pupils out of the 150 sightless citizens of the state. These also were new institutions, the School for the Blind opening in 1856 and that for the deaf in January, 1857.

On the average, each doctor would have had over four hundred patients. Many who listed medicine as a profession combined it with other callings, as did Dr. T. C. Hill, also a druggist, and Dr. N. D. Labadie, who advertised as an importer of drugs, medicine, dye-stuff, and paints. The Texas Medical Association was organized in 1853 to promote the welfare of the profession and to exclude from its ranks "unworthy and unqualified persons." Its membership, which incidentally did not have a second meeting for sixteen years, might not have cared for the advertisement in the *Almanac for 1860* by Dr.

Robert Kelly of Houston, whose card read: "Cures cancers, tumors, etc. and challenges the Medical Faculty to compete with him in his cures." He could not have referred to the faculty of the Texas Medical College, which was chartered in February, 1860, but was not really organized until 1864.

The newspapers and periodicals of the period were filled with notices of patent medicines. The *Almanac* cited Dr. M'Lane's Celebrated Liver Pills and his equally Celebrated Worm Specific or Vermifuge, Dr. Billings's Carminative and Astringent Syrup, Dalley's Magical Pain Extractor for healing burns and scalds, and Dr. Wright's Celebrated Rejuvenating Elixir, recommended for general debility, general irritability, low spirits and "confused ideas"—no doubt the 1860 counterpart for tranquilizers. E. P. Angell of Galveston dispensed homeopathic books and medicines. Texans despairing of adequate care at home might go to New Orleans to Dr. James's Dispensary "for the cure of all private maladies," or to Dr. L. C. Thomas of Southern Medical Hall for surgery.

An interesting—but somewhat confusing—advertisement was that for Vandevee's Schiedam Schnapps, "the only gin in Holland recommended by the Faculty there." This "GUARDIAN OF HEALTH" for the ladies was "more powerful than any vermifuge for the EXPULSION of worms in children of all ages and was recommended for the cure of debility, natural decay, colic, and decline." One begins to compare with Hadacol, but the ad goes on to say that as a drink it "counteracts the evil effects of overindulgence and excess ... is not an INTOXICATING beverage but the safest as well as the most harmless alcoholic drink in existence."

The census lists three professional booksellers, and the *Almanac* carried notices for three bookdealers: Julius Berends of San Antonio, James Burke in Houston, and, in Galveston, Francis D. Allen, who carried magazines, Bibles, lawbooks, valentines priced from five cents to fifteen dollars, and Henderson K. Yoakum's *History of Texas* (strongly bound in sheep at five dollars). Olmsted had found Austin well supplied with a number of drinking and gambling shops but not one bookstore. The druggist, who kept a small stock of books, sold him a copy of *Eagle Pass* for a dollar, the price elsewhere, according to Olmsted, being forty cents. Planters and professional families probably ordered their magazines and general reading material through New Orleans or direct from the East Coast. Whatever the absent soldier bought or read at home, he absorbed all the printed material he could find. John C. West wrote to his sister in Austin from his Confederate camp:

You will observe we have a good deal of time to think while in camp, . . . and some time to read, too. I have read lately, "The Autocrat of the Breakfast Table," "Aurora Leigh," "Davenport Dunn," "Les Miserables" by Victor Hugo, and innumerable articles in magazines, which I have picked up in waste places. I now have on hand "Tasso's Jerusalem Delivered," which belongs to our quartermaster. I have carried a Bible and Milton in my knapsack all the time, so you see we are not absolutely illiterate.

Austin was the capital, but it was still a frontier town. Amelia Barr described the life of the women there as a "joyous, genial existence," and commented on local culture:

In 1856, I knew of only two pianos in the city of Austin, one was in the Governor's mansion, the other belonged to a rich Jewish family called Henricks. I think there were certainly more scattered in the large lonely planter's houses outside the city . . . books were not obvious in private houses; and if there had been any literary want felt, there was wealth enough to have satisfied it.

The advertising section of the *Almanac* reveals that C. W. Yellowby of Parsons Female Seminary at Webberville had bought a piano from Albert Weber in New York. Yellowby liked the piano fine, but had failed to order a piano stool and "such a thing can not be bought here."

When Melinda Rankin reported on Texas in 1850, she deplored the scarcity of teachers and the deficiencies in the textbooks and advocated the choice of the Eclectic Educational Series as a "real service to the cause of education itself." At the time she wrote, there were in the state 360 teachers in 349 schools and 137 teachers in 97 academies, or 497 teachers for 446 institutions, meaning that most of the schools were one-teacher institutions. Other than personal collections of books, there were twelve libraries with a total of 4,230 volumes, the libraries being located in one college, five Sunday schools, three schools, and three public libraries. The enrollment of 7,949 children in school in 1850 meant that one child in five was getting an education. In the years following 1850 a number of factors stimulated interest in schools: a reaction against propaganda taught in the northern schools, the desire of private-school people to keep at home the money that was being spent sending Texas students to other states, the conviction that education in general had been a failure, and the possibility of securing a combination project of building railroads and supporting public schools. The result of the interest was the passage of the school law of 1854, which established the permanent school fund and provided for the organization of common schools. Actually little was done under the law, and of the 124 counties organized in 1861, only twelve filed a school report.

In addition to these common, or "Old Field" schools, by 1860 nine educational associations had been incorporated and 117 educational institutions had been chartered, including 7 universities, 40 academies, 30 colleges, 27 institutes, and 2 seminaries. The girls' schools were prepared to train in deportment and the refinements of life. Despite pretentious names, the work was chiefly elementary. These schools had granted two degrees in 1854, one in 1855, seven in 1856, three in 1857, two in 1858, eight in 1859, and seven in 1860. No degrees were granted in 1861; most of the members of the senior classes were in the army. New Braunfels Academy was the only free public institution. Interestingly enough, it ordered one thousand copies of the catalogue of its library printed in 1860, but the catalogue does not seem to be extant.

Except for those supported by the Masonic Order, the Texas schools were chiefly denominational institutions. In 1850 Texas reported a total of 341 churches with seating accommodations for 63,575 and property valued at $204,930. The Methodists had 176 churches, the Baptists, 82, and the Presbyterians, 45. In that year there were only 13 Roman Catholic churches represented, but their property valuation of approximately $80,000 was the largest. By 1860 the churches had increased to 1,034 in number, with accommodations for 271,000 members and property valued at over a million dollars. Only 758 clergymen were reported, indicating that many rode a circuit to serve a number of charges. Instead of 2 union churches there were 96. The Roman Catholic churches had increased to 33, but their property valuation at $180,900 was surpassed by both Methodists and Baptists and almost equaled by the Protestant Episcopal group, with only 19 churches.

The Methodists might have the greater number of churches, but the Ernest W. Winkler *Check List of Texas Imprints* indicates that the Baptists led in number of publications, probably because of the democratic and decentralized organization of the denomination. For the Methodists there were *Minutes* of the Texas Conference or of the East Texas Conference, and the Baptists published *Minutes* of the Little River, Mount Zion, Sister Grove, and various other associations. The Methodists began publication of their *Christian Advocate* in 1847. The paper changed both name and place of publication and was being printed in Galveston when the war started in 1861. *Proceedings* of the assembly to organize an Episcopal diocese in Texas were published in 1849, and the *Journal* of the first convention of the diocese was printed in 1850. The Presbyterians published the *Minutes* of the Synod of Texas first in 1856.

Miss Rankin had rejoiced in 1850 that "the hallowed influence of the 'Sons of Temperance' had spread its blisful light," and continued: "It is a fact worthy of note, that nothing is done imperfectly in Texas; if an object receives attention at all, the people enter into the spirit of it with enthusiastic devotion." The LaGrange Division of the Sons of Temperance printed its constitution and bylaws in 1849. In a similar field of publication were sermons (often eulogistic obituaries), doctrinal expositions, Masonic speeches, or addresses to urge Christian Education.

Closely related to denominational publications were those distributed by the educational institutions, particularly the church schools. Samuel McKinney's address at the laying of the cornerstone of Austin College was printed at Huntsville in 1851. The college's first catalogue appeared in 1854; the 1860 catalogue included the address at the inauguration of President Rufus W. Bailey in 1859. F. B. Sexton's address on "Human Progress," delivered before the literary societies of the college, was printed in 1858.

Baylor University was established during the days of the Republic, but its first catalogue was not printed until 1852, after which separate catalogues were issued for the male and female departments. Baylor's literary societies included the Erosophian and Philomathesian, as indicated by the publication of Robert H. Taliaferro's oration before those groups in 1854. Rutersville College, earliest institution of higher learning in the state, published its first catalogue in 1840. By 1858 the school was designated as the Texas Monumental and Military Institute and was involved with the Texas Conference of the Methodist church over a claim to the college lots and buildings.

Winkler's introduction to the *Check List*, from which these items have been gleaned, gives a history of printing in Texas. Between 1845 and 1861, printing establishments spread from eighteen to forty-one separate villages and towns. Job printing was done chiefly in San Antonio, Anderson, Houston, Galveston, and Austin. Almost one-third of the imprints listed were from Austin, which had a practical monopoly of public printing. The *Civilian* office at Galveston was the best-equipped plant in the state, but the *State-Gazette* and the *Southern Intelligencer*, both in Austin, competed in bidding for the public printing contracts. Government documents were the most numerous class of publication. The Baptists issued over one hundred titles in the fifteen-year period; the Freemasons were third in number of titles issued. Most of the printing was done on hand presses. The Galveston *News* had a power press in 1852, but it was a Hoe cylinder press operated by "equine and colored" power. The *Civilian* had a steam press by 1857, the Galveston *News* by 1859. The San Antonio *Herald* secured a steam engine in 1860 and combined operating its printing press and a grist mill. When big-volume printing was necessary, the Texas presses were not adequate. Albert Hanford's *Texas State Register* for 1856 was printed in New York. Willard Richardson's *Texas Almanac for 1861*, both editions, was set in type in Galveston but had to be stereotyped in New York.

The 1860 census shows that the number of newspapers and periodicals in Texas had increased from thirty-four, with a circulation of 6,737 in 1850, to a total of seventy-one in 1860. These included three daily papers, three triweekly, and sixty-five weekly papers, the last with a circulation of 90,615. In addition, there were nine weekly and three monthly literary magazines and four religious publications. Winkler's imprint list totals 205 for the year 1860. The list shows that Texans belonged—other than to the church, the Democratic party, the Masons, the Odd Fellows, and the Sons of Temperance—to such organizations as the Agricultural, Horticultural, and Mechanical Society of Collin County, the Cat Springs Agricultural Society, the Dallas County Agricultural and Mechanical Association, or the Smith County Agricultural and Mechanical Society. For entertainment, the Texan might attend dramatic productions or a program by the Swiss Bell Ringers at Buaas's Hall in Austin, go to a cotillion party at the Menger Hotel in San Antonio, or participate in a barbecue at Belton if he planned to support John C. Breckinridge and Joseph Lane.

Because of the tense political situation in 1860, many of the imprints of that year reflect the bitter differences of opinion between the regular Democrats and the Union Democrats, who supported Governor Sam Houston, who was nominated for the presidency of the United States at a mass meeting at the San Jacinto battleground on April 21, 1860. There were calls for convention, announcements from the Union Executive Committee that they were "for the government so long as the Constitution is maintained," requests that the governor state his position, and a plea from Dallas County citizens that the governor convene the legislature so that it might determine Texas's course in relation to the result of the presidential election—this after Abraham Lincoln's victory in November, 1860. So, the imprints of the year reveal the temper of the times. One Texas soldier, writing almost a half century later, reminisced:

The year 1860, my first in Texas, was a memorable one in several respects, not only to the newcomers but to the oldest inhabitants. The severest drought ever known in eastern Texas prevailed until after the middle of August. It was the hottest summer ever known in Texas, the temperature in July running up to 112 degrees in the shade. It was a Presidential election year, and political excitement was intense. . . . The excitement, apprehension, unrest, and vague fear of unseen danger pervading the minds of the people of Texas cannot be understood by persons who were not in the State at that time.

Amelia Barr depicted the friction generated in the summer heat of 1860:

They were furious with the United States Government's interference with their state's social and domestic arrangements. They would not admit its right to do so, and were as mad as their own prairie bulls, when compulsion was named. I heard arguments like these, both from men and women constantly; they talked of nothing else, and the last social gathering at my house was like a political arena. . . . There were bitter disputes wherever men were congregated, and domestic quarrels on every hearthstone, while feminine friendships melted away in the heat of passionate arguments so well seasoned with personalities. There were now three distinct parties: one for remaining in the Union; a second which demanded a Southern Confederacy, and a third which wished Texas to resume her independence and to fly the *Lone Star* flag again. It was a quarrel with three sides, and the women universally entered into it, with so much temper, that I could not help thinking they had all exercised too much long suffering in the past, and were now glad of a lawful opportunity to be a little ill-natured.

Amelia Barr was an Englishwoman who lived in Austin from 1856 to 1866. Less sympathetic than her depiction of Texans in 1860 is that of an Ohio school teacher named George Adams Fisher, who lived in Collin and Denton counties, where more recent settlers from the North expressed considerable Union sentiment. Fisher identified four classes of Texans: (1) the slaveholding aristocracy, gentlemanly in manner and honorable in dealings, but "unscrupulous champions of human bondage"; (2) a non-slaveholding class of respectable citizens—mostly northern men of "energy, enterprise, and intelligence"; (3) poor whites from the southern states, "an ignorant and degraded herd," few of whom could read or write and all the slaves of prejudice; and (4) scoundrels and blacklegs, "sharpers—men without principle and morality." Classes (1) and (4), he said, were the ones who exercised "a controlling influence over the ignorant white, who, for a dram of whiskey, would vote for the devil." Fisher attributed mortality in the Confederate army to the delicacy of young men unused to labor, even though he described Texans in the cavalry as among the best horsemen in the world.

Olmsted's *Journey through Texas* and other travel books left the impression that the mass of southerners were "poor whites" and that the planters were often equally crude and ignorant. Cadwell W. Raines's opinion of Olmsted's work—that there was "no better book yet written of travels in Texas; and by an intelligent student of our industrial system"—is in contrast with an article called "Texas" in *De Bow's Review* of August, 1857. The latter was a caustic review of Olmsted, who, according to the reviewer, found the opportunity "too tempting to be resisted to revile and abuse the men and the society whose open hospitality he undoubtedly enjoyed." What of the opinion of other travelers? En route to California in 1857, John C. Reid wrote of San Antonians:

I had no other opportunity of judging of the people than that afforded during the few hours of the middle of that day—hence in passing upon them, must suggest that the evidence induced in the belief that they were intelligent, patriotic, and as good looking as any assemblage on a like occasion, that I have witnessed.

Charles C. Nott of the 176th New York Volunteers, who was a prisoner at Camp Ford at Tyler during the war, classed the Texans in general as a "simple, half-educated people," but admitted his confusion about so-called wild Texans because his guards "did not drink; they did not swear; they did not gamble. They were watchful of us, but did everything kindly and with a willingness that greatly lessened our feeling of dependence." A. H. J. Duganne, another prisoner, was interested in the nonslaveholding laboring southerners who became the bulk of the rebel armies. He asked one such lad why he did not make his way to the Union lines. The boy answered that he never had a chance to get near the Feds for "They were always running away from us Texas boys." Duganne had to admit that it was no marvel that "those roughnatured, courageous men . . . should become vain and self-glorious concerning their invincibility."

Charles Anderson, resident of San Antonio in 1860, described the Knights of the Golden Circle as "mostly mere villainous desperadoes," chiefly responsible for disunion, and next to them in responsibility he blamed the Methodist Episcopal Church, South, which he described as being composed of the only "numerous, honest influential class of men in Texas, which did favor secession." R. W. Johnson of the United States army drew a contrast between the lawlessness he observed on the Texas frontier and the good order of the settled portion of the state, where the people were "educated, refined, and law abiding." Johnson was impressed by the fact that "every Northern officer married to a Southern wife joined in the rebellion against the United States, and every Southern officer whose wife was from the North remained loyal to the government." There is no exact measurement for the weight of the attitude of the Texas woman in demanding that her man live up to the speeches she made about him. There was no dearth of speeches as he left for the battle front in 1861, usually with a special flag made for his regiment. Miss Sallie O. Smith presented a banner to the Walter P. Lane Rangers in Marshall, and Miss Ida DeMorse of Clarksville presented a Bonnie Blue Flag to the troops there. Both gave reviews of all Texas history in their effusive speeches, and Miss DeMorse admonished:

You have a character to sustain, and a reputation to support—a McCulloch, a Travis, a Terry, and a host of God-like dead, whose actions we expect you to imitate, whose names you must never sully.

Texas in 1860 was a fast-growing, exuberant, young, hardy state. Its population had almost tripled in the preceding decade. The great mass of the population had originated in the Old South, and when the break came in 1861, the Texans' sentiment of states' rights conformed with the pattern of their ancestors.

Long before 1860 there was a Texas tradition of intense local loyalty, rugged individualism, pride in size, a history of independence, and a fearless fighting spirit. Not all Texans, not nearly all, were southern cavalier gentlemen; neither were all of them crude backwoodsmen or ruffians. They were the result of a frontier environment and of local legend born of battling Comanches, Mexicans, and variable temperatures, which reacted on pioneer American characteristics inherent within the people who composed the population.

Texas Under the Secessionists

STEPHEN B. OATES[*]

Following the election of Abraham Lincoln as president of the United States in 1860, Texas, along with her sister slave states of the Old South, withdrew from the Union and joined the newly formed Confederate States of America. For many Texans the decision to leave the Union was painful. Sam Houston, the old hero of San Jacinto who was serving as governor of the state, was bitterly opposed to secession. Houston refused to take the oath of allegiance to the Confederacy and was removed from office by the Texas secession convention.

In the essay that follows, Stephen B. Oates, professor of history at the University of Massachusetts and author of several major works on the Civil War period, describes Texas's role in the Civil War. Because of its length, only an abridged version of Oates's article has been included in this collection.

Readers seeking more information on the Civil War in Texas and the Southwest should see Oates's CONFEDERATE CAVALRY WEST OF THE RIVER (Austin, 1961), Harry M. Henderson, TEXAS IN THE CONFEDERACY (San Antonio, 1955), Alwyn Barr, "Texas Coastal Defense, 1861–1865," SOUTHWESTERN HISTORICAL QUARTERLY, LXV (July, 1961), and L. Tuffly Ellis, "Maritime Commerce on the Far Western Gulf, 1861–1865," IBID., LXXVII (October, 1973).

*Stephen B. Oates, "Texas Under the Secessionists," Southwestern Historical Quarterly, LXVII (October, 1963), 167–212.

Across the United States that eventful November telegraph wires carried the crucial news: on November 6, 1860, Abraham Lincoln, running on the Republican party ticket, had been elected president by a largely sectional vote. South Carolina, long known as "that hotbed of agitation and nullification," cried out that the Federal government, controlled by northern Republicans, would destroy southern institutions. On December 20, South Carolina adopted an ordinance of secession, imploring the other southern states to do the same. As the winter days wore on, Alabama, Mississippi, and Florida also passed secession ordinances. Georgia and Louisiana soon joined them. The signs were ominous, and an anxious nation turned to Texas, the Lone Star State.

Linked to the slaveholding South by sentiment and belief, Texans were united in opposition to Lincoln and his "Black Republicans." A few days after his election, the Lone Star flag was flying over a number of Texas cities. Fervid political leaders were clamoring for secession. Austin, especially, was a scene of feverish activity, as groups of secessionists marched up and down Congress Avenue, waving torches and carrying signs condemning Lincoln and his "abolitionist" government. The secessionists, led by Oran M. Roberts, Clement R. Johns, George Flournoy, and John S. ("Rip") Ford, broke up small Unionist meetings and denounced anyone who spoke for moderation. "Me and Old Rip had like to got to fighting the other night," Unionist Aaron Burleson told his cousin on November 19, "and dam him I will whip him if [he] does attempt to stop me from speaking my sentiments at any place or time in these United States God dam him."

"Damn the Union and Abraham Lincoln," chanted hundreds at a secession rally. On the platform Roberts and John A. Green spoke in favor of another Texas Republic, followed by others advocating a similar course. But over in the Capitol, Governor Sam Houston, in the face of statewide sentiment for secession, still refused to call a convention to consider it, still argued that as loyal Americans who believed in the democratic process, they must all submit to Lincoln's victory at the polls. So secessionists Roberts, Ford, Flournoy, and William P. Rogers, ignoring law and constitution, issued their own call for a convention to assemble at Austin on January 28, 1861. Delegates were to be chosen in a special election on January 8.

When word came that citizens in other towns across the state were also holding mass demonstrations by torchlight, Roberts, Ford, and friends planned a large parade in Austin for January 5. At midmorning it moved off from the Capitol, with parade marshal Rip Ford in front on a white stallion, followed by a blaring brass band, then a weaving line of carriages full of ladies who waved Lone Star flags, and finally a number of yipping political leaders and businessmen on horseback. Down Congress Avenue went the blatant demonstrators, swinging around the corner of Eighth Street and stopping at last at the intersection of Eighth and Colorado. There, while everyone shouted as loud as they could for a full ten minutes, a color guard ran the Lone Star flag up a 130-foot flagpole especially erected for the occasion.

Through the next three weeks some 174 delegates from most of the state's representative districts arrived in Austin in carriages and on horseback. They too joined in the almost interminable demonstrations until, on the prescribed day of January 28, they assembled in the Representative Hall in the capitol. One of their leaders recalling them take their seats wrote in later years that "lawyers of distinction, military men, farmers, merchants, physicians, preachers, were there" and were "a remarkable selection of men." The first business of the day was to elect a president. As men stood up to nominate their favorites, members of the legislature who were not delegates and a crowd of "interested spectators" gathered in the galleries. Soon they heard someone announce that Judge Oran M. Roberts, wise, methodical in mind and in manner, had been elected president, and "quick as an electric flash" the crowd cheered "triumphant, defiant, simultaneous," doing it "again and again with reverberations that filled the whole house."

When the shouting stopped at last, the delegates got quickly down to business. Through that afternoon and those of January 29 and 30 they discussed the constitutionality of secession, justifying it by an old political philosophy—the compact theory of government, better known in 1861 as states' rights. According to this theory, the United States Constitution was a compact among free, sovereign, independent states that had originally covenanted together of their own free will and in the same manner could dissolve that union whenever the central government tried to destroy a state's independence and ancestral institutions.

On February 1, the delegates, by a vote of 166 to 8, adopted a secession ordinance declaring that Texas "is a separate Sovereign State; and that her citizens and people are absolved from all allegiances to the United States or the government thereof." The convention submitted the ordinance to the voters, who would ratify it in a special election on February 23, and then proceeded to draw up a declaration of causes showing why Texas was impelled to secede. The central government, the Texans insisted, had violated the original compact of union in a number of ways. Chief among them was the fact that the government had failed miserably to provide adequate protection for settlers living on the Texas frontier. Furthermore, "the recent developments in Federal affairs"—the underground railroad, John Brown's raid on Harpers Ferry, the rise of abolitionism, to name a few—

make it evident that the power of the Federal government is sought to be made a weapon with which to strike down the interests and prosperity of the people of Texas and her sister slave-holding States, instead of permitting it to be, as was intended, our shield against outrage and aggression.

How lamentable, the Texans cried, that the North was so hostile to the "Southern States and their beneficent and patriarchal system of African slavery." How unnatural that the North should proclaim "the debasing doctrine of the equality of all men, irrespective of race or color—a doctrine at war with nature, in opposition to the experience of mankind, and in violation of the plainest revelations of the Divine Law." Ignoring the passion for equality that had been a moving force in the founding of the nation, the Texas delegates justified their pretext for disunion in self-righteous and then in pious terms:

We hold as undeniable truths that the governments of the various States, and of the confederacy itself, were established exclusively by the white race, for themselves and their posterity; that the African race had no agency in their establishment; that they were rightfully held and regarded as an inferior and dependent race, and in that condition only could their existence in this country be rendered beneficial or tolerable.

That in this free government *all white men are and of right ought to be entitled to equal civil and political rights;* that the servitude of the African race, as existing in these States, is mutually beneficial to both bond and free, and is abundantly authorized and justified by the experience of mankind, and the revealed will of the Almighty Creator, as recognized by all Christian nations; while the destruction of the existing relations between the two races, as advocated by our sectional enemies, would bring inevitable calamities upon both and desolation upon the fifteen slaveholding States.

The convention adjourned on February 4 to await the vote. On election day the ordinance passed by an impressive margin, 46,129 to 14,697, and the convention reassembled on March 2 to announce the returns and to pass an ordinance uniting Texas to the newly formed Confederate States of America.

In almost every town across the state Texans cheered and danced in the streets; militia units paraded noisily; cannon boomed. The sovereign state of Texas was once again free of tyranny and everywhere there was a feeling of buoyant optimism. Few thought violence would come. The Republicans surely would not risk a fight with the "blood-and-thunder men of the South." Most felt that northerners were cowards anyway; and one man suggested facetiously that southerners should "set out an immense trotline, bait the fish hooks with postage stamps, and 'catch all the Yankees.' " To Texans that stormy winter, war was distant, war was unreal.

While citizens were rejoicing, the reassembled convention was busily setting up the political machinery for Confederate Texas. On March 14, the delegates adopted an ordinance maintaining the present state government, whose officials, to stay in office, must declare their allegiance to the Confederacy. Governor Houston, who believed secession was treason, refused to take the oath. A Presbyterian minister, present at the convention, recalled that

the officer of the gathering up stairs summoned the old man three times to come forward and take the oath of allegiance.... I remember as yesterday the call thrice repeated—'Sam Houston! Sam Houston! Sam Houston!' but the man sat silent, immovable, in his chair below, whittling steadily on.

Still, because he loved Texas "too well to bring civil strife and bloodshed upon her," Houston rejected President Lincoln's proposal to help him oppose the secessionists with force and withdrew from his office peacefully. The convention promptly gave Lieutenant Governor Edward Clark the governorship; and Houston, humiliated and embittered, retired to his farm near Huntsville, remaining loyal to Texas but not to the Confederacy until his death on July 26, 1863.

Most of the other state officers took the oath; the convention, its work done, then adjourned *sine die* on March 26; and Texans moved with alacrity into what they considered a new experiment in nationhood. The legislature met briefly to designate an election for Confederate congressmen and to adopt constitutional amendments—one gave Texas the right to secede, the others related to "internal matters"—and then adjourned so that its members could volunteer in "The Army of Texas." After that, political matters "sank into comparative insignificance" as Texas leaders vied with one another to get military commands. There were no conventions, no political parties except the Democratic, and no choice in elections between issues or ideologies. Men like Francis R. Lubbock and Pendleton Murrah, the war governors after Clark, defeated the political opponents mainly because they were more convincing in their promises to prosecute the war with vigor and dedication. From April, 1861, on, said Judge Roberts, who himself took the field at the head of an infantry regiment, "both the people and the government" absorbed themselves "in measures relating to military operations."

The agency in charge of such operations was a fifteen-man Committee of Public Safety, whose members all had military experience. The secession convention had set it up back on January 30 to raise a state army with which to fight the Federals and to ensure the safety of citizens until the Confederate army should become effective in Texas. The committee had then named the McCulloch brothers, Benjamin and Henry E., and John S. Ford colonels of cavalry in the Army of Texas. They had orders to recruit volunteer cavalry regiments and to capture all Union forts and munitions of war for the state.

On the night of February 15, Ben McCulloch, a celebrated Texas Ranger who had led the charge on the Bishop's Palace at Monterrey during the Mexican War, secretly assembled a thousand volunteers on Cibolo Creek near San Antonio. Their objective was the historic Alamo, then a United States fort under the command of General David E. Twiggs. The next day at dawn, Colonel McCulloch, wearing a striking "uniform" of black velvet, led his Texans into town. They occupied the roofs of buildings surrounding the Alamo and, through their gun sights, drew beads on army sentries barely visible on the distant ramparts. Inside the Alamo, the soldiers who saw the Texans' blurred figures decided that to fight them was hopeless and surrendered to McCulloch without a shot having been fired.

The Texans were ecstatic. At the Grand Plaza later that day they celebrated their victory—for the South it was the first victory west of the Mississippi, won some two months before Fort Sumter and the opening of the Civil War. The celebration soon became a dazzling fiesta in which the Texans drank free liquor and ate free food—gifts from happy civilians who exactly one week later would vote in favor of secession—and danced with "beautiful señoras" to guitar and song of the cabellero. The volunteers regrouped later in the evening to cheer and wave their rifles overhead as their commander and other distinguished men gave talks about the glory of Texas and the South.

When official agents of the state took charge of the Alamo on February 19, the volunteers whose services were no longer needed disbanded and went home in groups and individually. Many of them, including Ben McCulloch, would join the Confederate army in the months that followed.

The next day, February 20, Henry E. McCulloch's regiment assembled in the Alamo City and prepared to ride north. Unlike his dashing brother, Henry was a taciturn, unassuming man, but he was a reliable cavalry officer and quite popular with his troops. That evening, as civilians again gathered in the streets to watch, Henry McCulloch's riders trotted through town and headed across mesquite country toward the Red River. Through the next month the outfit captured Camp Colorado, Fort Chadbourne, Camp Cooper, and Fort Belknap. Colonel McCulloch soon got a Confederate commission and rode back to San Antonio to recruit additional companies for his cavalry regiment. On April 15, 1861, ten full companies from Bexar, Travis, Gonzales, and surrounding counties organized as the First McCulloch Texas Mounted Rifles—the first military outfit from Texas to enter the Confederate army.

While Henry McCulloch worked in San Antonio, Rip Ford rode around the Houston area signing up recruits. On February 20, some five hundred eager volunteers reported for duty at Ford's Houston headquarters. The next day the colonel marched them over to Galveston, where they boarded the schooner *Shark* and the steamer *General Rusk* and sailed down the coast to an amphibious landing at Brazos Island, a United States stronghold a few miles up the coast from Brownsville. The island's twelve defenders surrendered almost at once. After locking these in the steamer's brig, the Texans beat the brush over the island looking for men who might have fled the stockade. Then the horsemen reassembled on the parade grounds to hear Colonel Ford warn them not to shoot an enemy soldier except in self defense, for the colonel had orders to avoid violence if at all possible. The Texans agreed, but grudgingly. They stood there in silence as a color guard ran the Lone Star flag up the pole while cannon boomed.

On February 22, Ford and his staff went onto the mainland for a talk with the Union commander at Fort Brown. The talk consumed weeks; winter turned to spring; back on Brazos Island the Texans, spoiling for a fight, began taking pot shots at flying brids or thrown rocks and sticks. On March 4, they sent Colonel Ford an angry note. That morning, the note said, the Texans had heard "the explosion of guns" in the direction of Fort Brown. Later they learned that "this noise" was nothing less than a Federal salute honoring Lincoln's inauguration. The Texans were outraged, the note continued, and were going down to Fort Brown "and avenge the insult offered to Texas." Ford knew the temperament of his volunteers well enough to believe them. He told the Federal commander what was in the air; the two officers quite soon reached an understanding; and Rip Ford on March 20 publicly announced the capture of all United States forts from Brownsville out to El Paso. Through the next month his hard-boiled Texans stood guard in the lower Rio Grande country as United States troops boarded their ships and sailed away to less hostile ports. On April 18, Ford lined his men up in Fort Brown and congratulated them for their bloodless victory and talked eloquently about their new nation born not of war, but of peace and a vision of destiny. That afternoon the news of Fort Sumter arrived.

The Texans were happy about it. At last they should shoot and shoot to kill. After they were sworn into Confederate service as the Second Texas Cavalry, they occupied the outposts along the Great River. During the next two years they spent most of their time in the saddle, fighting small bands of Union cavalry, renegade Comanches, and Mexican outlaws led by Colonel Ford's old enemy, Juan ("Cheno") Cortina, whose army of bandits had terrorized the border country in the so-called Cortina War back in 1859 and 1860. The cavalry chased Cortina up and down Webb County, fought several of his detachments in wild running battles, and finally drove the Mexicans across the border. Except for scattered Comanche raids, the river people then enjoyed a brief period of peace.

While his cavalry patrolled the border, Colonel Ford himself remained in Brownsville. Since Federal troops had gone, the town was almost without law and order. Gunmen and drunks roamed the streets and brawled in saloons. Controlling these demanded a great deal of the commanding officer's time and patience. The military police who soon garrisoned the town under Ford's orders were not altogether successful, for in 1863 Arthur Fremantle found Brownsville still "the rowdiest town of Texas, which was the most lawless state in the Confederacy." In Brownsville "the shooting-down and stringing-up systems are much in vogue."

Colonel Ford did all he could to maintain order in his district and to help the Confederacy. In December, 1861, he supervised the construction of coastal defenses in the Brownsville area and in the spring of 1862 negotiated a trade agreement with the Mexicans. This agreement was extremely important to Confederate armies, since Matamoros furnished a medium for Confederate-European trade as well as a good market for the sale of cotton and the acquisition of arms and war matériel. If it had not been for Ford's ability to deal with the Mexicans and for the cavalry patrols he detailed to guard the wagon trains that rolled back and forth across the border, the Confederate Trans-Mississippi Department might have collapsed early in the war. Except for a brief tour of duty as state conscript commander, Colonel Ford would continue to do good service along the river until the end.

So far almost all the Texas outfits raised had been cavalry. Back in April 1861, the War Department called on the state to furnish 8,000 infantry for Confederate armies fighting in Kentucky and Virginia. Governor Clark wrote back that he did not see how he could possibly get so many infantry but that he would try. He obtained commissions for prominent citizens and sent them into counties throughout the state to raise companies of foot soldiers. The recruiters soon found that Texans, well known for their peerless horsemanship, would have little to do with the infantry because they thought it unromantic and rather inglorious. Nearly every man, it seemed, wanted to join the cavalry and make a lasting impression on relatives and young ladies by riding off to war on horseback to the tune of "The Girl I Left Behind Me."

Governor Clark knew then that he had to do something and soon, lest the Richmond government reprimand him for failing to send along his quota of infantry. After much thought he got a bright idea. He directed that camps of instruction be set up around the state to show the men that infantry service was every bit as glorious as that of the cavalry. The results were twofold: one was that by the end of 1861 Clark's recruiters, with the help of infantry instructors, had raised seven regiments and four battalions of foot soldiers, a total of about 7,100 men; the other was that rivalry between the two branches of the service became rather severe if not downright vicious. Cavalry and infantry recruiters vied with one another to get volunteers; generals of the respective branches quarreled and quarreled over which one was the more effective in combat; and the men themselves, wherever they met, fell to name calling and fistfighting. "Wagon dogs!" the cavalry would growl, with an air of supreme condescension. "Webfeet!" "Mud sloggers!" At that the infantry would reply, with equal malice: "There goes the buttermilk cavalry." "A hundred dollars rward for just *one* dead cavalryman." "All those fellows do is to find Yankees for us to kill."

In terms of numbers, the cavalry of course came out the better in this rivalry. During the four years of war some 58,000 Texans joined the cavalry (though many of them were dismounted after 1862) as compared to roughly 30,000 volunteers and draftees in the infantry and artillery. This was to be expected, for Texans had, after all, had a long and intimate companionship with the horse, with the six-shooter and carbine. And that these horsemen should form the backbone of the Confederate cavalry in the Trans-Mississippi was also to be expected. They were splendid, if undisciplined, horsemen, whose performances as independent raiding forces, as scouts and reconnaissance patrols for the main army, and occasionally as foot soldiers alongside the regular infantry, played a large part in keeping the Trans-Mississippi Department Confederate to the last.

Texas also produced a number of highly regarded officers and outfits for Confederate armies fighting east of the Mississippi River. Perhaps the best-known officers who saw action outside the Trans-Mississippi were General Albert Sidney Johnston, who fell at Shiloh, General John B. Hood, and Colonel Benjamin Franklin Terry. Hood and Terry commanded Texas outfits that, whether on horse or on foot, fought with such valor that they became easily the most celebrated organizations from the state.

Terry organized his regiment of rangers in September, 1861, in Houston. The personnel of the outfit were "of the very highest," comprising sons of prominent families, college students, merchants, lawyers, bankers, farmers, and cowboys, expert with lariat and six-shooter. Wherever they went, these Texans impressed people by their determination "to get into the war in a crack cavalry regiment."

No one was more impressed than peaceful citizens of Houston. While waiting there for the order to ride, the rangers "kept the town in a continued bustle with their daring feats of horsemanship." To "show what they could do," the men formed in squads and rode at a maddening gallop down the streets, jumping off and back on their horses and picking sticks and pieces of clothing off the ground. This apparently was not exciting enough for several men, so they rounded up some wild stallions and, howling and firing their pistols in the air, proceeded to break them in the middle of town—much to the exasperation of storekeepers who feared for their lives and property. With all this showmanship, a newspaperman decided that the rangers, harened from encounters with "the stealthy panther and more savage Mexican hog, in our forests," would be the "pride of Texas" and would make "the enemy beware" when they "get on their track." And the rangers became the pride of Texas as they fought without regard for death and lost their commander and two-thirds of their numbers in engagements covering half a dozen states east of the Mississippi.

Like the rangers, Hood's Texas Brigade was a hard-fighting organization, composed of the First, Fourth, and Fifth Texas Infantry regiments. The brigade commander, John B. Hood, became the ranking Texan in the Confederate army and led the Army of Tennessee toward the end of the war. Unfortunately for the Confederates, he led that army to near destruction at Nashville, which earned him a song:

> You may talk about your Beauregard
> And sing of General Lee
> But the gallant Hood of Texas
> Played hell in Tennessee.

Confederates from other states thought him indecisive, but Texans admired the man in no uncertain terms and called him one of their own, though he was a Kentuckian by birth. He came to Texas as a young man, then went on to West Point, graduating in 1853. He served for a time in Missouri and California, then returned to Texas as a captain in the Second United States Cavalry. He remained in that capacity until war broke out, when he resigned to enter the Confederate service. Good fighting earned him a colonel's commission and his own command—the Fourth Texas Infantry Regiment. He soon rose to the rank of brigadier general in charge of the Texas Brigade, which became a part of James Longstreet's Corps of the Army of Northern Virginia. From then until the end of the war Hood had nothing but bad luck. At Gettysburg he received a bad wound which permanently disabled his left arm; later at Chickamauga, he lost his left leg. After the stump healed, he returned to active duty, but for a time he was so weak that he had to be strapped to the saddle. Then came that lamentable defeat in the battle of Nashville in December, 1864, which severely damaged his reputation and caused him to resign from the army.

The Texans who followed Hood in distant theaters of war were, like their fellow Confederates, rather short on military formality. When they had to attend parades, they usually displayed unmilitary notions. For example, in June, 1863, when Robert E. Lee's army gathered near Culpeper Courthouse in Virginia, James E. B. ("Jeb") Stuart's cavalry corps put on a review for the commanding general and assembled guests, including Hood's Texans. As the cavalry rode past, sabers drawn, eyes right, making a big impression on the top brass, the Texans looked on with scorn and one muttered: "Wouldn't we clean 'em out if old Hood would let us loose on 'em?" Bellicose to a man, these Texans saw some of the heaviest fighting in the war and sustained such frightful casualties that, when they surrendered, their brigade had only about 557 men left out of some 4,480 initial recruits and replacements.

Once formed, Texas outfits never knew when or where they would get their meals and changes of clothing. The Richmond government could barely supply its armies in Virginia, much less those in the far-off Trans-Mississippi region; the Texas state government was equally incompetent; and the troops finally had to subsist on whatever they could get, good or bad, if they could get anything. If they had money, they bought what they needed in nearby towns; if they had no money, they stole cows, pigs, chickens, clothing, and books to read at night by firelight. Probably their largest source of quartermaster stores was the innumerable women's committees that began to be formed around the state almost concurrently with the raising of the first regiments. These committees, or ladies aid societies, collected not only blankets, socks, shoes, hats, pants, and shirts, but also beef, ham, flour, salt, coffee, tea, desiccated vegetables, and candles and sent them to their men at the fighting fronts. It was not until late 1863 that a quartermaster department, established in the Trans-Mississippi the year before, began to do even a fair job of supplying the troops, and even then the "uniforms" it gave out varied impossibly in color and design. Arthur Fremantle, who visited with Texas troops stationed on the lower Rio Grande, found that "their dress consisted simply of flannel shirts, very ancient trousers, jack boots with enormous spurs, and black felt hats ornamented with the 'Lone Star of Texas.' They looked rough and dirty...." Those enormous spurs in the end attracted more attention than the rest of the Texans' motley outfits. "The masses of them wore spurs on their heels," Thomas North noted,

generally the immense wheel-spur, and though they were not born with them on, yet they might as well have been, for they not only rode in them, but walked in them, ate in them, and slept in them. Their clanking as they walked was like a man in chains. They wore belts around the waist, suspended one or two revolvers and a bowie knife; were experts in the saddle, had a reckless dare-devil look and were always ready for whisky and a big chew of tobacco, and the hand-writing of passion and appetite was all over them.

For armament, Texas soldiers had, as Thomas North suggested, revolvers, bowie knives, muskets, shotguns, and carbines, either brought from home, purchased, stolen from peaceful civilians, or captured from the enemy. The musket was the main infantry weapon; the revolver was the preferred arm for the cavalry; yet neither of these scared the enemy like those pernicious bowie knives carried by all Texas soldiers. Often three feet in length, these weapons, according to a trooper in the Third Texas Cavalry, were "heavy enough to cleave the skull of a mailed knight through helmet and all." Another man felt that the awesome appearance of the knives "might have made a Malay's blood run cold." Shotguns were popular short-range weapons for both infantry and cavalry. As a cavalryman put it, one did not have to aim with a shotgun; and one had, moreoever, a good chance of killing two, perhaps three, Yankees in a single blast.

Though the troops themselves furnished most of their arms, government and private firms did try to help. In May, 1862, a privately-owned factory at Tyler started making a .54 and .57 caliber rifle variously called the "Texas Rifle," the "Austrian Rifle," and the "Enfield Rifle." The government bought the factory in the fall of 1863 and ran it until 1865. Another private concern—Tucker, Sherrod, and Co. of Lancaster—made a .44 caliber revolver called the "Tucker-Sherrod Colt Dragoon." It appeared "in every respect quite equal to the famous Colt's six shooter, of which it is an exact copy, with the exception of an extra sight on the barrel which we think is a decided improvement." The makers of this "remarkable" six'shooter intended it to be used exclusively in Texas, "as it is notorious how deficient we are in arms for home defense."

The Texas government had its own plans and made efforts to manufacture arms for its troops wherever they were fighting. A government-owned arsenal at San Antonio produced small numbers of rifles, carbines, and revolvers. The Texas Military Board, set up by Governor Francis R. Lubbock to purchase military supplies, had another arsenal built at Austin, which made a few cannon. Powder and cap and cartridge for these weapons came from government factories at Austin and in Bexar County.

Yet, because so many men were away in the army, these factories could find almost no one except a few women and children to work in them and so could scarcely fill the requisitions they received. Texas governors had therefore to call on the Confederate Ordnance Bureau for help; Governor Lubbock on November 13, 1862, even asked for old guns that armies east of the Mississippi had discarded, if nothing else could be done.

But nothing could be done, nothing at all. The Ordnance Bureau had no guns for Texas; the state government itself soon had no money left to buy or make enough to matter; and once again the men had to furnish everything themselves. By 1864, they had such difficulty in obtaining weapons, horses, food, and other necessities that they resorted more than ever before to stealing them from nearby farms. The farmers of course complained angrily to the governor, describing vividly how "rough, uncivil" army bands without "responsible officers" ransacked their homes, took their flintlocks and mules and forage and rode away swearing and shouting insults. To placate the citizens the governor did what he could: he asked officers to punish any offender they caught, then called on all Texas soldiers to respect civilians' rights and to stand by the laws of the land. Yet, the pillaging only increased, for the soldiers were hungry and poorly clad and poorly armed. It became so rampant during the last winter of hostilities that Texas citizens swore they feared their own troops even more than they did the enemy.

This disposition among Texas troops to steal badly needed supplies was inherent in their character, for they were not—nor had they ever been in their lives—soldiers in the true sense of the term. They were frontiersmen who had a granitelike individualism, an open disregard for discipline, and a powerful tendency to do as they pleased, especially in times of severe privation. Like almost every Texan who had ever taken up his rifle to fight for his land and his beliefs, Texas Confederates never adjusted to the strict enforcement of orders, the gap between officers and men, the heel clicking and spit and polish so characteristic of the professional military. According to Major General Richard Taylor, Texans "had no more conception of military gradations than of the celestial hierarchy of the poets."

Because of their aversion to "military gradations," because they would respect an officer only when he proved a better fighter than the men he led, Texans took a long, critical, and often disapproving look at the officers sent across the Sabine River to command the district of Texas. They grew to like Earl Van Dorn, who was there from April to September 4, 1861, because Van Dorn was a splendid horseman, an enviable fistfighter, and a good shot with a six-shooter. Tall, wiry and stern of voice, he knew no fear, which made him irresistably appealing to the Texans. Besides, he respected their individualistic nature. Here was the kind of leader they would follow to their deaths. But the War Department, realizing his potential, promoted him to brigadier general with a field command in Virginia and later sent him back to head the Trans-Mississippi Department.

Van Dorn's replacement, General Paul Octave Hébert, transferred in from Louisiana, was a superb example of the type of officer Texans despised. No sooner had he assumed command than he declared the entire state under martial law. He issued orders, decrees, and proclamations; he demanded that the governor and other civil officers pay him homage; he ordered Texas troops to learn how to drill and parade and to study books on tactics and on military protocol. He wanted a single-line chain of command going from General Hébert down through everyone, including civilians. A graduate of West Point (first in the class of 1840) and an assistant professor of engineering there for a year, Hébert wanted a model military district as prescribed in his books and as outlined in his notes and lectures. He could not have picked a worse place than Texas to try it. Still, the Texans might have forgiven him for his administrative compulsions had he proved a fierce and gallant field commander. What they found most repulsive about him was the fact that he was "a man of no military force or practical genius" who "preferred red-top boots, and a greased rat-tail moustache, with a fine equipage, and a suit of waiters, to the use of good, practical common sense." Because they abhorred his "European red-tapeism" and because they suspected him of cowardice, the Texans became tired and disgusted with him and began to complain. They wanted a man to command them who liked to fight.

Largely because of his enormous unpopularity, the War Department removed Hébert from command on October 10, 1862, and finally, after some vacillation, transferred him into Louisiana to command the northern subdistrict. The officer who replaced him, though, seemed precisely the kind that "best suited Texas." His name was John Bankhead Magruder, and he was a tough, rugged man who could swear and drink and fight as effectively as any officer the Texans had ever seen. He too was a West Pointer, yet he commanded not from books but from long experience as a combat officer in the Comanche wars in Texas and in the Seminole and Mexican wars. Though he carried a reputation as being "restless and hot tempered," young warriors like Thomas Jackson had requested to serve under him because "if any fighting was to be done Magruder would be 'on hand.'" Magruder knew how to entertain as well as he knew how to fight; on duty in Rhode Island before the Civil War he entertained with such courtly bearing and such a "brilliant ability to bring appearances up to the necesity of the occasion" that he got a nickname, "Prince John," and most everyone in Texas soon agreed that it was rather appropriate. Still, at bottom, he was an aggressive soldier who won the respect and loyalty of his Texas troops. As a popular saying went among them, "the advent of General Magruder was equal to the addition of 50,000 men to the forces of Texas."

For Bankhead Magruder came to Texas determined to wipe out a black mark on his otherwise excellent military record. He had gotten it during the Seven Days campaign back in Virginia when he badly mismanaged a Confederate charge and afterwards denounced Robert

E. Lee, who had rebuked him for carelessness in command. The upshot was that Magruder got himself transferred to faraway Texas. A sensitive man beneath his tough exterior, he left Virginia with a promise to restore his reputation through bold and brilliant combat leadership.

Thus when he assumed command on November 29, 1862, he reviewed the military situation and made battle plans with a single-minded purpose that caused him to ignore his administrative duties. The first thing he had to do was recapture the vital seaport of Galveston. It had fallen back in October when eight Federal warships steamed into the harbor and demanded immediate surrender. Confederate defenses under the overall command of Colonel Joseph J. Cook answered with an artillery salvo, but then gave up after eleven-inch Federal guns disabled Fort Point and fired a few blasts at the city itself.

The Confederates were still evacuating Galveston when Magruder began to make plans to retake it. Before he could consolidate his scattered forces, though, the enemy boats landed troops of occupation on December 25. They would not stay there long, Magruder promised. He would drive them back into the sea and soon. During the next five days he gathered a motley assortment of horse and infantry—the Twenty-sixty Texas Cavalry under Colonel Xavier B. Debray, a sophisticated Frenchman who had been schooled at the famous St. Cyr Military Academy; several other cavalry groups, detachments, and companies under Colonel Tom Green of New Mexico fame; and some volunteer infantry. Magruder also had a battery of artillery and two battered river steamboats that had been converted into warships—the *Bayou City* and the *Neptune*. The plan of attack called for the land forces to move into the city under cover of darkness while the gunboats, descending from the mouth of the Trinity River, attacked and sank the Federal war vessels anchored in the harbor. Aboard the Confederate ships were a number of dismounted cavalry—"horse marines"—who would fire at the enemy from behind cotton bales stacked on deck.

A daring plan this was, yet one that might well succeed if the gunboats could disable the enemy vessels and gain control of the harbor. At 1 A.M. on New Year's morning, 1863, while the Federals slept after a night of heavy drinking, Magruder led his land forces quietly into the city; after the moon had set, they swept the wharves with howitzers, then stormed Federal camps there with pistols blazing. The Federals somehow rallied and drove them off, but the Texans, crying their famous yell, charged again and again. The fighting, begun as a surprise attack, soon developed into a respectable battle as the warships out on the water lowered their cannon and raked the streets where the Texans were alternately advancing and retiring.

When the Confederate sailors above the city saw the flashes of the Union guns, they steered their boats out into the choppy bay waters and began their rush toward the heavily armed *Harriet Lane*. As they approached in the dim morning haze, Tom Green's horse marines picked off Union sailors running along the *Lane's* decks; Green himself shot a courageous young officer trying to discharge a loaded cannon single-handed. Suddenly, the *Neptune* took a direct hit from the *Lane's* pivot gun, lurched dangerously, then veered off into shallow water where it sank. The *Bayou City* continued its advance, though, with Green's sharpshooters still peppering the *Lane's* deck. Their fire was so blistering that Union sailors, to save their lives, had to take cover below. At last he Texas vessel bumped into the *Lane's* starboard side, and the horse marines stormed aboard, captured what remained of the crew, and struck the colors.

The Texans found the *Lane's* deck strewn with dead and wounded and pieces of exploded shell. An early Texas major who came aboard to help the wounded saw "his own son"—a Federal lieutenant—"lying on the deck mortally wounded." The major did not cry or say anything, but simply took his son in his arms and held him through the long, agonizing moments until he was dead. Only then did the major cry, a brief, cry, wrenched from deep inside; then he went on, quietly, to help the other wounded and to watch the battle move into its final stage.

The other Texans on board the *Lane* had crowded along the rail to listen to the racket of cannon and musketry coming from the town and to see what the remaining Federal warships would do. The men let out a resounding cheer when they saw, quite suddenly, white flags go up over the other vessels. There was an exchange of shouts: the Texans demanded surrender, the Federals refused. But they had had enough and by mass consent agreed to withdraw. As they steered their boats out of the harbor, they passed the Union flagship, which had run aground earlier in the fighting; suddenly a terrific explosion blew the ship apart—a premature detonation which killed the Union fleet commander and several others. For the navy this was the final blow in a humiliating New Year's battle in which almost everything had gone wrong.

Yet it was even worse for the Federal infantry, still fighting on the wharves, who looked on in horror as the Federal fleet steamed around the burning flagship and headed toward the open sea. Without naval support, the infantry soon fell to Magruder's charging Texans.

And so a Confederate general who had come to Texas determined to prove himself had won an astonishing victory which dealt Union naval prestige a severe blow. His men praised him as a general who fought at the front of battle instead of at the rear. Civilians, too, all over the state, lauded him, and the legislature in a joint resolution commended him for heroism and then gave him a standing ovation. In the months that followed, political leaders would of course come to regard Magruder as a tyrant in his administrative capacities; yet, even then, they would concede grudgingly that as a field commander this Virginian was indubitably bold and effective.

Magruder himself had little time to enjoy all the praise. The Federal gunboats came back in a few days to blockade Galveston and to bombard Confederate installations all along the coast. The general feared that this might be the advance of an all-out invasion which Texans had been expecting since the opening of the war. He reinforced his batteries with a few guns from the interior and warned his field officers to expect the worst.

The long-awaited invasion came that fall. On September 8, 1863, a Federal force of four gunboats and twenty-two troop transports carrying some 4,000 men steamed into Sabine Pass, about sixty miles up the coast from Galveston. Confederate forces at the Pass, reinforced months before on orders from Magruder himself, consisted of forty-seven men with six cannon and two cotton-clad rams under the command of Lieutenant Richard W. Dowling. Despite the odds, the Texas artillerymen, firing at an incredible clip of one shell every two minutes, disabled two enemy gunboats, took 350 prisoners, and turned back the invasion.

Repelled at Sabine Pass, the Federals decided to invade Texas through the lower Rio Grande valley. On November 1, 1863, some

4,500 troops under Nathaniel P. Banks landed at the mouth of the Great River and overran Brownsville, cutting off the all-important Confederate trade route through Matamoros. The invading force then split into two columns: one drove up the river to occupy Rio Grande City; the other swept up the coast to capture Corpus Christi, Aransas Pass, and all of the Matagorda Peninsula.

As the Federals continued to advance against mild resistance, Magruder took the field himself, leaving his immediate staff to tend administrative functions. The general gathered a small force, including walking wounded, and went after the Federals around Matagorda Bay, but he was so badly outnumbered and outgunned that he had to retreat west of the Colorado River, wrecking long stretches of the San Antonio-Gulf Coast Railroad as he went.

Then, inexplicably, the Federals also retreated—back down to Matagorda Island. Unknown to Magruder, who was frantically collecting an army of home guard troops, old men, and anyone else who would fight, Federal commanders had decided to hold what they had along the coast and along the Rio Grande and concentrate most of their manpower on the Red River campaign, which would take Union forces up Louisiana and into Texas from the northeast.

Magruder, though, knew nothing of this. As far as he was concerned, the Federal withdrawal could mean any number of things. It could mean, for instance, that they had pulled back merely to regroup and would soon advance directly into the interior toward San Antonio and Austin. Aggressive soldier that he was, Magruder decided to counterattack and recapture as much of the valley as possible. On December 22, 1863, he named his conscript commander, Rip Ford, to command the operation, with orders to raise 2,000 men for three-months duty in the "Cavalry of the West." Because Ford had a brilliant record as a Texas Ranger and cavalry colonel, Magruder no doubt expected much from him. Yet, the colonel had considerable difficulty in getting money and men and supplies for the enterprise. He was not ready to move until mid-March, 1864, and even then most of his 1,300 troops were under eighteen and over forty and were all poorly armed.

On the march, new problems arose to impede Ford's progress: severe shortages of food and ammunition; attacks by Federal cavalry detachments and Mexican bandits operating along the Nueces River;

and the lack of water caused by a severe drouth during the past two years.

While Ford moved slowly toward the Rio Grande, Magruder over on the coast continued to strengthen his defenses in anticipation of a new Federal offensive. Then he received ominous news from Louisiana that Banks, with 27,000 men and a powerful flotilla, had launched a drive up the Red River toward Shreveport, that Texas for the first time in the war was in danger of being overrun by a truly large Federal army. Learning this, Magruder lost all interest in the Federal forces occupying the valley. On orders from E. Kirby Smith, he started what troops he had toward Louisiana, only to collide head-on with angry civilian leaders who refused to let their soldiers leave with the enemy still on Texas soil. In the midst of this civil-military conflict, Magruder again received news from Louisiana: Richard Taylor's army, including several Texas cavalry and infantry brigades, had stopped the Federals at Mansfield (April 8) and at Pleasant Hill (April 9) and thrown them back down the Red River. At about the same time, in Arkansas, three Confederate cavalry divisions had overtaken and turned back a second Yankee column from Little Rock.

The Federal threat in Louisiana gone, Magruder stopped feuding with civil officials and concentrated on regaining possession of the valley. He sent Colonel Ford, then at Rio Grande City, a few fresh troops and cannon and urged him to attack Brownsville. Ford was rather reluctant to do so, having heard that the enemy there outnumbered him two to one, but at last he moved forward.

Through the next few weeks, Ford, with some of his old fighting spirit, defeated Federal cavalry detachments and their Mexican guerrilla allies in several running engagements; then, on July 30, 1864, he captured Brownsville after a week of heavy skirmishing. By mid-August, Ford's Texans had forced the enemy to abandon all of the Rio Grande except Brazos Island. Once again the life-giving supply trains from Matamoros rumbled across the border, heading for Confederate armies in Arkansas, Louisiana, and beyond.

As the commander of Texas who had conceived the valley campaign, Bankhead Magruder took most of the credit for Ford's achievement. This brought him to the attention of E. Kirby Smith, commanding the Trans-Mississippi Department, who was looking for a good combat officer to head the Arkansas District, where

Confederates were planning a new offensive against the Union forces that held the northern half of the state. Though Magruder had a bad reputation as an impulsive administrator with "an utter disregard for the law," Kirby Smith nevertheless thought he had energy and ability and on August 4, 1864, transferred him to Arkansas.

The Texans viewed Magruder's transfer with mixed emotions. An administrative tyrant was gone, but so was a dependable warrior who had perhaps done more than anyone else to save their homes from the Yankee invaders. Would the new district commander, a reticent general named John G. Walker prove as effective once the Federals renewed their offensive against Texas? And another invasion would indubitably come, the Texans believed, since the enemy had retained a strong garrison on Brazos Island.

The fear of invasion continued to haunt Texans throughout the final year of the war. Every Confederate defeat beyond their borders—Sterling Price's cavalry disaster in Missouri that winter, the fall of Georgia and the Carolinas to Sherman's advancing army—forebode a new Federal offensive against Texas. By February, 1865, the invasion jitters had developed into a kind of statewide paranoia. Down in the valley, Rip Ford's cavalry kept a constant watch on Brazos Island, lest a Yankee striking force land there. All along the coast, from Corpus Christi to Sabine Pass, Texas sentinels scanned the moving Gulf waters for a sign of enemy ships. Over in Houston, at district headquarters, Walker and his staff studied the reports of Confederate losses on every front and wondered what was in store for them. Then, on the evening of March 6, a Confederate secret service agent fresh from New Orleans came to headquarters with alarming intelligence. At New Orleans a Federal invasionary army of 40,000 men, maybe more, was preparing to strike the Texas coast sometime in the next few weeks. His story was hardly substantiated, but Walker and his officers were in such a nervous state that they believed it without question. The next morning, March 7, Walker sent a frantic message to Kirby Smith at Shreveport; a huge invasionary force was coming across the Gulf toward Texas; Walker had to have reinforcements in a hurry. Apparently, Kirby Smith also had the invasion jitters. He took Walker at his word and moved swiftly to meet the impending danger: he ordered Joseph O. Shelby's cavalry to Shreveport, Thomas J. Churchill's infantry to Marshall, John H.

Forney's infantry to Huntsville, and Bankhead Magruder back to Houston to replace Walker as district commander. If an invasion were coming, then a fighting commander must be in Texas to meet it.

Through the weeks the Confederates waited, but they saw not a sign of invasion, not a single sign. April came and passed. Then on May 11, down in the valley one of Rip Ford's cavalry patrols spotted enemy troops coming off Brazos Island in a blinding rain storm. Was this the invasion? Had a Yankee army landed on the island undetected? At Brownsville, Ford and General James E. Slaughter, who the previous fall had taken command of the Rio Grande subdistrict, called on Magruder for reinforcements and fast. On May 13, while Slaughter waited for help to arrive, Ford, with nearly a thousand cavalry, rode southeast to Palmito Ranch, where the Texas patrol had already engaged the invaders. In an explosion of daring, Ford ordered an attack. His Texans charged fiercely and drove the Federals back to Brazos Island in a wild, running fight.

As it turned out, however, the Texans had not stopped an invasion, but had merely whipped the regular island garrison composed mainly of Negro troops. From a prisoner, the Texans learned that General Lee had surrendered at Appomattox over a month before and that the Federals on the island, having heard the news, had started for Brownsville, expecting the Texans to capitulate as well. The engagement at Palmito, the prisoner concluded, had been an awful mistake—a mistake, that, as it happened, was the last land battle fought in the Confederacy.

The reports of Confederate collapse east of the Mississippi River started a nervous, frightened ripple over the state. General Magruder called on his troops to stand by the colors in spite of what had happened in Virginia. Governor Pendleton Murrah also pleaded for loyalty in these dark moments:

Look at the bloody and desolate tracks of the invader through Georgia and South Carolina, and see the fate that awaits you. . . . Rally around the battle scarred and well known flag of the Confederacy and uphold your state government in its purity and integrity—*There is no other hope for safety for you and yours.*

In response, civilians and soldiers gathered in mass demonstrations to pledge their allegiance and their lives to the Confederacy. "If our people," cried a soldier in a meeting at Millican, Texas, "and our

TROOPS would come to the rescue as they should do; if they would unite as one man; the Trans-Mississippi could defy the combined powers of Yankeedom."

Then came the crushing news that the Army of Tennessee—General Hood's old command—had given up at Greensboro, North Carolina, and that Confederate forces in Arkansas and parts of Louisiana had disintegrated.

This seemed to take everything out of Texas troops. Their patriotism and tenacity gave way to fear—a fear of coming violence, a fear of the unknown. On May 15, troops at the Galveston garrison mutinied and took off for their homes in fear and panic; at the same time men at other garrisons all along the coast demonstrated an open disregard for discipline and organization. Magruder set out for Houston in a desperate effort to keep his military units together. But as he rode he was confronted every hour with the evidence that his district was crumbling to pieces around him. Fully half the troops in the western subdistrict had deserted. The remaining half refused to bring them back, thinking it "useless for the Trans-Mississippi Department to undertake to do what the Cis-Mississippi Department has failed to do." Magruder returned to Houston a bitter, defeated man. He wired Kirby Smith at Shreveport that all was lost, that to prevent further rioting the commander must let all the troops go home by regiments "with as little damage to the community as possible." "For God's sake," Magruder cried, "act or let me act."

Kirby Smith, though, wired him to hold on at all costs: the commander had decided to move his headquarters from Shreveport to Houston, where he would "fight to the bitter end."

But the end was already there. When Kirby Smith reached Huntsville, he found mobs of "disorderly soldiery thronging the roads"—the remnants of Forney's infantry division. Things were even worse at Hempstead, where cavalry outfits had disbanded so that the men could go home to protect their families from "roving bands of thieves and robbers." All across East and South Texas, these gangs of violent men—many of them draft dodgers and deserters and Unionists—pillaged towns and bushwhacked Confederate soldiers.

At last Kirby Smith reached Houston, but by that time everything in Texas had crumbled—all the cavalry and infantry had disbanded, and control over troops and jayhawkers and everyone else was gone.

On May 22, Kirby Smith and Magruder were generals without an army. Several days later they heard that on May 26 Kirby Smith's chief of staff had surrendered the Trans-Mississippi Department at New Orleans, and that a Federal steamer was bringing the surrender terms to Galveston for Kirby Smith's signature. There was little he could do but give in; and on June 2, with Magruder at his side, he boarded the ship in the harbor and signed away the last, lingering hope of the South.

Soon after, fearing that the Yankees might persecute them, the two men joined a column of diehard Southerners on their way to Mexico. In the ranks were cavalrymen from Missouri, including such reputable commanders as Joe Shelby and Sterling Price. Governor Murrah of Texas, too, was there. So were two other Confederate governors and several lesser politicians and private citizens. They moved on through Eagle Pass, stopped at the Rio Grande so that the troopers could bury their flags in the muddy waters, and then rode out of a land whose people had fought so hard and so sadly for a cause that was perhaps lost from the beginning. For those tired, empty men who crossed the Mexico plain toward Monterrey, as well as for thousands of southerners who remained in Texas, in Arkansas, Georgia, and everywhere else in the South, the "bright dream" of the Confederacy was over. Perhaps they could all—as a young soldier on his way home to Marshall expressed it—perhaps they could all "fall down in the dust and weep over our great misfortune, our great calamities."

Section III.

RECONSTRUCTION TO 1900

A Historiography of Reconstruction in Texas: Some Myths and Problems

Edgar P. Sneed [*]

From its inception Reconstruction generated controversy. Probably only the Texas Revolution and the institution of slavery stirred contemporary ideological clashes that continue with such vigor into the present. The historical issues raised in all three cases partially guaranteed the ferocity of the debate. Questions that demand moral judgments, such as racism and freedom, constitutional failure and political opportunism, poverty and corruption, can scarcely but spawn differing opinions.

In the case of Reconstruction, the defenders and detractors of the Radicals, then as now, lived on both sides of the Mason-Dixon line. Chronologically, however, most pre–World War II writers accepted the so-called southern view of Reconstruction. Many of the scholars who left graduate schools after 1945, however, have attempted to modify that interpretation. Edgar P. Sneed belongs to the latter group.

This essay, moreover, poses other questions for students of Texas history. It asks the readers to look at how a writer evaluates historical data. Furthermore, it implicitly warns that, by uncritically accepting white contemporary accounts of events affecting race relations, the

---

*Edgar P. Sneed, "A Historiography of Reconstruction in Texas: Some Myths and Problems," Southwestern Historical Quarterly, LXXII (April, 1969), 435–448.

true story cannot be told. Sneed closes his essay by urging historians to
revise the story of Reconstruction in Texas. Ten years after his
challenge, except in scattered articles, theses, and dissertations, that
history has not yet appeared. The two best works are probably James
Smallwood's "Black Texans During Reconstruction" (Ph.D. diss., Texas
Tech University, 1974) and John Carrier's "A Political History of Texas
During the Reconstruction, 1865–1874" (Ph.D. diss., Vanderbilt
University, 1971).

By and large, historians of Texas Reconstruction either have spoken
for themselves or, worse, have spoken for their ancestors. Down
through the years, other historians have not critically tested their
original assumptions about their subject. Therefore, their scholarship,
while rich in data, is in danger of losing substance. Reevaluation, as
well as new research, is mandatory to restore useful vigor to this major
field of Texas history.

Enduring value and relevance in historical literature depend upon
a work's significance for succeeding generations of historians and
readers. The historian must not speak for himself but must speak to the
continuing historical community and interested public.

A reevaluation of the Reconstruction history of Texas should fit
within the context of current historiographical examination of
American Reconstruction history. The two recent books of John Hope
Franklin and Kenneth M. Stampp demonstrate the degree to which
traditional Reconstruction history, national and local, has lost
consequence.

The fact that almost all histories of Texas Reconstruction have been
written by Texans in sympathy with their ancestors' views does not in
itself compromise the significance of their research and writing.
Sympathy for his subject is a legitimate mood for any historian. But
most Texas historians of this period have confused sympathy with
judgment. With few exceptions, they have accepted the conservative
bias and racial prejudice expressed during Reconstruction, not only as
facts relevant to the period, but as the assumptive basis for their own
scholarly interpretations of events. They have been too "understanding."

Texas historians have not realized (or have not pointed out) that the words and conduct of conservative southerners after the Civil War were the weapons used to continue the struggle against the liberal nationalism of the victorious North and West. Historical judgment can never be left unquestioned to the participants of a conflict. Antagonists rarely achieve disinterested viewpoints. Certainly conservative Texans, unbroken in spirit in 1865–1867, were not ready to quit the struggle and abandon what they considered their rightful way of life. They had lost the military war, and after 1866 they nearly lost the political war. Their last resort was a guerrilla resistance in which words were the principal weapons. Radical governor Edmund J. Davis called it "a slow civil war." Consciously or instinctively, the "old regime" Texans poured forth torrents of words on their adversaries. Ignoring reality, as well as their own faults and shortcomings, they vigorously denounced every real and imagined sin they could attribute to their enemies: Negroes, northerners, and Unionists. Most Texans did not really believe themselves sinless; they were waging a war with the only weapon available to them—bitter and truculent words. With regrettable results, sympathetic historians have often accepted these partisan feelings and exalted them to the level of historical judgment.

The real product of this habit has been the creation of "traditional history," in which folk myth stands equal to historical analysis. Like the medieval chronicler, many Texas historians seem to find their duty in the recording and conveying of folk experience, wisdom, and myth. Too often, they seem unaware that modern research methods alone do not suffice to produce modern historical literature. History emerged as an intellectual discipline in the past century, when critical analysis of the past began replacing attempts to recreate, merely to relate, or simply to preserve the past: Herodotus of Athens and Gregory of Tours sometimes accepted the myths of their ancestors as sufficient explanations of events; twentieth-century historians cannot. Yet myth is found in the historical literature of Texas Reconstruction.

An example is the assertion that the Ku Klux Klan appeared and functioned only in response to the physical and political dangers posed by freedmen and northerners; that the KKK played upon Negro "superstition" and seldom resorted to violent or illegal methods; and that the Klan largely disbanded in the late 1860s when military and civil authorities restored order. Yet at least three eminent Texas historians, Charles Ramsdell, Seth Shepard McKay, and William Curtis Nunn, let these stand as historical judgment. Nunn observes that "the record of Klan activities during the Davis administration in Texas is far from complete." Nevertheless, he accepts hearsay evidence supporting the Klan myth while disparaging conflicting hearsay reports. His one attempt to provide substantive evidence for the Klan's essential innocence is the statement: "No record has been found showing that the State Police ever arrested any man wearing Ku Klux Klan regalia. . . ." Such an assertion is about as conclusive as a claim that no spy resembling Ian Fleming's 007 has been caught, therefore the British government has no spies. The editors of *Documents of Texas History* prefaced a document on the Knights of the Golden Circle, another guerrilla conspiracy, with the claim that its members took up "the responsibilities of democracy." But according to the document, all members swore solemn faith in white supremacy and in the necessity of opposing all measures for Negro welfare. Moreover, members pledged to go to any extreme in protecting the Golden Cross and in promoting its aims. Such are the "responsibilities of democracy"?

The stuff of another myth is the euphemistic explanation of "black codes" in Texas. Ramsdell declares: "Even the labor law [one of the "black codes"], harsh and stringent as it seems, was almost universally regarded as necessary both to the good order and the protection of the negroes for whom alone it was intended." That this statement constitutes a historical fact—the public profession of almost all Texas at the time—cannot be doubted. But, that this statement as a historical judgment represents the true nature of the black codes and of Texan motives is subject to grave doubt. The general conduct of whites toward Negroes in 1866 simply will not substantiate the professed motives for enacting the codes. Against whom did Negroes require protection? Only conservative whites, for all their paternalistic presumptions, threatened Texas Negroes. Ramsdell does not defend the black codes, but his explanation does not withstand historical or logical analysis. He is reduced to assessing as "minor measures" one of the black codes "explicitly granting to freedmen all rights not prohibited by the constitution, except intermarriage with whites, voting, holding public office, serving on juries and testifying in cases in which negroes were not concerned."

"Carpetbag rule" is another myth accepted by uncritical Texas historians. Nunn implies this myth in *Texas Under the Carpetbaggers*, with the title and with occasional use of the term "carpetbag" in the text; but nowhere in the work is "carpetbag" or "carpetbagger" defined or demonstrated. Nunn ignores the findings of James R. Norvell, who has identified only two northerners (the historical figure of the word) holding responsible positions in the Radical government of Texas: a supreme court justice and a congressman. Neither of these men, incidentally, was ever accused of violating his public trust, the charge most frequently associated with the term "carpetbagger." Certainly such indicting evidence cannot support Marion H. Farrow's claim that Reconstruction in Texas was "a period marked . . . by carpetbagger and 'scalawag' influence."

Social scientist Alfred B. Sears has wrestled with this problem of traditional history and myth-making. In his presidential address before the Southwest Social Sciences Association convention in 1960, Sears suggested an explanation for the willingness of Texas historians to promote the myth of Negro inferiority:

Psychologically and sociologically, for the Southerner to have accepted the equality of the Negro after 1865 would have been an admission of guilt, not only for the injustice of the slave system but also for the disaster of a war which cost the lives of 600,000 white boys. The face-saving new article of faith had to be a racist social status which would continue the freedman "in his place"—his place of inferiority.

This is racism—the racism of guilt. When a competent historian can state in 1938 that "from slavery to freedom and citizenship was more than the limited intellect of the black could appreciate, and he was at a loss to know what to do with himself," that historian is not just in sympathy with his ancestors; he shares in their guilt.

Persistent recourse to these and other myths has reduced the reliability and permanent value of Texas Reconstruction history. There is sadness in this historiographical judgment, for most historians of Texas Reconstruction have pursued their profession with skill and fervor. Ramsdell's *Reconstruction in Texas* possesses most of the technical characteristics of work of enduring historical significance. Ramsdell obviously tried to be fair to unpopular men and events. Yet his work is marked as traditional history because Ramsdell, even if unconsciously, allowed his sympathies or his background to cloud his historical judgment. The fate of Ramsdell's work, and that of other "traditionalist" historians, depends upon historiographical reevaluation (supplemented by some new primary research).

A cursory inquiry into three of the major problems of Reconstruction history in Texas demonstrates the extent to which reexamination can depend upon research in traditional literature. A brief investigation of these three problems may provide inspiration in the task of rewriting Reconstruction history in Texas.

First, there is the question of the legality of Radical rule in Texas. This problem rests, finally, upon the interpretation of the "rights" of a state after an unsuccessful rebellion against its federal union. This matter, touched upon in several Supreme Court decisions and in the Fourteenth and Fifteenth Amendments, remains unresolved. Still, the legality of Radical government within Texas may be judged by investigating the allegation that the Radicals sought to violate or change constitutional, legal, and political traditions in Texas.

More recent articles in the *Southwestern Historical Quarterly* by J. E. Ericson, George E. Shelley, and Leila Clark Wynn offer convincing evidence that the Constitution of 1869 was almost entirely within the political traditions of Texas, both before the Civil War and after the end of Reconstruction. The Bill of Rights of 1869 was virtually identical to those in the constitutions of 1845 and 1861, and there was little change made in the Bill of Rights of 1876.

Moreover, Leila Wynn concludes that "the judicial system remained much the same, even under the new Constitution of 1869." The attacks by Texans against the contemporary Radical courts certainly had tactical advantage but virtually no substantive merit. Even the blanket condemnation of the judges proves to be more tactical than substantial. Of the thirty-five district judges appointed by Radical governor E. J. Davis, the "Redeemer" Thirteenth Legislature lodged formal charges against only twelve. Of those charged, "several of the judges were removed"; the overwhelming majority of judges continued in office. Even the state supreme court of the Radicals, derisively labeled the "Semicolon Court," does not deserve the universal condemnation heaped upon it. George E. Shelley, an outstanding Texas lawyer, carefully examines the composition and conduct of the Semicolon Court and finds it compared favorably with the state supreme courts before and after Reconstruction. Only in the famous *ex parte Rodriguez* case of 1874, and in the ensuing struggle for the statehouse, did the court (and everyone else involved, conservative and Radical) fail the state's legal tradition.

Conservative Texans did not immediately institute a wholesale purge of Radical laws, police officials, and judges, once Reconstruction ended, and this would seen to be testimony both to the common sense of Texans and to the general propriety of Radical conduct. To test this thesis will require an administrative history, as yet unwritten, of the Davis government and its Redeemer successors. In legislation and in public administration over such major concerns as ranching and the public domain, the shifting political currents had almost no effect. Certainly many distinguished Texas Rangers and Redeemer law officers had been members of the much maligned State Police of E. J. Davis.

There is even basis for the judgment that the Radical Constitution of 1869 was a more efficient and more democratic instrument of government than its 1876 successor. Governor Richard Coke, the succeeding governor, called for amendment rather than replacement of the 1869 constitution; and considering the course taken by the constitutional convention of 1875, his suggestion certainly merited attention. McKay describes the delegates to the convention as a singularly ordinary and undistinguished assemblage. These delegates made very few substantial changes in the form of state government, but they greatly encumbered efficiency and democracy in state government with a long series of negative and petty restraints. In the ratification election of 1876, many Texans expressed doubts about their new instrument. Despite the psychological and patriotic urge to repudiate Radical Reconstruction decisively, almost 30 percent of the Texas voters rejected the new constitution. At least one historian has attempted to expose the myth of infallibility connected with the 1876 constitution. In his judgment:

. . . the majority of the people living in Texas in 1876 realized that the Constitution which they adopted did not completely meet the needs of the State even then. Certainly at no time were they led to believe that it was particularly meritorious. They agreed to ratify it because they thought that it was preferable to the obnoxious instrument of 1869 and that its admitted defects could be overcome by amendment.

A second major problem in the history of Texas Reconstruction is the charge that Radical Reconstruction brought in its train an epidemic of unparalled violence and lawlessness. Again, available evidence suggests that the charge was exaggerated by conservative Texans to discredit Radicalism.

Frequently the Freedmen's Bureau is blamed for much of the violence and disorder during military rule. It is charged with freeing Negroes arrested by local authorities and with encouraging Negroes to hate their former masters and to break labor contracts. Indeed, specific cases are cited in which Freedmen's Bureau agents ordered the release of Negroes from local jails and courts. But in many such instances the bureau had justice, if not local law, on its side. There seems little doubt that white sheriffs, judges, and vigilantes cared little about the guilt or innocence of Negroes; their concern was keeping Negroes "in their place." These law officers and judges reflected the fixed belief of conservative Texans that the Negro was unfit to appear in court except as a defendant.

Also, the claim that the Freedmen's Bureau encouraged Negro idleness does not square with the facts. The bureau promoted the contract system of farm labor, and, while patently optimistic, bureau records indicate that by January, 1866, "nine-tenths of the former slaves were under contract, working steadily and soberly . . . theft, idleness, and vagrancy had almost become a thing of the past. . . ." Moreover, army officers "were instructed to encourage labor contracts" in the absence of bureau officials.

Indeed, Freedmen's Bureau records, supported by reports of federal military commanders and of loyal Texans, place the onus of lawlessness on conservative Texans. White duplicity and maltreatment in dealing with Negroes and their supporters is a constant theme in bureau and army reports to Washington. When federal troops first penetrated the interior of East Texas in September, 1865, they discovered most Negroes still bound in slavery. Masters had deceived their slaves by telling them that emancipation would not come until Christmas. Teachers for bureau schools, whether bureau-paid or missionary volunteers, were constantly subjected to "scurrilous and scandalous attack," no matter how "blameless" the conduct. These attacks ranged from social ostracism and KKK intimidation to beatings and murder.

Freedmen's Bureau and United States army reports of such violence usually charged Texans with disloyalty. Ramsdell agrees that "beyond doubt, most people [in Texas] were not enthusiastic in their loyalty," and that "alleged persecution and maltreatment of Union men and Freedmen... constantly occurred. ..." Otis A. Singletary, in his study, "Texas Militia During Reconstruction," declares that "the implacable hostility of many Southern whites" compelled Davis to create the State Police and militia. The success of these police forces in preserving the Radical government, far more than their abuses of power, incurred Texans' wrath.

The statistics on murder committed in Texas after the Civil War, compiled by a special committee of the 1868 constitutional convention, substantiate the charges of violent white hostility to Negroes and to Unionists. Ramsdell determines that about 500 whites and 500 Negroes were murdered in the first three postwar years; while 90 percent of the Negroes were killed by whites, only 1 percent of the whites were killed by Negroes. Probably the number of murders was far greater. These damnning statistics leave no doubt. Texas was the scene of a race war in which Negroes and their protectors suffered great loss of life.

Stark racial and rebellious motives account for most of the political crime and disorder in Texas during Reconstruction. Frontier lawlessness and the cowboys' celebrated "free spirits" had little direct link with the political violence of Texas's Reconstruction. Unfortunately, however, the general conditions of law and order in Texas after the Civil War have not been adequately studied.

A third major problem confronting historians of Texas Reconstruction is the chronic complaint of post–Civil War Texans that military and Radical rule resulted in great economic impoverishment and chaos. This may have occurred in some southern states, but a similar estimate of economic conditions in Texas is quite unfounded in fact. Still, major Texas historians continue to repeat the charge of contemporaries that military and Radical rule "proved woefully destructive to the private fortunes of many Texans." Nunn writes that

after the Civil War Southern capital had vanished; bank stocks and deposits had lost all value. Many plantation owners were unable to continue their operations. ... Mortgage sales were numerous, ... the recently freed Negroes, having a tendency toward shiftlessness, could not be depended upon as day laborers. ...

Yet, the undigested evidence marshalled by Nunn demonstrates just the opposite—an early, continuing, and expanding prosperity in Texas throughout Reconstruction.

The most often repeated "proof" of economic dislocation in Texas after the Civil War is the decline in the value of farms: in 1860, Texas farm property was worth an estimated $88,000,000; in 1870, the estimated value had fallen to $60,000,000. But this decline, whatever its actual extent, was largely due to the inevitable dislocation of agrarian institutions following emancipation and the resulting breakup of commercial plantation holdings. The Radicals were responsible for neither of these. It may be argued that the numerically tiny agrarian aristocracy in Texas suffered; but in the process a much larger number of yeoman and subsistence farmers greatly benefited from the breakup. The redistribution of land during Reconstruction furthered the democratization of Texas society and politics. Historians note the financial losses; they rarely account for the human gains.

Even admitting a loss in land values, the available evidence unveils a picture, not of "great economic impoverishment," but rather of a developing economic prosperity unparalleled in Texas history. In reality, Texas was little disturbed by war; her cotton, cattle, unsettled land, and natural resources became the foundation for a healthy, diversified economy that expanded rapidly until the panic of 1873. Even the 1865 flight to Mexico of a small but influential number of Texans, carrying with them a considerable amount of capital, did not seriously affect the state's economy.

Vera Lee Dugas's compilation of economic data on "Texas Industry, 1860–1880," from the United States census returns provides an initial examination of Texas's postwar economy. Miss Dugas cites, for example, the rapid growth of industry in Texas during the late 1860s. Factories more than doubled, and the value of their products rose from $6,500,000 to $11,500,000. Most of this industrial expansion came at the height of military and Radical rule.

The rise of the cattle kingdom was a major, if not primary, reason for Texas's prosperity. "Texas in 1865 was a vast reservoir fairly overflowing with . . . fat cattle which were worthless at home but of great value in the North and East," writes Edward Everett Dale, in his colorful history of *The Range Cattle Industry*. He demonstrates that cattle provided Texas, in the two decades of 1865–1886, with great wealth, stimulating related industries, immigration, and a lawlessness born of greed. Seth Shepard McKay also comments that "some remarkable profits were made in Texas at farming and stockraising during the E. J. Davis régime."

Even those alleged "excessive costs" for military and Radical governments were returned to Texas with handsome interest in the form of federal gifts, subsidies, improvements, frontier defense, and federal payrolls.

Undoubtedly, McKay's study of "Social Conditions in Texas in the Eighteen Seventies" is the best available expression of material well-being in Texas during Reconstruction. Texans were a people satisfied with and proud of their economic and social progress. Their sense of well-being is demonstrated in population statistics; the population rose in the 1860s by one-third, while that of the nation increased by one-fourth. Their economic stability is witnessed by the size of Texas's middle and substantial classes; based upon 1870 census data, fully 60 percent of all Texans "gainfully employed" were property-holding farmers, businessmen, members of professions, or skilled tradesmen. Their faith in the future is reflected in the rapid growth of the Texas cities of Galveston, San Antonio, Houston, and Jefferson; Galveston acquired its first paved streets in 1869, several theaters in 1870, the Tremont Hotel ("considered one of the finest in the entire South") in 1872, and gas lights on the streets soon after. Texans were not a people crushed under despotic, alien rule!

These are but three of many problems in Texas Reconstruction that should occupy Texas historians. Some problems will require little more than reevaluation; the scholarship of Ramsdell, McKay, and others is graced by extensive research. Historiographical reevaluation of this scholarship, reinforced with basic research into those topics still untouched, will save much of it from an unfortunate fate—insignificance.

Wealthy Texans, 1870

RALPH A. WOOSTER[*]

Historians have turned recently to what many students would consider unlikely sources for reconstructing America's past. These scholars have searched out many types of statistical data to describe and analyze leaders or common folks, and, indeed, communities and institutions such as slavery. One cache of valuable statistics for this kind of historical research has been the manuscript returns of the United States census. Ralph A. Wooster, a professor of history at Lamar University, was among the first historians of Texas to use that valuable data base.

"Wealthy Texans, 1870," can serve as a short introduction to this type of historical methodology. Furthermore, Wooster's descriptions of the rich Texans of 1870 will acquaint students with important, yet, relative to pre–Civil War reputations, little-known leaders of the state. A careful look at Wooster's conclusions accents the changes occurring in Texas after the Civil War. As a result of these changes, merchants and bankers replaced planters and farmers of means as the largest class of wealthy Texans.

Students interested in statistical methodology and history should read the pioneering article by Barnes F. Lathrop, "History from the

[*]Ralph A. Wooster, "Wealthy Texans, 1870," *Southwestern Historical Quarterly*, LXXIV (July, 1970), 24–35.

Census Returns," SOUTHWESTERN HISTORICAL QUARTERLY, *LI (April, 1948). In addition, a perusal of Wooster's "Wealthy Texans, 1860,"* IBID., *LXXI (October, 1967), would add to the comparisons he draws in this selection.*

A recent study based upon the manuscript returns of the 1860 federal census showed that the census listed 263 Texans who held over $100,000 each in total property on the eve of the Civil War. These wealthy Texans, highly successful lawyers, merchant capitalists, railroad developers, and plantation owners, were leaders in the social and economic life of the state prior to the Civil War. Many of them held positions of responsibility and trust during the war itself; and, like others in the South, many of them suffered great personal loss as a result of the war and the economic dislocation that followed during the years of Reconstruction.

The economic loss was greater for some Texas capitalists than for others. Especially hard hit were the sugar and cotton barons of the lower Brazos and Colorado rivers. David G. Mills of Brazoria County, for example, the largest slaveholder in antebellum Texas, lost over 300 slaves as a result of emancipation. His real and personal property holdings dropped from $614,234 in 1860 to $50,000 in 1870. His neighbor John McNeel lost almost as heavily. In 1860 McNeel was listed in the federal census with 136 slaves and a total property holding of $316,550; in 1870 no property was listed for him in the census enumeration. Similar losses were suffered by planters W. B. Davenport of Jackson County, who owned 55 slaves and $115,660 in 1860, but held only $2,600 in 1870; John Rugeley of Matagorda County, who owned 62 slaves and $117,000 in 1860, but only $6,400 in 1870; Charles W. Tait of Colorado County, who owned 63 slaves and $119,026 in 1860, but only $6,545 in 1870; and Thomas Clictt of Austin County, who owned 100 slaves and personal property of $150,000 in 1860, but only $500 in 1870.

The loss of property which occurred during the war years and Reconstruction was not confined to planters and farmers. New York-born merchant John Adriance of Brazoria County, for example, had a total property holding of $112,326 on the eve of the Civil War.

In the 1870 census, however, he was listed with only $600 in total property. Ammon Underwood, native of Massachusetts and a resident of Brazoria County, was another of the northern-born Texas merchants who suffered heavily from the war, losing over $200,000 in property during the 1860s. Merchant J. H. Muckleroy of Nacogdoches County also sustained major economic reverses in the decade, his total property listed at $129,000 in 1860 but only $980 in 1870. George N. Phillips, a physician in Montgomery County, was yet another of Texas's antebellum wealthy who sustained heavy personal losses. In 1860, he held $180,000 in property, but in 1870 he possessed only $16,000.

This is not to imply that all of the antebellum wealthy Texans suffered major economic reversals in the war decade. While the war had ended the institution of slavery, cotton was still a major money crop in the state and many planters and farmers were able to make the transition from bonded to free labor without a devastating economic loss. The opening up of the cattle industry with the great drives north to market allowed stockmen and ranchers such as Richard King and Mifflin Kenedy to expand their activities beyond the limits of the state. The rapid increase in population after the war as a result of heavy migration from the older South afforded ambitious merchants new opportunities for profit in wholesaling and retailing, particularly in hardware and grocery commodites. And the expansion of various types of milling—grain, lumber, textiles—in the Reconstruction period provided new areas of investment for those willing either to diversify their economic activities or to break completely from the agrarian pattern.

Eleven of the Texans who held $100,000 in property in 1860 (Elijah Robertson of Bell County, Nathaniel Lewis and Samuel A. Maverick of Bexar County, William J. Bryan of Brazoria County, Fletcher S. Stockdale of Calhoun County, Thomas J. Perryman of Guadalupe and Comal counties, Ebenezar B. Nichols of Galveston County, William R. Baker, Thomas W. House, and William J. Hutchins of Harris County, and Jabez D. Giddings of Washington County) still possessed over $100,000 in 1870. Three of the wealthy prewar Texans, builder Nathaniel Lewis of Bexar County, lawyer J. D. Giddings of Washington County, and farmer Thomas J. Perryman of Comal County, actually increased their property ownership in the war decade. Several others, notably Levi Jordan and Stephen S. Perry of Brazoria County, José San Román of Cameron County, B. A. Shepherd and A. Groesbeck of Harris County, David R. Wingate of Jefferson and Newton counties, and Thomas O'Connor and John H. Wood of Refugio County, lost economically during the decade but still possessed $30,000 or more in total property.

By 1870, the midpoint of political Reconstruction in the state, the number of Texans possessing $100,000 had dwindled to fifty-eight. Eleven of the fifty-eight were individuals who possessed $100,000 in 1860. The other forty-seven were newcomers to the ranks of those with great wealth, although most of them had resided in the state prior to the Civil War.

As in 1860, the wealthy Texans of the Reconstruction era came from all of the geographic areas of the state, although one-half of them lived in the major cities of Galveston, Houston, and San Antonio. Galveston County, where eleven of these individuals lived, was the home of more wealthy Texans in the Reconstruction period than any other county. Seven individuals with $100,000 lived in Harris County and five in Bexar. The only other counties with more than three wealthy Texans in 1870 were Travis, in which the state capital is located, and Marion, in which the town of Jefferson, then at the height of its economic and social prosperity, is located.

The loss of individual wealth in the 1860–1870 decade was particularly evident in the counties along the lower Brazos and Colorado rivers. Brazoria County, center of the rich cotton-sugarcane complex in the antebellum period, had twenty-six residents with $100,000 or more in 1860; one person was listed for the county in 1870. Other counties in the area were similarly affected by the war. Austin County had twelve individuals with $100,000 in 1860; Colorado, ten; Fort Bend, sixteen; Matagorda, ten; and Wharton, seven; in 1870 there were no individuals with $100,000 living in any of these counties.

The economic decline was of course not confined to the coastal area. Washington County, just to the north, suffered a similar decline. In 1860 there were eighteen persons with $100,000 residing in the county; by 1870 J. D. Giddings was the only one. Grimes County, northwest of Washington, had eight wealthy Texans in 1860, but none in 1870.

Several individuals with $100,000 in property in 1870 lived in counties not previously represented in the lists of wealthy Texans. Three of the wealthiest individuals of 1870, for example, resided in Comal, a county not mentioned in 1860. Collin, McLennan, Nueces, and San Patricio were other counties where wealthy Texans resided in 1870 but not in 1860. Two counties in which wealthy Texans resided in 1870, Davis and Duval, had not even been organized as counties in 1860.

As in 1860, the majority of wealthy Texans of the Reconstruction decade were between forty and fifty years old. Seven were in their thirties, twenty-three in their forties, eighteen in their fifties, and seven in their sixties. Twenty-four-year-old Charles E. Phillips of Marion County was the youngest of the group and the only one under the age of thirty. John D. Andrews of Harris and W. W. Downs of McLennan, each aged seventy-four, were the only wealthy Texans over the age of seventy. The median age for the whole group was forty-eight years, exactly the same as for the wealthy Texans of 1860.

The percentage of wealthy Texans born in slaveholding states was lower in 1870 than it had been a decade earlier: 31 of the 58 wealthiest Texans of 1870 (53.4 percent) were born in slaveholding states, compared to the 207 (78.7 percent) of 1860. The percentage of affluent Texans born in the North and in foreign countries doubled during the 1860s. At the beginning of the decade, 34 of 263 individuals (12.9 percent) were born in northern states; at its close, 15 of 58 individuals (27.6 percent) were born in northern states. In 1860, some 22 individuals, or 8.4 percent of the total, were born outside the United States; in 1870, the number was 11 individuals, or 19 percent of the total. These figures, while perhaps not surprising, seem to confirm the generally held belief that nonsoutherners (in terms of birth) occupied a more prominent position in southern economy and society during Reconstruction than in the prewar period.

A higher percentage of wealthy Texans of 1870 were merchants than was true in the antebellum period. In 1860 only 41 of 263 individuals (15.6 percent) were merchants. In 1870 the number was 23 of the 58 wealthy Texans (39.6 percent). The majority of those were individuals—such as Henry Rosenberg of Galveston County, William Headin of Nueces County, and William Hutchins of Harris County—engaged in the wholesale dry-goods business, or, as in the case of Frank Moureau of Comal County, George Butler, J. J. Hendley,

Isadore Dyer, and Robert Mills of Galveston, commission merchants dealing primarily in cotton. Some merchants, such as J. P. Davis, Edward Wood, and James M. Brown of Galveston, specialized in handling hardwares, and others, such as Houston merchant Thomas House, were both wholesale grocers and commission merchants.

In 1860 farmers and planters constituted over half (65.2 percent) of those individuals having $100,000 or more. In 1870, however, only ten, or 17.2 percent, of the fifty-eight individuals having $100,000 in total property were farmers or planters.

Seven of the 1870 wealthy Texans listed their occupations as lawyer, three were stock raisers, two were physicians, and two were bankers. The two women among the fifty-eight wealthiest, Mary Alexander of Fannin County and Amanda Cartwright of San Augustine County, both listed their occupation as housekeeping. Joseph R. Morris was mayor of Houston; Joseph A. Richardson was a beef packer in the same city; William Baker, a railroad president; and Frederick Stanby, a cashier and bookkeeper. Charles Phillips of Marion County, youngest of the group, listed his occupation in 1870 as "gentleman."

Many of the affluent Texans engaged in more than one occupation. John Sealy, prominent businessman from Galveston, for example, was listed in the census as a banker-merchant, but other sources indicate he also had been president of the Galveston Wharf Company, an organizer of the Galveston Gas Company , and codeveloper of several railroads. Joseph Landa of Comal County, successful immigrant from Germany, was listed in the census simply as "miller," but other accounts show that he was also developer of a cotton gin, sawmill, electric plant, ice-manufacturing plant, and cotton oil mill. And Thomas House, onetime Houston confectioner, was a wholesale grocer, cotton and wool factor, hardware and dry-goods dealer, as well as developer of the Houston Board of Trade and Cotton Exchange and the Houston and Texas Central Railroad.

Forty-three of the fifty-eight wealthiest Texans of 1870 held more real than personal property, nine held more personal than real property, and six held an equal amount of each. Median real property holding for the group was $70,000, compared to the median personal property holding of $35,000.

Table 1 shows the breakdown of real and personal property holding of the wealthy Texans of the Reconstruction period. It may be noted that the extremes in real-property ownership ranged from the six individuals who owned less than $25,000 to the eight individuals who owned $200,000 or more. In personal-property holding the extremes ranged from twenty-seven individuals who owned less than $25,000 to the four individuals who owned $200,000 or more.

Table 1
Property Holding of Wealthy Texans
1870

Number of Individuals

Amount of Property Held	*Real Property*	*Personal Property*
None listed in census	2	3
Less than $25,000	4	24
$25,000 and less than $50,000	2	5
$50,000 and less than $100,000	11	16
$100,000 and less than $200,000	31	6
$200,000 and over	8	4
Totals	58	58

Only three Texans, Richard King of Duval County, and John Sealy and J. J. Hendley of Galveston County, held half a million dollars in property in 1870. King, the great cattle baron of South Texas, was the wealthiest person in the state, possessing $200,000 in real and $365,000 in personal property in 1870. Hendley and Sealy, commission merchants in Galveston, each held $250,000 in real and $250,000 in personal property in 1870. All three of the wealthiest Texans were born in the North: King, a native of New York, Hendley, a native of Connecticut, and Sealy, a native of Pennsylvania.

Most of the wealthy Texans of the Reconstruction period appear to have lived in the state prior to the Civil War. All twenty-two of those with biographies in the *Handbook of Texas* lived in the state before 1860. Of this group, merchant-banker Robert Mills of Galveston was the earliest arrival, having come to Texas in 1827. Eight others migrated to Texas in the 1830s, ten in the 1840s, and two in the 1850s. One—South Texas rancher Thomas M. Coleman—had been born in Texas. Many were listed in the federal census with children born in

Texas prior to the Civil War, and several were listed on tax rolls of the Republic.

The majority of the wealthy Texans of the Reconstruction period were self-made men who came from humble family backgrounds and who had had little formal education. Some—such as William S. Herndon, who graduated from Mackenzie College; John C. Robertson, who attended Harvard Law School; Samuel Maverick, who received a B.A. degree from Yale; and George W. Paschal, who completed course work at the Georgia State Academy—were college trained, but the majority were not so well educated. English-born Thomas W. House started his career as a baker in the old St. Charles Hotel of New Orleans; John Sealy and Henry Rosenberg were clerks in mercantile stores; and Richard King went to sea as a cabin boy after only eight months of formal schooling. At least three of the group, William J. Hutchins, J. D. Giddings, and Mifflin Kenedy, were onetime school teachers, although their own formal education had been limited to the common schools.

Some of the wealthy Texans of the Reconstruction period played active roles in public life. Four—E. B. Nichols, John C. Robertson, E. S. C. Robertson, and F. S. Stockdale—were members of the secession convention of 1861, and one, Samuel Maverick, was a member of the Texas Convention of 1836. Two of the group, E. S. C. Robertson and F. S. Stockdale, later served in the constitutional convention of 1875. William J. Hutchins had been mayor of Houston; Joseph R. Morris was serving as mayor of Houston in 1870; and William R. Baker would become mayor of Houston in the 1880s. William S. Herndon of Smith County was a member of the Forty-second and Forty-third United States Congresses, and F. S. Stockdale of Calhoun County was lieutenant governor of the state during the last two years of the Civil War. Henry Rosenberg of Galveston served not only as a city alderman, but also as the consul for his native Switzerland for several years. George W. Paschal of Travis County was a distinguished jurist and writer, having served as chief justice of the Arkansas Supreme Court prior to moving to Texas in 1847. During the 1850s Paschal was editor of the Unionist newspaper the *Southern Intelligencer;* and after the Civil War he wrote *A Digest of Laws of Texas* and *The Constitution of the United States Defined and Carefully Annotated.*

All in all, the wealthy Texans of the Reconstruction period had much in common with their prewar contemporaries. Like the wealthy Texans of 1860, they were men who had become wealthy largely through their own talents and hard labor, by taking advantage of "a developing economic prosperity unparalleled in Texas history." They were also leaders who combined economic achievement with public service. Most of them had resided in Texas for many years prior to the war, although there was a larger percentage of nonsoutherners (in terms of birthplace) among the 1870 group than among the earlier group. The greatest difference between the two groups was the nature of their occupations. In prewar Texas a majority of the wealthy individuals were farmers or planters; in 1870 they were merchants and bankers.

Wealthy Texans, 1870
With a Summary of Biographical Data
Taken from the Manuscript Returns of the Ninth U.S. Census

County	Name	Age	Place of Birth	Occupation	Real Property	Personal Property
Anderson	Thomas Adams	55	Tennessee	Physician	$108,500	$ 800
	Benj. Hollingsworth	68	South Carolina	Farmer	100,000	1,877
Bell	E. S. C. Robertson	50	Tennessee	Farmer	100,000	30,000
Bexar	Francis Guilbeau	59	France	Merchant	100,000	15,000
	James Honco	54	Ireland	Merchant	100,000	
	Nat. Lewis	64	Massachusetts	Builder	70,000	50,000
	Samuel Maverick	67	South Carolina	Lawyer	160,000	5,000
	John Twohig	62	Ireland	Banker	90,000	50,000
Brazoria	William Bryan	55	Missouri	Farmer	100,000	10,000
Calhoun	F. S. Stockdale	43	Kentucky	Lawyer	100,000	20,000
Collin	Madison Bullion	46	Alabama	Merchant	250,000	2,000
	G. Foote	46	Virginia	Merchant	100,000	20,000
Comal	Joseph Landa	52	Germany	Miller	150,000	10,000
	Frank Moureau	44	Germany	Merchant	15,000	90,000
	Thomas Perryman	59	Georgia	Farmer	20,000	100,000
Davis	William Lambert	48	Georgia	Farmer	100,000	2,000
Duval	Mifflin Kenedy	52	Pennsylvania	Stock Raiser	21,000	139,600
	Richard King	44	New York	Stock Raiser	200,000	365,000
El Paso	Samuel Shantz	42	Germany	Merchant	50,000	75,000
Fannin	Mary Alexander	43	Kentucky	Housekeeper	180,000	2,400
	John Dale	45	Tennessee	Farmer	90,000	10,000
	John R. Russell	47	North Carolina	Merchant	78,000	55,000
Galveston	J. M. Brown	47	New York	Merchant	175,000	100,000
	George Butler	40	New York	Merchant	50,000	50,000
	J. P. Davis	53	Virginia	Merchant	100,000	30,000
	Isadore Dyer	52	England	Merchant	50,000	50,000

County	Name	Age	Birthplace	Occupation		
	J. J. Hendley	62	Connecticut	Merchant	250,000	250,000
	Robert Mills	62	Kentucky	Merchant	100,000	
	E. B. Nichols	54	New York	Merchant	100,000	
	Henry Rosenberg	46	Switzerland	Merchant	144,000	49,000
	John Sealy	47	Pennsylvania	Banker-Merchant	250,000	250,000
	J. L. Sleight	58	New York	Merchant	125,000	125,000
	Edward Wood	54	New Jersey	Merchant	175,000	75,000
Harris	John D. Andrews	74	Louisiana	Planter	100,000	3,000
	William R. Baker	49	New York	Railroad Pres.	218,000	8,000
	Thomas House	56	England	Merchant	158,000	80,000
	William Hutchins	57	New York	Merchant	200,000	12,750
	Joseph R. Morris	42	Connecticut	Mayor	155,400	10,000
	Joseph A. Richardson	51	Massachusetts	Beef Packer	250,000	12,000
	Frederick Stanby	35	England	Cashier-Bookkeeper	100,000	11,000
Liberty	Charles D. Cleveland	46	Kentucky	Lawyer	56,000	50,000
McLennan	W. W. Downs	74	North Carolina	Planter	150,000	3,000
Marion	James Bemis	32	Mississippi	Banker		200,000
	Perry M. Graham	46	Tennessee		75,000	30,000
	Charles E. Phillips	24	Arkansas	Gentleman		100,000
	Fred A. Schluter	52	Tennessee	Wholesaler Dealer	100,000	15,000
Nueces	William Headin	32	Ireland	Merchant	50,000	50,000
Red River	W. B. Aiken	65	North Carolina	Farmer	70,000	50,000
Rusk	S. W. March	46	North Carolina	Physician	100,000	30,000
San Augustine	Amanda Cartwright		Tennessee	Housekeeper	343,281	75,529
Smith	William Herndon	33	Georgia	Lawyer	122,000	55,000
	John C. Robertson	46	Georgia	Lawyer	100,000	20,000
San Patricio	Thomas Coleman	36	Texas	Stock Raiser	25,000	75,000
Travis	Eugene Bremond	40	Maryland	Merchant	12,000	100,000
	George W. Paschal	58	Georgia	Lawyer	110,000	6,000
	George W. Samspon	40	South Carolina	Merchant	25,000	75,000
	William H. Sinclair	32	Ohio	Planter	100,000	12,000
Washington	J. D. Giddings	55	Pennsylvania	Lawyer	100,000	15,000

Retracing the Chisholm Trail

WAYNE GARD *

Probably no other figure in American history is so enshrouded in myth and romance as the cowboy. He has become a symbol of individualism and a nostalgic image of a lost America. Historians of the American West, consequently, devote long hours and write numerous lines of prose attempting to create an accurate portrayal of cowhands and the cattle kingdom. Their undertaking is a difficult one, because they must overturn impressions drawn from folklore, fiction, and films.

Wayne Gard, a well-known authority on western history, undertakes such a task in his essay "Retracing the Chisholm Trail." As he points out, the Chisholm Trail has been identified by various people as every small, winding cattle trail in a plethora of Texas counties or, for purists, as simply Jesse Chisholm's wagon road. Gard sets the record straight in both cases.

In doing so he writes of the history of the famous trail as well as describing its path. Moreover, the reader can share with the author in this essay that brief period of Texas history when cowboys herded cattle north to market. Interested students can buttress this accurate account with other articles by Gard, such as "The Impact of the Cattle Trails," SOUTHWESTERN HISTORICAL QUARTERLY, *LXXI (July, 1967), and "The Shawnee Trail,"* IBID., *LVI (January, 1953). Among many other*

* Wayne Gard, "Retracing the Chisholm Trail," *Southwestern Historical Quarterly*, LX (July, 1956), 53–68.

additional fine selections, a good overview is Clara M. Love's "History of the Cattle Industry in the Southwest," IBID., *XIX (April, 1916).*

The Chisholm Trail, in 1956 the path of a historical tour, is something that Texans have been reminiscing about, and even singing about, for three generations. It almost could be carpeted with the pulp stories and the Hollywood films it has inspired. It has become a byword for the romance of the open-range era.

For the frontier cowhand, on "a ten-dollar horse and a forty-dollar saddle," the trail stood for something more real. It meant long hours in dust or rain. It spelled the dangers of river crossings, of midnight stampedes, of raids by marauding Comanches. Yet, even for him, the route of the Longhorn herds to Kansas markets was a road to high adventure.

> I woke up one morning on the old Chisholm Trail,
> Rope in my hand and a cow by the tail.
> Feet in the stirrups and seat in the saddle,
> I hung and rattled with them Longhorn cattle.

This winding trail, over which several million Longhorns plodded north, made history. It carried the greatest movement of cattle ever known. Yet it was neglected by serious historians for so long and was so distorted by writers of fiction that its name came to have widely varied meanings to different people. Local historians have applied the Chisholm name to cowpaths in almost every Texas county, with confusing results.

To some, the Chisholm Trail denotes any cattle trail that led from Texas northward, or perhaps even westward. Others, going to the other extreme, say the name should be used only for the road that Jesse Chisholm followed, with his wagons, from his trading post on the North Canadian River to the one he established at the mouth of the Little Arkansas, in southern Kansas. Those who accept this narrow definition say there was no Chisholm Trail in Texas.

Use of the term in the period of the great Longhorn drives, though, shows that the Chisholm Trail was a fairly definite route from the Texas ranges to Kansas markets. Both on the map and in time, it was

the middle one, and the most used, of the three principal cattle trails
pointing north. To its east was the earlier Shawnee Trail, and to its
west was the newer Western Trail. Use of the Chisholm Trail, which
existed from the middle of 1867 through 1884, overlapped, in its
earlier years, with that of the Shawnee Trail, and, in its later years,
with that of the Western Trail, opened in 1876.

Red River Station

Ft. Worth

T e x a s

Waco

Austin

San Antonio

The Chisholm Trail
in
T E X A S

Like the other trails, the Chisholm was a means of solving an
economic problem. Texas had an overabundance of wild and half-wild
Longhorn cattle, especially after the Civil War had disrupted
marketing. There were no railroads to haul the cattle to market, and
Gulf shipping could handle only a small fraction of them. The one
means available was to walk the cattle to distant cities or railroad
shipping points. This method called for time, patience, and courage;

but it took little cash outlay, since the cattle could sustain themselves on the grass along the trail.

The tough Longhorns, descended mainly from Spanish cattle brought over by the conquistadors but with some blood from British breeds, were well adapted to the hardships of the long tramp. "As trail cattle," said Charles Goodnight, "their equal never has been known. Their hoofs are superior to those of any other cattle. They can go farther without water and endure more suffering than others."

These cattle were in strong demand in the North, not only for stocking new ranges but for increasing the beef supply. A Longhorn steer worth only six or eight dollars in Texas might bring twenty dollars or more in Kansas. Butchers might discount the beef as less tender than that from the Midwest farmer's barnyard, but many thrifty housewives viewed it as a bargain. Too, a few months of feeding on corn helped the quality of the Texas product that came up the trail.

Some of the confusion over the Chisholm Trail arises from mistaking for it one or the other of the trails on it flanks. Some comes from the nature of the trail. It did not follow an exact route, year after year; nor was it a line from a single starting point to a single destination. It might be compared to a tree with many roots and several large branches. The roots were feeder trails coming in from every part of Texas that raised beef cattle in the trail period. The trunk was the route through North Texas and the Indian Territory, now Oklahoma. The branches were the extensions to various railroad towns in Kansas in which the cattle were sold and shipped.

As Thomas C. Richardson of Dallas has pointed out,

We shall get rid of a good deal of geographical difficulty at once by recalling that the trails originated wherever a herd was shaped up and ended wherever a market was found. A thousand minor trails fed the main routes, and many an old-timer who as a boy saw a herd of stately Longhorns, piloted by bandanaed, booted, and spurred men, lived with the firm conviction that the Dodge or Chisholm Trail passed right over yonder.

In its parts south of Waco, the Chisholm Trail was identical with the earlier Shawnee Trail. Drovers had begun to use this older route in the early 1840s, determined to take their cattle to markets even though they had no railroads. From Austin past Waco and Dallas to the Red River, this route followed the military road that Colonel William G. Cooke had surveyed in 1840. From the site of Dallas north, the trail followed high ground and came to be called the Preston Road. The trail crossed the Red River at Rock Bluff, near Preston.

Northward through the eastern end of the Indian Territory, the Shawnee Trail followed an old Indian trail past Boggy Depot and Fort Gibson. Southbound emigrants had begun to use and widen this trail, which some of them called the Texas Road.

In southeastern Kansas, at a point near the present Baxter Springs, the Shawnee Trail split. Some of the drovers took their herds on north to Independence, while others pointed northeast to St. Louis, Sedalia, Quincy, or Chicago. Later, as settlement pushed westward, some drovers went around to the west, then north to Junction City, Kansas City, or some point in Nebraska or Iowa.

The Shawnee Trail served Texas drovers well until a few years before the Civil War, when they began to have trouble with Kansas and Missouri farmers over what then was called Texas fever. Then the war virtually put a stop to the northward trailing. After the war, with the ranges crowded with half-wild cattle and with money scarce, the Texas cowmen took up trailing on a larger scale than ever. In 1866 they crossed the Red River with herds estimated to total 200,000 to 260,000 head.

But that year they ran into more trouble than ever. Midwestern farmers were more determined than before that the Longhorns, themselves immune to the fever carried by the ticks on their hides, should not infect the farm cattle along the trail. Gathering in armed mobs, the farmers stampeded many of the herds and killed several of the trail hands. They caused other drovers to follow roundabout trails or to hold their herds in the Indian Territory until they could find some way to take them to market.

This conflict made it clear that a new trail and a new market were needed. The Texas cowmen realized this need but were not in a good position to meet it. A group of Kansans proposed a new trail and a new market, but their plan fell through. It remained for a young Illinois stock dealer, still in his twenties, to take the initiative.

This was Joseph G. McCoy, who, with his older brothers, was engaged in the livestock business in Springfield, in the heart of the feeder country. Young McCoy had talked with several Illinois cattlemen just back from Texas, and with one of his friends who had helped string an army telegraph line across the state. He was aware of the vast reservoir of cattle in the Lone Star State and of the need for a new market that would be free from the trouble that had disrupted trailing over the old Shawnee route.

McCoy first considered establishing a market at Fort Smith and shipping the cattle down the Arkansas River, but he gave up that plan as impractical. Then he visited some of the Kansas towns on the new Union Pacific Railroad—towns west of most of the farm settlements and near or beyond the quarantine line drawn for trailing. In the summer of 1867 he decided on the village of Abilene and, after making arrangements with the railroad, began building stockyards, a hotel, and other facilities there. He sent notices to the Texas cowmen of his new market and advised them how to reach it over a new route.

Since most of the trailing was done in the spring and early summer, when the grass is most lush, the principal season was over by the time McCoy was ready. But he received several fall herds and others owned by drovers who had come up earlier and who had been marking time in the Indian Territory or in southern Kansas. He began shipping in September and prepared for a big business in 1868.

The trail to Abilene was new only above the crossing of the Brazos River near Waco. Below, it followed the beaten paths of the Shawnee Trail. Some of the herds came from ranges along, or even beyond, the Rio Grande. Drovers bought or stole cattle from Mexico and swam them across the border stream. They trailed them northward through the brush country, either following the old Beef Trail past Beeville, Gonzales, and Lockhart to Austin or bending westward to San Antonio.

In San Antonio the trail hands could find entertainment as long as their money lasted. While the bosses put up at the staid Menger Hotel, the others could find cheaper lodging elsewhere. They could lose their money at monte or other games, watch rooster fights in the streets, attend a bull fight on Sunday afternoon, or take in a horse race on the prairie turf at the edge of town. If the chili and enchiladas at the Mexican stands were too peppery, they could be diluted at any corner bar. At night there always were girls at the dance halls and in half-dark doorways.

Above San Antonio, feeder trails came in from each side, one of the most heavily used leading from the fertile grasslands of Matagorda County. At Austin the drovers took their herds across the Colorado

River, most of them using the Montopolis ford, a little below the town. Plodding on northward, the herds kept below the Balcones escarpment on their west. Usually they found abundant grass and ample water as they crossed Brushy Creek and the San Gabriel and Lampasas rivers.

Sometimes the muddy, reddish water of the Brazos gave the drovers trouble and caused delays. In the earlier years, most of the herds were swum across at Waco. Later it became more common to trail on upstream and cross at Fort Graham or Kimball. By the time the cattle reached Fort Worth, most of them were well broken to the trail.

Fort Worth, although without a railroad until the summer of 1876, quickly became an outfitting point for the drovers. It offered saddles, rope, six-shooters, groceries, and other supplies. It also provided entertainment as lusty as any cowhand could want.

At Fort Worth, where hogs still roamed in the streets, cowboys primed with firewater could shoot up the town on Saturday night without much fear of penalty. In 1876, Fort Worth had a two-gun marshal, T. I. Courtright, better known as Long Hair Jim. On Saturday nights he and his two policemen might crowd twenty-five to thirty hilarious cowhands into the two cells and dungeon of the log jail at Second and Commerce streets, but usually the miscreants stayed only long enough to recover their sobriety.

From Fort Worth, where some of the herds changed hands, the Chisholm Trail crossed the West Fork of the Trinity River, veered a bit to the northwest, and led north along the border of Wise and Denton counties. Crossing Elizabeth and Oliver creeks, it passed east of the village of Decatur, then across Denton Creek and Clear Creek. Beyond, it entered the breaks of the Red River.

Some of the early herds crossed the Red River at Sivell's Bend, in Cooke County, or at old Spanish Fort. But most of them were trailed farther upstream and put across at Red River Station, in northeastern Montague County. This crossing, just below the mouth of Fleetwood Branch, took its name from a Civil War outpost of the Texas Rangers. Soon after it became a heavily used crossing, it acquired a store and a saloon.

The Red River, often flooded during the spring trailing season, was one of the worst streams to swim a herd across. Some times several herds were held up on the Texas bank, waiting for the water to subside.

At best, the crossing was made dangerous by quicksands and by the tendency of the Longhorns to start milling in the middle of the river instead of going on across.

On the rolling prairies of the Indian country, the trail outfits were subject to the constant hazard of redskin raiders. Comanches, Kiowas, and others would try to stampede the cattle and drive off the horses. Night guards had to heed every sound. But usually the Territory offered plenty of grass and water. The trail led almost straight north on a route now closely hugged by U.S. Highway 81. Trees along the streams provided firewood for the trail cook, except in the northern part, where he had either to carry wood or to rely on cow chips.

About twenty-seven miles north of the Red River was a landmark that many of the trail drivers remembered. This was a mesa that became known as Monument Hill or Monument Rocks. Situated just east of the present village of Addington, it offered a fine view of the surrounding country. Cowboys on its summit could spot cook wagons and strung-out herds for ten to fifteen miles in either direction. The almost flat top of the hill was strewn with slabs and boulders of reddish sandstone. Early drovers gathered some of these rocks into two piles as markers for the trail. The piles were about three hundred feet apart, and each was about ten feet across and twelve feet high. Cowboys who climbed the hill later used their knives or spurs to carve their initials or brands on the soft stone.

In the Indian country the trail outfits had five rivers to cross—the Washita, the South Canadian, the North Canadian, the Cimarron, and the Salt Fork of the Arkansas. They entered Kansas just south of the present Caldwell and pointed on north. Usually they had little trouble with the Kansas stream crossings, which included the Chikaskia River, Slate Creek, the Ninnescah River, Cow Skin Creek, and the Arkansas River. Sometimes, in the northern part of the Territory or in southern Kansas, they met herds of buffaloes. They had to avoid trailing too close to them, lest some of their cattle, or even their spare horses, join the shaggies.

On the trail the cowmen followed the routine that had been developed on the Shawnee and other earlier routes. The size of the trail herd varied from a few hundred to several thousand; but it seldom ran above three thousand, since a large number meant delays in watering the cattle and in crossing streams. To avoid crowding and overheating, the herd was strung out, often for half a mile or more.

On each side of the lead cattle was a bowlegged cowboy on horseback. This pair, the pointers, kept the herd headed in the desired direction. They did not drive or hurry the cattle but barely stayed close enough to keep them from wandering from the trail. Behind the pointers, at intervals on each side of the herd, rode the swing men, the flankers, and finally the drag men with buckskin poppers for laggards. As the dust became much worse toward the rear of the herd, the trail hands usually rotated their positions from day to day.

The cook, who drove and presided over the chuck wagon, roused the men for an early breakfast; and the wrangler brought the horses into camp. After the men had eaten and the Longhorns had grazed for a short time, the herd was put on the trail. As the cattle moved slowly, the cook in his wagon could pass the herd and have dinner ready when the outfit stopped before midday. The afternoon drive usually ended at a stream that offered water for the cattle and near a place the foreman had chosen for a bed ground. The boss usually tried to have the cattle bedded away from timber that might hide Indians or wolves, and on high ground that would catch the breeze.

The cook, with the back end of his wagon turned down for use as a work table, soon had ready an appetizing meal. Beef, beans, and sourdough biscuits were the staple items, though sometimes stewed tomatoes or canned or dried fruit gave variety. The hungry men ate from tin plates as they sat cross-legged on the grass. They washed down their food with Arbuckle's coffee, strong and steaming hot.

As darkness fell, the men quietly pushed the cattle into a more compact mass on the bed ground. The two punchers assigned to the first hours of night guard began riding slowly around the herd, in opposite directions. Often they hummed or crooned lullabies to soothe the cattle and make them less likely to stampede. When the Big Dipper showed that their stint was done, they wakened the pair to take their places and slid into their bedrolls.

The indefinite, virtually unblazed route that the Longhorn outfits followed from the Texas ranges to Abilene had, in its early years, a great variety of names. Some cowmen called it merely the trail, the cattle trail, or the Kansas Trail. Others, a bit more specifically, called it the Abilene Trail or McCoy's Trail. Kansans called it the Great Cattle Trail, the Texas Cattle Trail, the Great Texas Cattle Trail, or later the Wichita Trail.

The name Chisholm Trail, which probably was used orally long before it appeared in print, began to pop up in Kansas newspapers in the spring of 1870 and in Texas papers four years later. For several years Jesse Chisholm, a Scotch-Cherokee trader and guide, had been traveling back and forth between his trading post on the North Canadian and the one he had set up on the Arkansas, at the future site of Wichita. Other traders followed his wagon tracks and called the route Chisholm's Trail.

When the first Texas herds were trailed to Abilene in the fall of 1867, it was convenient for the drovers to use the Chisholm ruts as a guide for part of their route. Although Jesse Chisholm died in the following spring, he was so strongly associated with that part of the trail that it came to bear his name, not only among Kansans but among the Texas drovers. With the Chisholm name applied to part of the trail, its extension to the whole route was easy and natural.

In the early days of the Chisholm Trail, the drovers included some of the most prominent Texas cowmen. One was James M. Daugherty of Denton County, who had been tied and whipped by a band of Jayhawkers on the Shawnee Trail in 1866. Others were William H. Day and his brother-in-law, Jesse L. Driskill, who would leave an Austin hotel as his monument. From Caldwell County went Colonel John J. Myers, who had gone to California with John C. Frémont, and Mark A. Withers, one of the most expert in handling a trail herd. From Brushy Creek, in Williamson County, two brothers, Dudley H. and John W. Snyder, took herds north almost every year. From the coastal plains of Matagorda County came Abel H. ("Shanghai") Pierce, whose booming voice and salty stories were known in many a cow camp.

For the men who rode the trail, it was long and tiring. By the time they reached Abilene, they were ready to celebrate. They had been perhaps two months in the saddle, with monotonous diet, no women, and no entertainment byond the nightly howling of the coyotes. So Abilene, which had been a sleepy village of a dozen log cabins, roofed with dirt, and a few business buildings, became in a few weeks a riotous cow town. Soon it had eleven saloons with gambling rooms in the back, several dance halls, and a whole colony of bagnios.

The frontier Texas cowboy liked to wear his pistols wherever he went and to use them whenever the spirit moved him. Abilene residents soon became aware of this habit. Young J. B. Edwards, who delivered ice to the saloons, saw much of this revelry. "When a man from Texas got too much tanglefoot aboard," he recalled, he was liable under the least provocation to use his six-shooters. Not less than two were always hanging from his belt. If his fancy told him to shoot, he did so—into the air or at anything he saw. A plug hat would bring a volley from him at any time, drunk or sober.

With the Abilene cattle business doubling every year, the town fathers soon had to do something to check cowboy exuberance. For the summer and fall shipping season of 1870, they hired as marshal Tom Smith, a husky Irishman from New York who had gone west and worked at railroad building in Nebraska. Later he had been a marshal in Wyoming. Smith turned out to be one of the best peace officers on the frontier. With amazing courage, he thrashed the town bullies and enforced the ordinance against carrying guns. But Smith was murdered in the fall when he went out to a dugout in the country to arrest a killer.

For the 1871 season, with a peak drive of 700,000 Texas Longhorns being pointed north, Abilene hired as marshal the celebrated pistoleer James B. ("Wild Bill") Hickok. In his suit of fringed buckskin and with his hair down to his shoulders, Wild Bill made a picturesque figure; but as a law officer he fell short of Tom Smith.

In Abilene that summer were several widely known Texans, including Ben Thompson and Phil Coe, who ran the Bull's Head Saloon and its profitable gambling room. Another was John Wesley Hardin, who had come up with a trail herd and who already had put many of the figurative notches in his deadly gun. Wild Bill made his headquarters at the popular Alamo Saloon and made frequent rounds of the others. But despite his fame as a marksman, he did not always keep the ebullient cowboys in rein.

By the fall of 1871, the permanent residents of Abilene and the farmers in the surrounding country were fed up with the cattle trade. This section of Kansas was becoming more thickly settled, and the farmers did not want their fences destroyed and their crops trampled by Longhorn herds. Nor did the parents in town want to rear their children in an atmosphere dominated by saloons, gambling rooms, dance halls, and brothels. So, in February, 1872, they asked the Texas drovers to market their cattle elsewhere.

For the next four years the chief Kansas markets for cattle taken up the Chisholm Trail were Ellsworth and Wichita, though some were sold at Newton and other towns. Ellsworth was on the Kansas Pacific—originally and again now the Union Pacific—about sixty miles west of Abilene. It had begun to ship some cattle in 1871, and it took over much of the Abilene business the next year. Several Abilene businessmen even took down their buildings in sections and moved them to Ellsworth. With them went some of the gamblers, including Ben Thompson.

Wichita, which split with Ellsworth the business of shipping Texas trail cattle, was a new town at the mouth of the Little Arkansas. It had just been reached by the Santa Fe Railroad in May, 1872, and it hastened to build loading pens and to hire agents to persuade the drovers to use its market. It also engaged Joe McCoy to go north and east to persuade cattle buyers to come to Wichita. This new market had an advantage in being on the trail and in being much nearer to Texas than was Ellsworth.

With the peak of trailing past and the business divided, neither Ellsworth nor Wichita matched Abilene as a trail's-end town. Yet each did a flourishing business from 1872 through 1875, and each had its share of vice and crime. As at Abilene, steers from the beef herds were shipped mainly to feeders in Illinois, while cattle from the mixed herds were trailed on, often by new owners, to stock virgin ranges in the Northwest.

The 1875 season marked a peak in the practice of some of the big cowmen in buying herds on the range or on the Texas part of the trail and sending them on under their own road brands. One successful partnership in such ventures had been that of Captain Eugene B. Millett and Major Seth Mabry. Another was that of John O. Dewes and Colonel James F. Ellison. In 1875 all four combined in a partnership that owned or controlled two-thirds of the whole Texas drive.

Yet the fringe of farmer settlement kept pushing farther west as the buffaloes were cleared from the plains and as railroads extended their tracks. Kansas lawmakers kept edging westward their quarantine line, only beyond which trailing was lawful. This trend virtually ended the shipping of trail cattle at Ellsworth and Wichita after the 1875 season.

The spring of 1876 marked the opening of a new major cattle market at Dodge City, on the Santa Fe, west of Wichita. Dodge, which has been the chief headquarters for the Kansas buffalo hunters a few years earlier, had shipped a few cattle in 1875. Now that the older markets were closed to trail drivers by the quarantine law, this new one began to boom. It offered not only shipping facilities but the kind of entertainment that quickly gave it the name of Gomorrah of the Plains.

As in the case of Abilene in 1867, the new market meant a new trail. While many drovers continued to go up the Chisholm Trail to the Cimarron and then cut across northwest to Dodge City, others followed a more direct route. Leaving the Chisholm Trail at Belton, they followed the Leon River upstream to the northwest, then pointed north to Fort Griffin, outfitting point and hide market for most of the Texas buffalo hunters. Heading on north, they crossed the Red River by a ford beside which Jonathan Doan had built a picket house with a roof of mud and grass and a buffalo hide flapping in the doorway. From there they pointed almost straight north through the Indian country to Dodge City.

Thus the Chisholm Trail, which only a few years earlier had become free of the rivalry of the Shawnee Trail to its east, now had competition from the new Western Trail on the other side. Fort Worth, which had most to lose from this shift, gave it scant attention at first. But Fort Griffin merchants were making the most of their new opportunity. "Cattle from the south are coming in rapidly," wrote a correspondent there on April 22, 1876. "It is estimated that 125,000 head will be on this trail this season."

Many have asked why the Texas cowmen continued to trail their cattle after railroads were available for hauling them. Beginning with the season of 1873, cattle could be shipped north from Dallas or Denison or east from Dallas. Beginning early in July, 1876, they could be shipped from Fort Worth.

Some cattle did go by rail from all three towns. Fort Worth shipped 51,923 head in 1877, the first full year that it had a railroad. But the rail shipments were only a small fraction of the trail herds. The railroads did not have enough stock cars to carry them all. Too, rough roadbeds, protruding horns, and inexpert handling often led to injury of the cattle.

The major factor, though, was that of cost. Walking the cattle north was much cheaper than shipping them by rail. A Texas stockman with a herd of two thousand cattle had to pay $10,000 to ship them to St. Louis by the Missouri, Kansas, and Texas, or $11,500 by the Texas and Pacific. But he could trail them to Kansas for $1,000 and ship them from there to St. Louis for $7,500, making a total of $8,500. In trailing, of course, he risked losses from river crossings, stampedes, and Indians; but most of the cowmen were willing to take those chances. The differences in cost, declared the Fort Worth *Democrat,* "are altogether too great. So long as they exist, we may certainly look for the trade to go where it has always gone—to Kansas."

So the trailing continued. Fort Worth handled twice as many cattle as did Fort Griffin in 1876, but in the next two years the larger town began to feel the pinch of competition. In the summer of 1878 the Fort Worth *Democrat* berated local merchants for letting much of the cattle trade slip away from them. In the early spring of 1879, Fort Worth leaders sent a man down the trail to persuade the drovers to use the old route. The Fort Worth and Fort Griffin newspapers engaged in much bantering and boasting on the size of their cattle drives. When the season ended, the figures showed that nearly half of the cattle had followed the new trail.

In 1880 the Chisholm Trail gained a temporary advantage when the town of Caldwell, near the south edge of Kansas, obtained a railroad connection and began shipping cattle in June. Caldwell, which was directly on the Chisholm Trail, was closer than Dodge City for many of the drovers; and it did a flourishing business. In 1880 it shipped more cattle than did Dodge City, though the latter received many more—the others being trailed on to Nebraska or beyond.

But barbed wire was narrowing the old cattle route, and after the trailing season of 1884 it barred the beaten path. Even on the Western Trail, the drives were diminishing and lasted only a few years. Not only was fencing a factor, but Texas railroads were beginning to offer better facilities for carrying the cattle to market. Cattlemen asked Congress to establish a National Trail along the eastern edge of Colorado, but the lawmakers declined to take this action.

Except for a few sporadic drives, trailing from Texas northward ended with the 1880s. As rain beat out the prints of Longhorn hoofs and grass spread over the bare ground, cowmen adjusted themselves to a new economy of fenced ranches and shipments by rail. But they knew that the Chisholm Trail had served them well. It had given them a market when they were overstocked with cattle and short of cash. It had spurred the settlement and stocking of the northern ranges. It had brought down the price of beef for the housewife and helped beef to displace pork as the chief meat item on the dinner table. It had hastened the building of western railroads, had increased exports of beef, and had given impetus to the industries of meatpacking and refrigeration.

Too, the trail had brought together people from different sections of the country and thus helped to lessen the animosity left by the Civil War. It had shown Texas cowmen the need for improved breeds and had given them the means to bring in blooded stock, as well as to improve their ranches. And, like the Crusades of the Europeans in earlier centuries, the trail drivers had given thousands of young men an opportunity for adventure and had provided subjects for epic literature and art.

Today few physical traces are left of the Chisholm Trail. Even most of the river crossings are hard to pinpoint exactly; and at Red River Station a change in the channel has altered the appearance of the stream from trail-driving days. In Oklahoma, where the trail followed a more definite route than in Texas or Kansas, the State Highway Department has traced and mapped the route and that of the Western Trail with commendable detail. This task was completed in 1936, carrying out the instructions of a legislative act of 1931.

Texas and Kansas have a number of markers, but they leave much to be desired. One difficulty in marking the trail is that no highway in Texas or Kansas follows much of it closely as does Highway 81 in Oklahoma. This is especially true of the river crossings. An ideal trail crossing was one that offered low, gradual slopes on each side, making it easy for the cattle to enter and leave the stream. But an ideal site for a highway bridge is just the opposite—it is a place where the river is narrow, with high banks on each side. Thus a marker at the exact site of a trail crossing is likely to be in a cotton patch or a cow pasture and remain unseen by the public. One along a highway might be miles from the scene it is supposed to mark.

Even at Abilene, the first terminus of the trail, nearly all the marks of the cattle drives have been erased. Instead of the rip-roaring town it once was, Abilene is an almost Puritan city of white houses and shady streets. Its citizens are proud of the Dwight D. Eisenhower home and museum and seeming willing to foget the exciting days of the Texas cattle trade. As one stands in front of an ice-cream store of yellow brick on Cedar Street, it takes a bit of imagination to realize that this is the site of Wild Bill's hangout, the big Alamo Saloon, with its long bar and polished brass fixtures, its large mirrors, its paintings of nudes in the style of the Renaissance masters, its brightly labeled bottles of joy juice, and its clinking spurs and ribald laughter.

In Texas the Chisholm Trail lives in song and story and in many an outstanding canvas. Yet the last word on this great trail and the men who rode it has not been said. It still offers grist for many forms of art above the level of the gun-smoke writers who thus far have exploited it in pulp stories and on the movie screen. It could be a backdrop for a musical show as satisfying and as successful as *Oklahoma!* or for a great novel. Perhaps the 1956 tour or some later one will strike a spark for some immortal epic of the trail.

What James Stephen Hogg Means to Texas

JAMES P. HART*

Currently many observers look upon Texas as a potential leader in a new political coalition that may guide the country toward neoconservatism. Texans, thus, now project a conservative image. It was not always so. Texas politicians, for example, wrote the first liberal homestead act, pushed for national and state regulation of railroads and corporations, ratified quickly the Seventeenth, Eighteenth and Nineteenth Amendments, and became an integral part of the William Jennings Bryan-Woodrow Wilson wing of the Democratic party. Many historians look upon James Stephen Hogg as the spokesman for these progressive Democrats in Texas.

James P. Hart, former Texas Supreme Court judge and chancellor of the University of Texas, agrees. In this article, first presented as an address for James Stephen Hogg Day at the State Fair of Texas, he expresses his unabashed admiration for the former attorney general and governor of Texas. Furthermore, Hart subscribes to the great-man theory of history. He sees men, not events, as that which determines the future. And this essay not only describes Hogg's career and praises his leadership, but it celebrates those whom Hart considers to be men of political principles.

The major biography of Hogg, Robert C. Cotner's JAMES STEPHEN

*James P. Hart, "What James Stephen Hogg Means to Texas," *Southwestern Historical Quarterly*, LV (April, 1952), 439–447.

Hogg *(Austin, 1959), was published after this article. Cotner's lengthy and sympathetic biography will remain the definitive one for quite a few years. The best account of the interworkings of politics in the period is Alwyn Barr's* Reconstruction to Reform: Texas Politics, *1876–1906 (Austin, 1971). Although appreciative of Hogg's contributions, Barr gives a somewhat more balanced account of the accomplishments and political aspirations of the governor.*

That state is fortunate which can look back into its history and find examples of great citizens to inspire it in times of trouble. Texas is rich in its heritage of courageous public leadership. Problems change as the world changes, but the qualities that make men great remain constant. So we look to our past, not to find specific solutions to particular problems that vex and puzzle us, but to remind ourselves of the virtues that our forefathers possessed that enabled them to master the difficulties they met—virtues that we may aspire to realize in ourselves so that we may not be overwhelmed by the waves of perplexity and adversity that beat against us. In any list of great Texans, James Stephen Hogg will be among the foremost. So we may with profit reexamine and reflect on the story of his life, in order that thereby we may gain the wisdom and strength to follow his example.

The life of James Stephen Hogg spans a series of revolutionary changes in Texas life. He was born near Rusk in Cherokee County on March 24, 1851. At that time, Texas was just becoming accustomed to its status as a member of the American Union after a decade of precarious independence as a Republic. Mexican rule had ended only fifteen years previously. The heroes of the Texas Revolution—Sam Houston, Thomas Jefferson Rusk, and others—were still active leaders in Texas public life. For all that it appeared at the time, Texas was due for a period of rapid growth and prosperity. Certainly, so far as the Hogg family was concerned, the prospects seemed bright.

James Stephen Hogg's father, Joseph Lewis Hogg, was a prosperous lawyer, landowner, and public servant. He had moved to Texas during the days of the Republic and had served as a member of the Texas Congress, as a delegate to the annexation convention in 1845, and as a state senator after annexation. He had seen active service in the army in the Mexican War. When, shortly after the victorious termination of this war, his third son was born, it must have seemed to General Hogg that this boy would surely grow to manhood in an atmosphere of peace and security.

For a few years this hope seemed to be well founded. With peace restored, pioneers poured into Texas from the older states of the Union and from the British Isles and Western Europe. In the decade between 1850 and 1860 the population of Texas virtually tripled. The great natural resources of the state were beginning to be developed and utilized. Under the able administration of such wise men as Governor Elisha M. Pease, the state's financial situation was strengthened to such an extent that in 1858 the Texas legislature was able to appropriate $100,000 for the establishment of a state university and to provide for a landed endowment to sustain the expense of building, maintaining, and operating it.

The bright prospects of peace and prosperity were, however, soon blotted out by the dark clouds of Civil War. General Joseph Lewis Hogg was a member of the convention which gathered in Austin in 1861 and voted to withdraw from the Union. It must have been with a heavy heart that General Hogg made this decision to vote for the dissolution of the ties that he had personally helped to create some sixteen years earlier. Whatever his misgivings and forebodings may have been, he assumed the full burden of sustaining his action. He immediately volunteered to serve in the Confederate army, in which he received a commission as a brigadier general. Only a little over a year later, in May, 1862, he was killed in action while leading his troops at the defense of Corinth, Mississippi. So ended the career of a courageous leader and public servant, and so ended the hopes of James Stephen Hogg for a secure and peaceful boyhood and the guidance of a wise father to start him on the path of manhood.

Sad and hard as it was, the youth of James Stephen Hogg was very much like that of other young boys in the South of his day. The material destruction that was caused by the war was made many times worse by the instability and misgovernment of the Reconstruction period. The property which General Hogg had left his family became relatively worthless and soon disappeared through sales which were made in order to pay taxes and to sustain the living expenses of the family. No opportunity for public education was afforded young Jim

Hogg. The appropriation to establish a university had been diverted for the defense of the state. A year of private schooling in Alabama was all that the family could afford to give Jim Hogg.

Returning to Texas in 1866, Jim Hogg at the age of fifteen set about as best he could to earn a living and at the same time to educate himself. He worked as a typesetter in Rusk, where he perfected his spelling and enriched his vocabulary, being encouraged by the example of the literary accomplishments of his brother, Thomas E. Hogg. The Reconstruction period was one of lawlessness, but Jim Hogg fearlessly attacked the lawless element. As a consequence he was ambushed and shot in the back, but he recovered and continued his campaign against law violators with renewed vigor. He published his own newspapers in Longview and Quitman, in which he attacked the subsidies to the railroads and the flagrant corruption of the Ulysses S. Grant administration in Washington.

At the age of twenty-one, Jim Hogg entered upon his public career, being elected justice of the peace in Quitman, in Wood County, in 1873. While he was serving in this office he studied law and was admitted to the bar in 1875. In the meantime, in 1874, he married Miss Sallie Stinson, the daughter of Colonel James A. Stinson of Wood County, a most fortunate and happy union which saw the birth of three sons and a daughter and which lasted throughout Jim Hogg's career as a public officer and until his wife's untimely death in 1895.

Jim Hogg's political career saw only one defeat, in 1876 when he was an unsuccessful candidate for the Texas legislature. In 1878 he was elected county attorney of Wood County, and two years later he became district attorney of the Seventh Judicial District of Texas, where he earned a reputation as a vigorous prosecutor. After four years' service as district attorney, he retired to the private practice of the law in Tyler. In 1886 he was made the Democratic nominee for attorney general. His speech of acceptance before the Democratic Convention at Galveston is remarkable for its candor and brevity. Among other things, he said:

My nomination is a compliment, coming as it does from the greatest political organization in Texas. I have sought, obtained, and now accept with thanks the high trust.

Jim Hogg was an aggressive and diligent attorney general, devoted and active in his efforts to see that the people's rights were fully protected. At that time Texas was almost wholly dependent upon the railroads for transportation. The railroads exercised a tremendous influence on the political life of the state, but Jim Hogg fought them fearlessly when he was convinced that they were not complying with the law. He was successful in breaking up the Texas Traffic Association, which was designed to pool traffic and to eliminate competition between different lines in rates and other matters. He enforced laws requiring railroads and other corporations to dispose of their lands within statutory time limits. In this way he aided in bringing about a wide distribution of land ownership. He prosecuted suits which caused wildcat insurance companies to leave the state and other suits which led to the recovery of over one and one-half million acres of land for the state. In his every action he displayed courage and integrity, fearlessly discharging his duty regardless of political consequences.

While he was serving as attorney general, it became apparent to Jim Hogg that it would be a hopeless task to attempt to regulate the railroads through only legislative action and the bringing of lawsuits, and that it would be necessary to create a railroad commission that could exercise a continuous power of supervision, with members and a staff who, through a full-time devotion to the task, could become experts in the matters within their jurisdiction. Accordingly, in 1890 Jim Hogg sought and obtained the nomination for governor principally upon the plank of the creation of a railroad commission. Following his election as governor, he succeeded in having the Railroad Commission created through constitutional amendment and, what is of probably equal importance, he assured the success of the commission by persuading United States Senator John H. Reagan to resign his office at Washington in order to be the first chairman of the new commission.

At this time, almost sixty years later, we are not so much interested in the specific accomplishments of Governor Hogg's administration as in its general objectives and overall effects. Governor Hogg's administration was a part of an epoch of almost unrestrained corporate expansion and reckless exploitation of our natural resources. Governor Hogg's view was that this almost boundless expansive energy should be guided by wise laws to insure the public

208 Texas Vistas

good rather than the enrichment of only a favored few. He was not, however, in any sense an opponent of the sound growth of commerce and industry. In order to encourage eastern capital to come to Texas, he journeyed to Philadelphia, New York, and Boston, where he made eloquent speeches pointing out the natural riches of Texas and explaining its laws.

Governor Hogg was deeply interested in public education, although he himself had been denied its benefits. In this, as in other matters of importance, his clarity of vision and his willingness to state the facts plainly were truly remarkable. In his first message to the legislature, in 1891, he said:

The proposition, narrowed down to the line of candor, is that if the people ever expect to have an efficient system of public free schools, they must prepare to pay for it. Resort to sophistries and subterfuges may disguise the truth, but its essence and effect will nevertheless remain. Unmask the facts, deal candidly, let the truth be known, and if the people revolt at the situation, they alone have the power to change it. No greater principle was ever uttered than when our fathers said that "unless the people are educated and enlightened, it is idle to expect the continuance of civil liberty or the capacity of self-government." ... An efficient system of public schools is the growth of years, the work of ability and experience, and above all depends on the pride and generosity of a progressive, enlightened people.

Referring to the University of Texas, Governor Hogg said:

The University is within, a part of, and belongs to the public free school system of this State—a fact that can be admitted with pride. The Constitution requires the Legislature to provide for the maintenance, support, and direction of this institution so that it shall be first class for the promotion of literature, the arts, and sciences. ... To the ambitious of both sexes who aspire and wish to become educated in general literature and the arts and sciences connected with the professional as well as agricultural and mechanical pursuits, the University and its branches (including the Agricultural and Mechanical College) ought to afford, in a great State like this, all opportunities and facilities they may desire. They are both the creatures of the pride of a great and generous people and deserve to be maintained to the full standard fixed by the Constitution.

At the end of his administration, in his message to the legislature in 1895, Governor Hogg closed his discussion of the University of Texas with these words:

... this great institution of learning, now fast reaching the hearts of the rich and poor alike, should receive that legislative encouragement and support commensurate with its inestimable importance in the educational fabric of our State.

Parenthetically, I think it is appropriate to say here that the sons and the daughter of Governor Hogg have repeatedly manifested their intense and entirely unselfish interest in the university, and it is deeply indebted to them for their munificent gifts which have greatly broadened and extended and for many years will continue to broaden and extend the scope of the service which the university is able to render to the people of Texas.

Aside from his devotion to the welfare of the people of Texas generally, and his special interest in the university, the most notable and perhaps an even more fundamental characteristic of the administration of Governor Hogg was his outspoken devotion to our constitutional form of government. The Constitution was for him a living guide for the conduct of our government, in bad times as well as in good, and even in the face of overwhelming popular clamor demanding in effect that it be disregarded. The tone of his whole administration in this respect was expressed in this sentence in his speech of acceptance of the Democratic nomination for governor in 1890:

Recognizing the principles that "fidelity to the fundamental law is the one indispensable condition upon which the safety and success of every free government must depend," and that "public office is a public trust, that must be administered for the benefit of the people," I pledge myself to stay with our Constitution under all circumstances. . . .

This pledge was for Governor Hogg a commitment of his sacred honor; it was not a statement lightly to be disregarded when political expediency seemed to dictate that it should be ignored. Two examples may be cited to establish the truth of this statement. Sixty years ago it was not popular in the South to support the constitutional rights of the Negro. Nevertheless, Governor Hogg did so openly and fearlessly. Defending his action in offering large rewards for the arrest and conviction of members of a mob guilty of lynching a Negro, Governor Hogg said, in a speech at Dallas in 1892, in the middle of a hard campaign for reelection:

This horrible execution violated every guarantee of the constitution. My duty was plain. I performed it and have no apologies whatever to make for it. It is a precedent set up on due delibration which, so long as I am Governor, will be adhered to. We had about as well understand this in advance.

Remember that these forthright and courageous words came from a native Texan, the son of a Confederate general killed in battle, a man who had witnessed at firsthand the disorders, abuses, and corruption of Reconstruction, and who was deeply imbued with the traditions of the South.

Another example equally striking of Governor Hogg's intellectual and moral independence and integrity was the attitude he took in regard to President Grover Cleveland's action in sending federal troops to break the Pullman strike in Chicago in 1894. Stating that he was "not unmindful of the almost universal sentiment at the back of the President in his martial law measure against Chicago," he nevertheless denounced the use of military force by the president over the protest of the governor of Illinois and in the absence of any actual state of insurrection. Referring to the president's action, Governor Hogg said:

To let it go unchallenged now will give it root and strength beyond the power of the Constitution. A bad precedent, like anarchy, if not crushed in its incipient state, will grow too strong for a constitutional government.

The two examples I have cited are only typical of the consistent attitude Governor Hogg took throughout his life toward the Constitution. Governor Hogg was a firm believer in American constitutional government, and at the same time he was a practical politician, in that he frankly sought and fought for public office and was entirely aware of the popular temper of his time and the people's reaction to what he did and said. Nevertheless, he failed neither to see his duty nor to do it, regardless of what the consequences to him might be. For a man weaker intellectually or morally it would not have been difficult to wink at lynch law as the best way to subdue the lawless elements in the Negro race. It would have been easier to condone the use of the army to break a strike when the popular feeling was against the strikers. But to Governor Jim Hogg, who thought clearly and spoke bravely, the Constitution was a guide for rough weather as well as smooth sailing. And it may be noted that while he suffered the abuse that all public officials must endure, even his political enemies respected his integrity and the people of Texas loved him for his uncompromising honesty.

After serving two terms as governor, Jim Hogg retired from public office. He did not, however, relinquish his active interest in public affairs. He was busy in an active law practice and in building up a comfortable estate to leave his children, but he always took time to throw his influence on what he regarded as the right side of important public issues.

He was the vigilant opponent of all attempts by large corporations to control the government of the state for their selfish aggrandizement. In a speech made in Austin in 1904, he closed with these words: "Let us have Texas, the Empire State, governed by the people; not Texas, the truck patch, ruled by corporate lobbyists."

Governor Hogg was a national as well as a state leader; he was a close friend of William Jennings Bryan and other Democratic leaders of national importance; he was invited to New York to address a meeting in Tammany Hall; and he greeted President Theodore Roosevelt upon his visit to Texas. Up until the day of his death, in the prime of his life in 1906, before he had reached his fifty-fifth birthday, he continued to be a potent factor in the public life of Texas and the nation.

Every person who knew Governor Hogg testified to his greatness. A man impressive in physical appearance, he dominated any gathering, large or small. He was an overpowering stump speaker. To a naturally acute and penetrating mind were added the outstanding moral traits of courage and honesty. Today, in an epoch when the ultimate goal which most persons seem to be seeking is temporal, material security, it should serve to bring us back to reality to contemplate the career of James Stephen Hogg. Never, except perhaps in the last few years of his life, was he in a position of security, financial or otherwise. In his boyhood, he witnessed the tragedies of war and civil disorder and the wiping out of his family's personal fortune. He had to struggle to earn enough to clothe and feed himself and his family, and all of his education he gained through his own individual study. In his early youth he entered politics, that most insecure and uncertain of all occupations, with the purpose not of getting a job to make a living but of being a real leader of his fellow citizens. Throughout his political career he was violently opposed by the most highly organized special groups with their highly paid lobbyists. He fought them unceasingly but fairly, and so far as the record discloses, he never compromised his principles or yielded to the dictates of mere expediency. He left public office poor in material wealth but rich in the respect and admiration of the people of Texas. His life may be truly characterized as the story of the triumph of strong and independent character over adversity and unrelenting opposition.

Texans have boasted with good reason of their material resources. All about us today in this great State Fair are exhibits which give graphic demonstration of the agricultural, commercial, and industrial wealth we have attained. But our greatest asset has been and always should be the character of the people who live here. So long as the people of Texas can produce leaders like James Stephen Hogg, we can face the future with confidence. May God grant that we may have the guidance of men like him in the awesome days that lie ahead.

Nineteenth-Century Farmers, Cotton, and Prosperity

Robert A. Calvert[*]

The history of nineteenth-century Texas must include farmers and cotton. Cowboys and cattle kingdoms were more romantic; industrialism spoke for the future of the state. But it was cotton in the Gilded Age that brought to Texans their major source of income and dominated their search for economic well-being. Prosperity never came, however. Instead, tenancy and poverty grew. Farmers tried to improve their lot through scientific agriculture, blamed their plight on others, joined third parties, and stayed with the cash crop of cotton. They had no other choice. The struggle of cotton farmers then was in large measure the story of Texas.

This essay offers a brief overview of cotton farming in the Gilded Age. It attempts to amplify and to elaborate on the above themes. Robert A. Calvert, of Texas A&M University, views the impact of capitalism on the family farmer as both exploitative and inevitable. Students might wish to compare this explanation with that offered by John S. Spratt in THE ROAD TO SPINDLETOP *(Dallas, 1955). Furthermore, both Robert McMath,* THE POPULIST VANGUARD: A HISTORY OF THE SOUTHERN FARMERS' ALLIANCE *(Chapel Hill, 1975), and*

*Robert A. Calvert, "Nineteenth-Century Farmers, Cotton, and Prosperity," *Southwestern Historical Quarterly*, LXXIII (April, 1970), 509–521.

Lawrence Goodwyn, DEMOCRATIC PROMISE: THE POPULIST MOMENT
IN AMERICA *(New York, 1976), argue that a more benevolent and
concerned federal government could have improved the lot of
agricultural Americans in the age of industrialism. Their books will
add significantly to a student's understanding of the problems faced
by rural Texans.*

"Let us crown our snowy white monarch King again!" exulted a
southern newspaper in the agricultural boom of 1867. Texans
endorsed this proposal heartily. After the Civil War farmers flocked
to the frontier regions of the state, and by 1889 Texans led all others
in the production of cotton. The monarch proved to be a fickle one,
however, because prosperity for the farmer did not necessarily follow
the king's growth. Indeed, from 1870 to 1930, the proportion of
tenant-operated to owner-operated farms grew steadily. Tenancy cast
its economic blight upon black and white impartially. In the famous
black-waxey lands of Texas in 1929, for example, 55.7 percent of all
farms were tilled by white tenants. The growth of tenancy and the
poverty of the state caused agricultural experts to bemoan the
southern attachment to cotton culture and to blame the king for its
peasants' woes.

Throughout the Gilded Age agricultural reformers offered
explanations for the increasing poverty of the cotton farmer. Most saw
his plight as growing from the single-crop economy that sharecropping and the crop-lien system buttressed. They thought, too, that
these systems began as an answer to the unwillingness of the Negro to
work. One expert explained that,

It [the sharecropping system] was devised by the planters in the days when
politicians and fanatics were drawing the attention of the freedmen from
their work in the cotton fields, and the employers found some means
necessary to make the laborers feel the effects of their own idleness.

Consequently the reformers began with the wrong assumption:
reliance on cotton produced poverty. Actually, it was the other way
around: poverty produced reliance on cotton.

The crop-lien system developed as a way to provide the sharecropper with the necessary supplies. Landlords and lienholders

demanded that their debtors plant cotton, the only commercial crop to guarantee some return on their investment. One way to wed labor and the land and to produce the mythical happy yeoman, many Texans thought, would be to eliminate the no longer needed crop-lien and sharecropping systems and to destroy the single-crop economy.

Agricultural reformers blamed other villains for the Texas farmers' plight, too. A handy one, of course, was the ubiquitous "furnishing" merchant, whose store seemed to exist at every crossroads, whose wealth seemed to be claiming all the land, and to whom most crop liens were owed. They sympathized, too, with the farmers' charges that the merchant not only marked the price of his goods too high, but that he falsified his account books so that his debtors were cheated. Few reformers realized, as later scholars demonstrated, that the merchant lost a great deal of his profits to those who defaulted on their debts; that he paid interest in turn to wholesale hourses which extended credit to his store; and that illiterate farmers who kept no books never knew how much credit they actually used.

Instead, reformers charged that the merchant bought cotton at the cheapest price, encouraged credit to increase profits, and used crop liens to maintain the sharecropper system and to hold the farmer in bondage. When Texas Grangers told farmers that "There are an Army of intermediate nonproducers . . . that stand between the producers and consumers that are unnecessary links in the chain of trade and should be dispensed with," they spoke of the furnishing merchant.

The crop-lien and the sharecropping systems did not develop, as farmers supposed, either because of the perniciousness of merchants or the shiftlessness of the freedmen. Necessity produced them and necessity kept them alive. Texas farmers lacked capital. Consequently, by necessity, they bartered their knowledge; they promised that their farming techniques could grow a commercial crop for a profit. That commercial crop was, of course, cotton. On the basis of this promise, the storekeeper financed the farmer. The creditor demanded that the debtor plant enough cotton to retire the debt; if that debt was not retired the first year, the answer was to plant more cotton the next. It was not the system but the lack of liquid capital that doomed the cotton farmer. Texas had too few banks which could grant long-term loans. Thus the farmer paid high interest rates on short-term loans. He needed the facilities to borrow money over a long period of time, so that his debts could be retired piecemeal, while capital improvements were made on the farm.

Agricultural reformers might not have agreed that Texans needed banks: they suspected banks, bankers, and credit. They suggested that farmers, instead of seeking credit, should reduce their cotton planting and diversify their farms. In urging diversification, however, farm experts probably did not mean to increase the number of commercial crops. Rather they asked that the farmer return to subsistence farming—that is, plant less cotton and produce all possible necessities on his own farm. A noted Texas economist has argued that such a proposal sailed against the tides of history. Industrialization demanded specialization; and to ask the farmer to forsake his most lucrative cash crop, cotton, was to ask him to look backward to nineteenth- and not forward to twentieth-century Texas.

Economic methods alone, agricultural reformers asserted, could not end the farmers' poverty. They bewailed his poor tilling methods that ravaged the soil and limited its yield. One spokesman for the Department of Agriculture lamented that:

Cotton is now cultivated under a very slovenly system, if it can be called a system. No manures are used, the first plowing scarcely exceeds two inches in depth, and after [later] cultivation is often delayed until the crop is materially injured by being crowded by grass.

Farm organization spokesmen believed that the farmer could increase his crop yields by employing fertilizers, by studying scientific agriculture, and by learning to keep accurate account books so that he could determine the costs and profits of farm commodities.

Despite admonitions of agricultural writers, farm organizations, and farm journals, Texas farmers planted more cotton each year. By 1879, some 2,176,000 acres were devoted to cotton, and by the close of the century the acreage tilled by cotton farmers had increased to 6,961,000. In 1880 most of this farming was done by manual labor, with the average expense of 167 hours and 48 minutes of man-labor per acre. Undoubtedly farmers continued to use methods deplored by proponents of scientific agriculture.

The rural population suspected scientific agricultural techniques. For example in 1880, many farmers would not use paris green, a well-known insecticide designed to control the army worm that destroyed cotton, because it contained arsenic trioxide, and laborers feared that it would poison them as well as the insects. Besides, it was difficult to disseminate agricultural information to illiterate farmers, and for them to keep books—when they neither knew how nor understood why—was an almost impossible task. Furthermore they thought, with some justification, that fertilizers often were too expensive or did not live up to their expectations. Guanos, the generic name that farmers used for manures, frequently contained weed seeds, and many farmers believed that their use increased farm problems rather than crop yields. Commercial chemical fertilizers contained additives such as brick dust, that prompted Granges and Alliances to denounce their use and to adopt resolutions condemning them throughout the late nineteenth century. This suspicion, the fertility of the comparatively virgin soil of the state and the farmer's illiteracy caused Texas to rank at the bottom of the list in 1880 in the amount of fertilizer used per acre of improved land.

Thus the Texas cotton farmer in the Gilded Age began his cotton farming each year schooled in little but past experience. If the field previously had been cleared, he in all likelihood planted on land that had had a cotton or a corn crop grown on it the last season. Crops seldom were rotated, and when they were, no particular order was followed. Land was rarely "turned out" or allowed to lie fallow. Since he usually did not practice fall plowing, the farmer began each spring by removing the previous year's cotton stalks. Before the advent of mechanical stalk cutters, he knocked these down with a heavy drag, a hoe, or club, or pulled them by hand. Sometimes farmers raked the stalks into piles and burned them, even though such a practice was known to destroy humus in the soil. In the 1880s farmers began using a mechanical stalk cutter. This machine, a two-wheel device that straddled the rows, pulled sharp blades or knives that cut the stalks into bits and enabled one man to clean five to nine acres in a ten-hour day.

When the stalks were removed the farmer prepared ridges in the fields—called rows or beds. To do this, he plowed out the depression between the previous year's rows with a "bull-tongue" plow. When this was completed, he replaced this implement with a turning plow, and plowed first on one side of the furrow and then on the other until he had built a row about four feet wide and six inches high. The distances between the rows varied from three to four feet in the uplands areas to four to five feet in the bottoms, where the soil was richer and the plants had a more luxuriant growth. The elevated bed permitted better drainage, allowed extra plants and weeds to be hoed out more easily, and, since the bed was warmer, caused more successful germination of the seed.

After the farmer had prepared his ridge, he usually pulled a log across it to smooth the bed and to pulverize the soil. Then he plowed a single trench down the middle of the bed and deposited seed into it. In 1880 he probably planted the seed by hand and covered it by dragging a log afterwards. Mechanical planters, which trenched the bed, deposited the seed, and covered it in one operation, saw only limited use that year. Their employment varied from area to area. Wood County land contained too many stumps and roots for their effective use. A farmer in Nacogdoches County reported, "they have been laid aside for the next generation," but Cooke County farmers seemed to have utilized them readily. The types of mechanical planters employed varied from homemade ones to the manufactured keg-type machines. By 1885 the Champion and Standard machines boasted widespread popularity in the state.

Farmers began planting in early March in the southern part of Texas, and most throughout the state had completed the operation by mid-May. Tender cotton plants cannot survive frost, but they need to mature before the usual summer drouths. After the appearance in 1893 of the cotton-boll weevil, farmers planted as early as possible, because the infestation of the insect grew worse toward the end of the season. In short, the farmer relied on experience to pick a planting date.

He planted between one-half and two bushels of seed per acre, depending once more on his location and previous experience. In 1880 most Texas farmers preferred the Schubach or "storm-proof" variety of seed, but farmers also expressed faith in the Dixon, Petit Gulf, Cheatham, Hurlong, Meyers, Sugar-loaf, Hefley, South American, and other varieties of cotton. These seeds produced cotton with the length of the staple between ⅞ and 1⅛ inches. Because of public gins and cross-fertilization by insects, farmers seldom acquired superior seed, and complaints that a particular variety had "run out" were common.

The new plants came up in from three to ten days. After the plants had grown for about two weeks, the grower "barred off" or plowed on either side of the row, leaving the cotton plants on a ridge about six inches in height and three inches in width. "Choppers" followed the "plowing off," and hoed out surplus plants and weeds. They left bunches of three to four plants spaced, depending upon the farmer's preference and the fertility of the soil, from ten inches to four feet apart. No work in the cotton field was harder. A tenant farmer, the main character in a novel by a Texas writer, explained the arduous chore:

Through the warming days chopping. Sending the blade slicing through the dark, hilled crumbles of earth. Killing weeds. Thinning cotton. Up, down, swing the hoe into a sort of limbo, a Nirvana, in which only a few muscles remain aware, and they not sharply. Sweat-wet clothes dragging cooly, cooly galling. And time no longer exists in minutes and hours, but in rows and acres. And even this is vague. A sea of up and down. Of bad meals. A back that aches in your sleep.

After chopping, the crop was cultivated. First the planter "dirtied up" the cotton by using a turning plow to throw dirt lost in "barring off" back on the ridge around the young plants. This action gave the plants ample soil to develop strong root systems. The farmer continued cultivation of the crops, usually three plowings and two to four hoeings, until about a month or six weeks before harvest. A man could hoe from one-half to something over an acre per day. The cultivating processes kept down weeds and grass, aerated the soil, and made it more capable of absorbing moisture. Then the cotton was "laid by," or allowed to remain idle until time to pick.

After 1885, the walking or riding cultivator came into use, eliminating much of that hand labor. Farmers not only welcomed its advent, but advertisers promised miraculous results. One company told the farmer that:

1st. The man who buys a 'Standard' Cultivator or Planter gets the full worth of his money.
2nd. His crops are always well worked.
3rd. He takes pride in paying his debts.
4th. His daughters are comely and helpful, and his sons respected and popular.
5th. His wife always cheerful and obliging.

6th. He is accounted a man of sound judgment.
7th. About 40,000 'Standard' Cultivators have been sold in Texas.

In about thirty days, early May in the southern counties and late June in the northern ones, the cotton sprouted blooms. From the time of blooming until the harvesting, the cotton plant was threatened by diseases and insects. Farmers lacked the knowledge to cope with these evils. Many thought "sore shin," a fungus, was caused by either laborers carelessly nicking the stalks while hoeing or by high winds blowing the plant and breaking its bark. Another fungus, root rot, was reputed to occur because of poison soils.

In addition to these and other diseases, cotton plants fell prey to such dread insects as the cotton caterpillar and, by 1895, the boll weevil. Farmers hunted desperately for cures. For the caterpillar, the scourge of the eighties, they hung lanterns or pots of molasses and vinegar in the fields to attract and kill the moths, dusted the plants with ashes, and experimented with supposedly caterpillar-resistant strains of cotton.

No insect did as much damage to cotton, of course, as did the boll weevil. In 1902 it was estimated that the southern states had lost from 235,000 to 500,000 bales, valued at between $8,000,000 and $25,000,000, to the weevil's depredations. In 1895 no insecticides were known to destroy the insect. It was suggested that the farmer plant early, have workers pick the affected bolls, or cultivate select plants at convenient parts in his fields, which with care would mature before the regular crop and attract the earliest beetles. These plants could then be destroyed and the damage done to the remainder lessened. Given the seeming hopelessness of the situation, the farmer was more than his usual easy mark for all sorts of spurious cures or machines that promised to eradicate the insect.

At times farmers faced the insect plight with grim humor. The suggestion that the United States government might import a natural predator such as a particular species of ant from Guatemala to attack the weevil elicited an ironic anecdote from H. L. Stringfellow, a Texas horticulturist. He told readers of *Farm and Ranch* that he had put a boll weevil and a native species of red ant under a glass jar and observed the following episode through a magnifying glass:

Finally, seeing that neither showed any desire for a closer acquaintance, I moved the glass backward and forward, so as to bring them into contact repeatedly, a proreeding [*sic:* proceeding] for which the ant seemed to blame the weevil, for in a few minutes he seized his snout, close to his head, with his mandibles and a rough and tumble fight ensued for more than an hour without a single break. Over and over they turned, the ant repeatedly bringing the rear of his body in contact with the weevil's back in what seemed to be a vain attempt to sting him, just as a wasp would, but the magnifying glass showed no sign of a wound. In the meantime my sympathy was all with the weevil, of whom the ant had taken undue advantage by seizing him by the snout without warning . . . sometimes lifting him clear off the board and then slamming him down on his back, a position occupied by the weevil during the greatest part of the fight. Of course I thought it would soon be all over with the weevil, for his only effective weapon was in his enemy's possession and all he could do was to kick and scratch the ant's stomach, which he did vigorously from start to finish.

Finally, after about an hour, to my surprise, the ant suddenly relaxed his grip of the weevil's snout, and doubling himself up in a ball, rolled over dead.

A careful examination of the ant's body showed no wound of any kind, while the weevil also was apparently uninjured, except the loss of his left hind leg, which had been broken off close to his body in the struggle. . . I at once gave him a fresh cotton square and the next morning found him sitting contentedly upon it just as if nothing had happened.

After such a contest, I could not kill him, so, after several days, holding him between finger and thumb, on my front gallery, I said to him: "Boll weevil, brave boll weevil, Fly away to Washington; And tell the entomologists, Killing ants is only fun!"

Cotton had to survive inclement weather as well as insects and diseases. Too little rain, of course produced a drouth; but too much rain, or rain falling in mid-summer, caused cotton to exceed the desired height of from three to four feet and "run to weed." Farmers combatted the excessive height by plowing close to the roots on either side of the plant or by pruning out the topmost branches. Rain did by far the most damage, however, after bolls had split open and exposed the lock of cotton. This lock, which became fluffy as it dried, was attached only at the stem end. After the boll opened, rain could cause the boll to stain the cotton, lowering its grade, or, if accompanied by high winds, could blow and beat the lock to earth, causing a near-total crop loss. For this reason Texans preferred a variety of cotton called "storm proof."

The lock of cotton was the most vulnerable at the time of harvest. Consequently, at picking time, which began in July in the southern counties and early September in northern ones, all available manpower came to the fields and picked until the harvest ended. Since the bolls opened progressively, hands usually harvested the cotton two or three times per field, the picking continuing well into December and sometimes into the new year. Even then some cotton was left in the field.

The necessity of quickly gathering the crop demanded that the farmer utilize all of his family and frequently hire additional labor to pick the cotton. The amount gathered by each worker depended on his ability. In 1895, in the prairie regions of the state, it was reported that six-year-old children had picked 100 pounds per day and that first-class pickers gathered between 400 and 600 pounds per day. The writer added that the workers took so little care that the cotton was mixed with trash and bolls. A more realistic appraisal by a later student states that in Texas a good picker averaged around 250 pounds of seed cotton in a day. In 1880 it cost a farmer between fifty cents and one dollar per hundred pounds to gather cotton.

The picker dragged a sack strapped to his shoulder that held a capacity of around 25 pounds of seed cotton. When the sack was filled, the cotton was weighed, deposited in a basket or wagon, and credited to the picker's account. When a farmer had enough cotton picked for a bale, he usually sent the staple to the gin. In some cases, however, cotton was stored in the fields in wagons or in cribs, giving only limited protection from the weather, until the entire crop was picked or until prices rose.

The cotton was now ready for the gin and ultimately for the market. When the farmer took the seed cotton from the field to the gin, the town began to claim its share of Texas's $100,000,000 cotton crop. In 1870 farmers estimated that it cost them anywhere from 3.5 cents to 10 cents per pound to produce the cotton lint, excluding the merchants' commission and the cost of transportation, storing, and insurance. The average annual yield per acre of lint cotton in Texas, 1874 to 1894, was computed by the United States Department of Agriculture at 229 pounds, with the minimum range (1884) of 142 pounds and the maximum (1894) of 383 pounds. In this same period the average price per pound of cotton ranged from a high of 13 cents in 1874 to a low of 4.6 cents in 1894.

Such estimates told nothing of, and could not total, the wear and tear of hard work on the farmer and his family. Even with the wide differences in costs and production per acre, and assuming that the farmer used all the by-products of the cotton—such as hulls and seeds—few family farmers became prosperous. The Texas farmer realized that prosperity was not automatically rewarding his hard work. Instead his labor produced all sorts of urban enterprises that seemed to him to prosper while he grew poorer. He undoubtedly saw the phenomenal rise in this period of industries based upon cotton processing. By 1900, for example, Texas had 4,514 gins within its borders, and these gins averaged 589 bales each year, handling 34 percent of the nation's total cotton crop.

Besides gins, the farmer witnessed the rise of kindred businesses—cotton compresses and mills. A cotton compress was easily dismantled and moved. When cotton production declined in one area or increased in another, the industry followed the production, and by 1890 the shipping areas of the state were served by over 40 cotton compress companies. In addition, the same period saw an increase from 7 to 103 in the number of oil mills that pressed cotton seed. Indeed, the investments in Texas in 1900 in businesses that were related to cotton processing probably ran to something around $25,000,000. These enterprises were not so much to serve the farmer as they were tools of the entrepreneur.

Texas farmers resented the fact that they did not receive what they considered to be their just share of profits from the production and sale of cotton. All other industries, they pointed out, were just auxiliaries of agriculture. "The soil is the source from which we derive all that constitutes wealth," an agrarian leader told Texas farmers. They particularly disliked the transportation companies and middlemen who, they believed, grew rich off of the farmers' toil. The poorer the farm population became, the more agrarians attacked these "abuses." Thus, many of the same farmers who supported the 1874 statement of Grange Worthy Master William W. Lang—that he was "unable to discover any antagonism to railroads or to transportation companies by the Patrons of Husbandry"—cheered wildly in 1888 when the Farmers Alliance demanded "that the state establish maximum freight and passenger rates on railroads."

It took fifteen years of poverty to turn the conservative Granger into the radical Allianceman. Yet Texas farmers always denounced the city. Lang, who felt farmers and railroads could cooperate, said in 1878 that

Great cities are beginning to be plague centers of the social system. Debasing pleasures there have temples overcrowded with devotees; depravity finds cordial friendship . . . . and, as filth generates a pestilence, so this congregation of all that is offensive to virtue corrupts society.

He unconsciously explained the reason for rural opposition to urban areas by calling on farmers to join the Patrons of Husbandry, win status, and end "the reckless yearnings of the young men of the country" for the city. Farmers wondered how to keep their sons "down on the farm" long before World War I and Paris.

Thus the Texas farmer must have considered as the ultimate irony the fact that the cotton he grew not only supported subsidiary industries, but was shipped to those "plague centers of the social system" and caused their growth. He saw Galveston become by the twentieth century the number one cotton port in the nation, handling at the height of the cotton season 40,000 to 50,000 bales a day. He saw the city prosper while he starved. Consequently Texas farmers joined Alliances and Granges and experimented with economic coopera-tives. Some ultimately bolted the Democratic party and formed a third political party. Yet farmers stayed with cotton: it was their only cash crop, and it could always be sold. The selling, though, seemed to bring prosperity only to others; and the hopelessness this fact engendered caused the attack of agricultural reformers upon the money crop.

Cotton continued to be the king of the state's economy, however, until events at Spindletop dethroned it. But except for a brief period before and during World War I, the cotton farmer never received many economic benefits from the monarch. History almost foreor-dained it that way. Industrialization processes exploit someone, and in the United States a large portion of that exploitation fell upon the farmer and worker. In the case of agriculture, industrialization meant the end of the family farm and of King Cotton. George Sessions Perry in 1934 had his fictional character Sam Tucker sum it up this way:

Land just catches the culls that can't do no good in cities. Cept me. I wasn't culled here. I blong. But there's too much cotton and too much corn. We go on raisin it cause it's all we know. Ain't worth enough in money to keep us alive, but the government's a-doing for us what it done for the arrow-makers

[Indians]. When their kind of work got useless and in the way. Farms ain't farms no more; not no real business. Just reservations where the government gives men money to stay there and keep off the relief. . . . An it seems strange when you know this year's cotton'll be just as good, just as white, and a better staple than it ever was; just as much work to raise. Except there ain't no use for but about half of it. Ain't nobody's fault, I guess, but ourn for raisin cotton. More of us got to crowd into factories, looks like.

Section IV.

TWENTIETH CENTURY

The Galveston Storm of 1900

John Edward Weems[*]

On September 8, 1900, the greatest natural disaster to ever strike North America hit Galveston, Texas. The Galveston hurricane killed approximately 6,000 people, impoverished more than 50 percent of the island's citizens, and called into question the location of the city itself. The aftermath of the hurricane witnessed a rebuilding of the city, a remodeling of city government, and an engineering feat—the seawall—then unparalleled in modern history. John Edward Weems, a well-known Texas author, conveys the story of human tragedy and survival, and chronicles an important event in Texas history.

Among the best accounts of the Galveston hurricane are Murat Halstead's GALVESTON: THE HORRORS OF A STRICKEN CITY (New York, 1957), Clarence Ousley's GALVESTON IN NINETEEN HUNDRED (Atlanta, 1900), and Weems's A WEEKEND IN SEPTEMBER (New York, 1957). The aftermath of the story can be found in Herbert M. Mason's DEATH FROM THE SEA (New York, 1972), and for governmental reform check Bradley R. Rice, "The Galveston Plan of City Government by Commission: The Birth of a Progressive Idea," SOUTHWESTERN HISTORICAL QUARTERLY, LXXVIII (April, 1975).

[*]John Edward Weems, "The Galveston Storm of 1900," Southwestern Historical Quarterly, LXI (April, 1958), 494–507.

The morning of Saturday, September 8, 1900, was dark—perhaps even foreboding—as readers of the Galveston *Daily News* scanned their papers. Most attention was focused on the Boxer Rebellion in China, but on page 3 of the *News* many persons noticed a telegraph story concerning a tropical hurricane in the Gulf of Mexico.

Some Galvestonians had been hearing about this storm for several days; the United States Weather Bureau office in Galveston had received its first notification of the hurricane on September 4, when it was moving northward over Cuba. Few persons, however, concerned themselves to any great extent with this latest storm. They were familiar with tropical hurricanes. The city was built to withstand them, and it had indeed withstood many Gulf storms in the past. First floors of residences and business buildings were elevated several feet above the sandy ground to provide for "overflows"—storm-tide inundations of the city. These overflows were frequently an occasion for a holiday; most businesses closed, and the clerks went home. Young Galvestonians splashed in the flooded streets. The festive atmosphere that prevailed in the island city during these inundations was not unlike that common to a city farther north during a snowstorm; there were outdoor sports to suit the occasion.

So it was that Galvestonians who saw the *News* item about the storm were generally unconcerned.

"Storm in the Gulf," the one-column headline announced. Under that, a small subhead proclaimed, "Great Damage Reported on Mississippi and Louisiana Coasts—Wire Down—Details Meagre."

Then came the story:

SPECIAL TO THE NEWS
New Orleans, La., Sept. 8, 12:45 A.M.—A terrific storm is now raging on the Louisiana and Mississippi gulf coast. Great damage has been done to shipping, but owing to the prostration of the wires, no details are obtainable.

That was all. There were other weather stories scattered through the Saturday edition—in those unhurried days the *News* editor could be pretty certain that his readers would eventually notice all the items—but the other weather stories were of even less prominence than the one on page 3.

On page 2 was an earlier storm story, weakly headlined "Storm on Florida Coast," telling of near-100-mile winds there from the same hurricane, which had battered Cuba and Jamaica even earlier. And on page 10 was the local weather story:

Early yesterday morning the United States weather bureau received storm warnings from Washington, announcing a change in the course of the storm that has been playing in the South Atlantic for several days. The notice stated that the storm, instead of moving north, had changed its course, and reaching the gulf, was moving westward in a northwesterly direction. The early indications were that the storm would probably strike land somewhere east of Texas, and make it way across land westwardly. Up to 5 P.M. the latest advices stated that the storm center was in the gulf, south of Louisiana, and headed northwest. Storm signals were hoisted early in the day and warnings sent out to shipping and the coast country, and in fact all stations in this district.

The storm struck the Florida coast on Thursday [September 6], and all communication with Key West was interrupted for several hours. It was reported that considerable damage was done there. From the Florida coast the storm went to sea again and has been plowing up the gulf. Yesterday afternoon it was between stations; that is, between the New Orleans and Galveston weather stations, and reports were hard to obtain until the blow reached farther west. At 5 P.M. it was moving slowly westward, with prospects of reaching here some time in the night. The weather bureau officials did not anticipate any dangerous disturbance, although they were not in a position to judge just what degree the storm may reach or develop when it strikes Texas.

This storm is of West Indian origin, such as are looked for during the months of August, September, and October. The weather bureau does not recognize any such classification as "equinoctial storms." The weather bureau records show that these three months usually produce these West Indian storms.

Immediately below that story was another paragraph, written and inserted shortly before the *News* went to press in the early hours of that Saturday morning:

At midnight the moon was shining brightly and the sky was not as threatening as earlier in the night. The weather bureau had no late advices as to the storm's movements and it may be that the tropical disturbance has changed its course or spent its force before reaching Texas.

The newspaper readers were unaware of it, but many of them were in fact reading their own obituaries in the Saturday edition of the *News*. Later that same Saturday, September 8, the West Indian hurricane blew inland at Galveston—the eye passed only a few miles to the southwest of the city—and it left the proud seaport a shambles.

This was a disaster that currently few can imagine; for in 1900 Galveston, with more than 37,000 residents, was Texas's fourth largest city. It was a commercial center, a tourist resort, a seat of culture. Yet, when the Sunday morning sun came up on September 9, the southern part of the city (nearest the Gulf) was swept clean of buildings, and at least 6,000 persons were dead. After that, many residents were in favor of abandoning the city forever. The tragedy is still known as the worst recorded disaster ever to strike the North American continent.

Ironically, for months Galvestonians had been debating when the twentieth century began. The Vatican (and some other authorities) said that it would begin on January 1, 1901, and Catholic Galveston largely accepted this. But the nineteenth century actually came to an end, an abrupt end, for the island city on September 8, 1900; the changing of the centuries was nowhere more noticeable than at Galveston.

The United States Weather Bureau office in the Post Office Building in Galveston still has the original weather records of September, 1900. In faded ink, on yellowing pages, precise writing tells the impersonal story of the storm. (It is important to remember, when considering these records, that all time stated in them represents seventy-fifth meridian, or eastern standard time. Galveston time was one hour earlier, and this has resulted in unnecessary inaccuracies in some newspaper and magazine stories.)

The weathermen—Isaac M. Cline, in charge; his brother, Joseph L. Cline; and John D. Blagden, a man on temporary duty there at the time—recorded a consistently falling barometer from 8:00 EST (7:00 Galveston time) Thursday morning, September 6, until the storm had passed. The barometer that Thursday morning stood at 29.974; the temperature was 80 degrees; there was a slight wind of six miles an hour from the north, and the sky was clear.

These weather conditions seemed anything but ominous; yet there was a storm in Florida. It was the one that had passed over Cuba on September 4 (after having been conceived in late August somewhere in the easterly trades between South America and Africa—5,000 miles from Galveston). Isaac Cline noted in his journal that same September 6: "Advisory message in regard to the tropical storm central over Southern Florida received and distributed at 2:59 P.M."

A tropical hurricane frequently is preceded by hot weather, and the temperature on September 6 became unseasonably high for Galveston; a maximum of 90.9 degrees was registered during the afternoon.

The next day was even hotter: 91.1 degrees. (The daily mean for both days was 86 degrees). Joseph Cline, who made the 8:00 P.M. EST readings on September 7, recorded a barometer of 29.687 falling, a maximum wind velocity during the day of nineteen miles an hour—from the north—and a sky completely covered with stratocumulus clouds, coming from the northeast. Meanwhile, during the day Isaac Cline had made the following journal entry:

> Broken cumulus and strato-cumulus. Fresh to brisk northerly winds. Special observations taken at noon and 3:00 P.M. [EST] Order to hoist storm northwest 10:35 A.M. [EST] received at 11:30 A.M. [EST] and hoisted at 11:35 A.M. [EST] Rough sea with heavy southeast swells during afternoon and evening.

The storm, then, had turned northwestward from Florida. Since the winds from a tropical hurricane blow counterclockwise around a low-pressure center (in the Northern Hemisphere), the central office in Washington, D.C., which had sole authority then for issuing storm warnings, evidently had predicted the hurricane would strike the coast to the east of Galveston. This would have put the island city in the storm's left semicircle, where the winds are not so destructive.

When the 8:00 A.M. EST readings were made Saturday morning, September 8, the sky was still covered with clouds—stratus by then—coming from the north. The wind had risen. Joseph Cline observed, to a velocity of twenty-three miles an hour; it was also from the north. (This official velocity represented a five-minute average; at times it blew with greater force.) The barometer was still falling gradually.

In Isaac M. Cline's official report to the Weather Bureau, written a few days after the storm (and reprinted in full in Clarence Ousley's *Galveston in 1900*, the most accurate of several books published in the months following the disaster), Cline made this comment:

> The usual signs heralding the approach of hurricanes were not present. A brick dust sky was not in evidence. This feature, distinctly observed in other storms in this section, was carefully watched for, both on the evening of the seventh and the morning of the eighth. There were cirrus clouds moving from the southeast during the afternoon of the seventh, but by noon only alto-stratus from the northeast were observed. About the middle of the afternoon the clouds were divided between cirrus, alto-stratus, and cumulus, moving from the northeast. During the rest of the seventh, strato-cumulus

clouds prevailed, with a steady movement from the northeast. A heavy swell from the southeast made its appearance in the Gulf of Mexico during the afternoon of the seventh. The swell continued during the night without diminishing, and the tide rose to an unusual height when it is considered that the wind was from the north and northwest.

Isaac Cline's daily journal for September 8 relates the impersonal facts of the storm. There were strato cumulus, then low-hanging nimbus (rain clouds), covering the city that Saturday. A "light rain" began falling at 8:45 A.M. (EST); it "continued into the night." The rain gauge atop the Levy Building, where the Weather Bureau office was located, was blown down about 2:30 P.M Galveston time. Only 1.27 inches had then been recorded, but weathermen—basing their guess on statistics of nearby stations—later estimated that ten inches of rain fell on Galveston that day.

Isaac Cline, in his daily journal for September 8, also noted that special observations were taken at noon and at 3:00 P.M.(EST) and telegraphed to Washington. He stated:

Order to change northwest storm warnings to northeast to 10:30 A.M. [EST] received at 11:10 A.M. [EST] and warning northeast hoisted at 11:15 A.M. [EST] The warning only remained up a few hours until it was blown down.

The direction of the wind—from the northeast—forecast in this newest warning indicated that Galveston, after all, could expect to be in the right semicircle of the storm, where the violence was greatest.

The instrument shelter atop the Levy Building, 2223 Market, was blown away at the height of the storm. The four-cup anemometer whirled to pieces at 5:15 P.M. Galveston time, and the weathermen never knew the velocity of the wind that battered Galveston after that. Shortly before the wind gauge was carried away it had registered an 84-mile-an-hour average velocity for a five-minute period, but gusts of 100 miles an hour were recorded in that interval.

The Galveston weathermen later estimated the force of the wind as "110 or 120 miles per hour," and it is likely that this was a conservative estimate indeed. Many survivors recall seeing timbers, bricks, and other pieces of debris blown almost horizontally.

In his official report, Isaac Cline elaborated on the direction and force of the wind that Saturday. (Again, it should be remembered that the times he gave were one hour ahead of Galveston.)

The wind during the forenoon of the eighth was generally north, but oscillated, at intervals of from five to ten minutes, between northwest and northeast, and continued to do so up to 1:00 P.M. After 1:00 P.M. the wind was mostly northeast, although as late as 6:30 P.M. it would occasionally back to the northwest for one or two minutes at a time. The prevailing wind was from the northeast until 8:30 P.M. when it shifted to the east, continuing from this direction until about 10:00 P.M. After 10:00 P.M. the wind was from the southeast, and after 11:00 P.M. the prevailing direction was from the south or southwest. The directions after 11:00 P.M. are from personal observations. A storm velocity was not attained until about 1:00 P.M., after which the wind increased steadily and reached a hurricane velocity at about 5:00 P.M. The greatest velocity for five minutes was 84 miles per hour at 6:15 P.M., with two minutes at the rate of 100 miles per hour. The anemometer blew away at that time, and it is estimated that prior to 8:00 P.M. the wind attained a velocity of at least 120 miles per hour. For a short time, about 8:00 P.M., just before the wind shifted to the east, there was a distinct lull, but when it came out from the east and southeast it appeared to come with greater fury than before. After shifting to the south at about 11:00 P.M. the wind steadily diminished in velocity, and at 8:00 A.M. on the morning of the ninth was blowing at the rate of 26 miles per hour from the south.

Cline's reference to the "distinct lull" might make it appear that the eye of the hurricane passed directly over Galveston. At the end of Cline's official report, however, is this paragraph:

From officers of the U.S. Engineer Tug *Anna*, I learn that the wind at the mouth of the Brazos River went from north to southwest by way of west. This shows that the center of the hurricane was near Galveston, probably not more than thirty miles to the westward.

The tide commenced coming in over low portions of the city, Isaac Cline said in his daily journal, early Saturday morning. He sent the following telegram about 7:30 A.M. EST to the central office in Washington.

Unusually heavy swells from the southeast, intervals one to five minutes, overflowing low places south portion of city three to four blocks from beach. Such high water with opposing winds never observed previously.

The tide continued rising all day, Cline noted, and a sudden rise of four feet occurred at 7:30 P.M. EST. This was a storm wave, frequently referred to as a tidal wave in historical accounts of the disaster. It was swept ashore in advance of the hurricane's vortex; it smashed many houses left standing, and it may be assumed that it took hundreds of lives. Cline stated that by 8:00 P.M.EST the entire city was under eight to fifteen feet of water, and that the entire south, east, and west portions of the city from two to five blocks inland were "swept clean" of buildings and residences. Cline also wrote:

The following special barometer readings were taken during the rapid fall during the late afternoon:

5:00 [P.M., EST]	— 29.05
5:11	— 29:00
5:30	— 28.95
5:55	— 28.88
6:06	— 28.86
6:20	— 28.82
6:40	— 28.73
6:48	— 28.70
7:15	— 28.69
7:40	— 28.62
8:00	— 28.55
8:10	— 28.53

The lowest barometer apparently occurred between the two last observations, when the barograph stood at about 28.44. The barometer began rising at about 8:30 P.M. [EST] and rose as rapidly as it had fallen.

Thousands were injured and killed by flying timbers, slate, and bricks while endeavoring to save themselves, Cline observed in his journal. He estimated property damage at $30,000,000, and said that the tide began to fall slowly at 11:00 P.M. EST and that "comparatively no damage resulted after this time."

Then Isaac Cline added a short paragraph to the end of his September 8 journal:

I. M. Cline, local forecast official, and Joseph L. Cline, observer, badly injured in wreck and drift, being on and among drifting houses from 7:30 to 10:30 P.M. [EST]

What actually happened was this: Isaac Cline, between quick trips to the Weather Bureau office downtown (in rooms 308 to 311 of the Levy Building), began warning residents nearest the Gulf to leave their houses for safer refuge shortly after 6:00 A.M. EST that Saturday. He continued to do this until midafternoon, when he finally made his way through the ever-rising water to his home, at 2511 Avenue Q, to be with his family—his wife and their three young daughters.

About 6:30 P.M. EST, Joseph L. Cline joined his brother's family in their two-story frame residence. Joseph Cline had been in the Weather Bureau office most of the day handling the special observations, and he had telephoned a 3:30 P.M. EST observation to Houston for telegraphing to Washington just before the last wire link with the mainland was ruptured, shortly after 4:00 P.M. EST.

By 6:00 P.M. EST Joseph Cline had decided to go to his brother's residence on Avenue Q, in case its occupants should need help, and he left the Weather Bureau office in charge of one man, John Blagden, who remained there during the rest of the storm, despite the trembling and creaking of the battered building.

Joseph Cline staggered through the water, being blown completely off his path at times by the wind, to his brother's residence. He had been there about two hours when the house fell.

Isaac Cline lost his wife, but he, his three daughters, and his brother survived. For three terrifying hours, as Isaac Cline stated at the end of his September 8 journal, they clung to floating wreckage, carried out into the Gulf and back, not knowing whether they would live or die. Hundreds of other survivors had similar personal experiences.

There have been many more violent storms than the one which struck Galveston in 1900. Winds of much greater velocity than that estimated for this one have been registered in tropical hurricanes since then, and much lower barometric readings have been recorded. Why, then, did this storm take the most lives? There are several reasons.

Many of the 6,000 deaths and countless numbers of injuries can be blamed on Galveston's familiarity with hurricanes. Most residents, including Isaac Cline himself, believed that their houses could withstand any Gulf storm. When they finally realized the ultimate fury of this one, it was too late. Because of the water and the high wind, which were flinging deadly objects about like so much paper, occupants could not leave their residences for the comparative safety of the downtown section, where most of the brick buildings stood. Some of these buildings, however, were flattened.) Residents were trapped in their houses, and when the residences fell many of the occupants died.

Another reason for the terrible toll was the water. The wind alone would not have done nearly so much damage to the city. But the waters of the Gulf completely covered Galveston Island that day, and the racing, wind-whipped current helped undermine buildings that could have withstood the wind's fury.

But even the wind and water would not have caused so much

destruction except for something else. When the Gulf came surging in that Saturday, it felled many weak structures comparatively early in the afternoon. The wreckage from these buildings was hurled against other stronger ones, and it helped collapse them. Buildings in the block nearest the Gulf generally fell first, and this debris acted more or less as a battering ram against the second block of buildings. When they fell there was even more wreckage for the Gulf to throw against the third block. Some of the sturdier structures might indeed have stood, as many occupants expected them to, except for the pounding of the wreckage.

Finally, the debris—piled up in some sections as high as a two-story building—acted somewhat as a seawall in stopping the Gulf's totally destructive advance toward downtown Galveston (which was located on the bay side).

But on Sunday morning after the storm, it appeared to most stunned citizens that nothing was left. Thomas Scurry, adjutant general of Texas and the officer in command of Texas guardsmen during the martial-law period at Galveston, described the city's plight:

Galveston has passed through an ordeal of wind and water, of wreck, ruin, desolation, and woe seldom if ever known in the history of the world. In the twinkling of an eye its homes have been demolished, its industries crippled, at least one-seventh of its population killed, and more than 15,000 of its surviving citizens made absolutely destitute. From a condition of splendid wealth it has been reduced to absolute poverty. Three-fourths of its estimated valuation has been totally destroyed. Two weeks ago there was but one city in American—Providence, Rhode Island—wealthier in proportion to its population. Today there is scarcely a city in America poorer than Galveston.

James Hays Quarles, a reporter for the Houston *Daily Post,* left for Galveston as soon as the extent of the disaster was realized. He departed Houston at 4:00 A.M. Monday (September 10) on a Galveston, Houston, and Henderson train, which reached a point about one mile from Texas City when washouts of the track ahead forced it to stop. The railroad bridges linking Galveston with the mainland, however, had already been obliterated.

From there Quarles traveled on foot, seeing "bodies everywhere."

When we neared Virginia Point, we came up with E. Gerloff of Galveston. He and his father were the only survivors of his family. He told how when the storm reached Galveston, he and his family left in a sailboat. It capsized and all drowned but the two. Gerloff was hungry, and one of the crowd gave him a package of lunch.

Martial law was proclaimed Monday in Galveston [actually it was not officially proclaimed until Thursday, September 13] Every soldier has been called to duty. Mayor James was appointing special policemen when I found him on Tremont Street, and the orders were to protect the dead. Military authorities gave orders that when a person was caught looting the dead he was to be shot, and before I left the city at 4:00 P.M. reports said four had been executed by soldiers. A citizens committee established a number of morgues about the city, and during the morning of Monday bodies were carried to these places. A large number were collected before noon, and burial began, but it was found impracticable to dig graves on the island for this purpose. Messrs. McMaster and Morrissey then took charge of the duty, and engaged a tugboat and barge. They began making arrangements to send the bodies to sea. Center Street wharf was used for loading and every wagon, dray, float, or cart to be found was impressed. [Later the bodies, which had been weighted and dropped overboard, began reappearing on the beach at Galveston, and burial and cremation was resorted to.]

The island did not escape the fury of the storm in any part of it, and every house is damaged and nearly one-half are total wrecks. The business portion suffered to a great extent. Provisions could not be used because of the damage by salt water. From what I could learn I consider that more than 5,000 lives were lost. I hesitate to say 7,000 because I am told that I am placing the number too high, but I do not think so.

The conditions of the minds of the people is such that they can not remember who were their friends and neighbors, and they are thinking only of their own. Thus a great many will be lost sight of. I never saw people in such a condition.

John Blagden, the observer who was on temporary duty at Galveston at the time of the storm, also wrote a description of the city after the storm.

Weather Bureau
Galveston, Texas
September 10, 1900

TO ALL AT HOME

Very probably you little expect to get a letter from me from here, but here I am alive and without a scratch. That is what few can say in this storm swept city. I have been here two weeks to take the place of a man who is on a three months leave, after which I go back to Memphis.

Of course you have heard of the storm which passed over this place last Friday night [it was actually Saturday night] but you cannot realize what it really was. I have seen many severe storms but never one like this. I remained in the office all night. It was in a building that stood the storm better than any other in the town, though it was badly damaged and rocked frightfully in some of the blasts. In the quarter of the city where I lodged (south part) everything was swept and nearly all drowned. The family with whom I roomed were all lost. I lost everything I brought with me from Memphis and a little money, but I think eighty dollars will cover my entire loss: I am among the fortunate ones.

The Local Forecast Official, Dr. Cline, lives in the same part of the city and his brother (one of the observers here) boarded with him. They did not fare so well. Their house went with the rest and they were out in the wreckage nearly all night. The LOF [*sic*] lost his wife but after being nearly drowned themselves they saved the three children. As soon as possible the next morning after the waters went down I went out to the south end to see how they faired [*sic*] out there. I had to go through the wreckage of buildings nearly the entire distance (one mile) and when I got there I found everything swept clean. Part of it was still under water.

I could not even find the place where I had been staying. One that did not know would hardly believe that that had been a part of the city twenty four hours before. I could not help seeing many bodies though I was not desirous of seeing them. I at once gave up the family with whom I stopped as lost which has proved true as their bodies have all been found. But the Clines I had more confidence in in regard to their ability to come out of it. I soon got sick at the sights out there and returned to the office to put things in order as best I could. When I got to the office I found a note from the younger Cline [Joseph] telling me of the safty [*sic*] of all except the Dr.'s wife. They were all badly bruised from falling and drifting timber and one of the children was very badly hurt and they have some fears as to her recovery. Mr. Broncasial [T. C. Bornkessell, who was lost in the storm], our printer, [who] lives in another part of the town that suffered as badly is still missing and we have given him up as lost. There is not a building in town that is uninjured. Hundreds are busy day and night cleaning away the debris and recovering the dead. It is awful, every few minutes a wagon load of corpses passes by on the street.

The more fortunate are doing all they can to aid the sufferers but it is impossible to care for all. There is not room in the buildings standing to shelter them all and hundreds pass the night on the street. One meets people in all degrees of destitution. People but partially clothed are the rule and one fully clothed is an exception. The city is under military rule and the streets are patrolled by armed guards.

They are expected to shoot at once anyone found pilfering. I understand four men have been shot today for robbing the dead. I do not know how true it is for all kinds of rumors are afloat and many of them are false. We have neither light, fuel or water. I have gone back to candles. I am now writing by candlelight.

A famine is feared, as nearly all the provisions were ruined by the water which stood from six to fifteen feet in the streets and all communication to the outside is cut off.

For myself I have no fear. I sleep in the office, have food to last for some time and have water and means of getting more when it rains as it frequently does here, and besides I have made friends here who will not let me starve.

We had warning of the storm and many saved themselves by seeking safty [*sic*] before the storm reached here. We were busy all day Thursday [without much doubt Blagden meant Friday] answering telephone calls about it and advising people to prepare for danger. But the storm was more severe than we expected.

Dr. Cline placed confidence in the strength of his house. Many went to his house for safty [*sic*] as it was the strongest-built of any in that part of the town but of the forty odd who took refuge there less than twenty are now living.

I have been very busy since the storm and had little sleep but I intend to make up for sleep tonight. I do not know how or when I can send this but will send it first chance. Do not worry on my account.

Write soon,
Yours truly
John D. Blagden

It was after the 1900 storm that Galveston built its seawall. The city actually raised its sea level, by pumping ashore sand. This first required raising structures in the area; one building raised was a three-thousand-ton church.

A reorganization of the municipal government after the storm resulted in the city commission form of government, which quickly spread to other cities in the United States.

Galveston made an amazingly rapid recovery from the storm. General Thomas Scurry was so impressed that he made this statement:

I do not think I exaggerate when I say that at no time in all history have there been examples of nobler loyalty or more heroic determination. The credit for what has been done belongs in an overwhelmingly large measure to the brave people of this city.

Progressives and Prohibitionists: Texas Democratic Politics, 1911–1921

LEWIS L. GOULD[*]

To post-1960s America, it seems incongruous that liberalism and prohibitionism might be synonymous. Moreover, that southern reformers might endorse the Ku Klux Klan and preach religious fundamentalism seems even more odd to the modern student. Lewis L. Gould, however, urges that students and scholars not be misled. Rather, he suggests that many Democrats of predepression Texas, who embraced the values of what we now call middle America, also rallied to the call for reform. For progressive Democrats the dividing line in Texas was liquor, and the issue of wet or dry determined if one joined the conservative or reform wing of the Democratic party.

Gould later published a monograph, PROGRESSIVES AND PROHIBITIONISTS: TEXAS DEMOCRATS IN THE WILSON ERA *(Austin, 1973), in which he expanded the thesis first ventured in this article. James H. Timberlake's* PROHIBITION AND THE PROGRESSIVE MOVEMENT, 1900–1920 *(Cambridge, Mass., 1963), and Joseph N. Gusfield's* SYMBOLIC CRUSADE: STATUS POLITICS AND THE AMERICAN TEMPERANCE MOVEMENT *(Urbana, 1963) document like opinions held by reformers in other states. In that sense those authors support Gould's contentions.*

*Lewis L. Gould, "Progressives and Prohibitionists: Texas Democratic Politics, 1911–1921," *Southwestern Historical Quarterly*, LXXV (July, 1971), 5–18.

During the past decade, students of American politics have devoted much attention to the turbulent history of the Democratic party in the 1920s. The struggles between the prohibitionist, old-stock southern, and western wing of the party, and the urban, wet, new-stock, northeastern portion of the Democrats have been effectively explored in state and national contexts. Perceptive local studies, incisive articles on voting behavior, and comprehensive monographs have traced the emergence of the New Deal coalition. In the process, the fortunes of the northern and urban faction of the party, and especially key leaders like Al Smith and Franklin D. Roosevelt, have received particular emphasis.

The ultimate success of the policies that the northeastern Democrats championed has more than warranted this historical concentration. No clear understanding of twentieth-century politics would be possible without a grasp of the attraction of a figure like Smith for the city voter in 1928, or the way in which Roosevelt created a majority coalition after 1932. But it is also true that these Democrats have enjoyed an intrinsic appeal to liberal academicians. They stood for cultural pluralism and a tolerant view of alcohol, and opposed organizations like the Ku Klux Klan. To those who assert that the party harbored competing provincialisms in the 1920s, other scholars respond that the northeastern version of this phenomenon does not compare with "the cultural 'provincialism' of the 100 per cent American nativists."

Modern historians may shrink from an endorsement of the aims and goals of prohibitionism, fundamentalism, and the Ku Klux Klan between 1910 and 1930, but the movement deserves at least sustained examination. The views that Klansmen expressed, for instance, mirrored the attitudes of many who never wore a hood. It is too easy to dismiss the qualms that citizens felt about the liquor traffic as cranky and narrow bigotry. One must then explain why a generation of Americans found the issue of alcohol control so compelling. The cluster of ideas that made up the rural and prohibitionist wing of the Democratic party have lost their force, but they gave a sizable number of party members a conceptual structure upon which to base participation in public life. Most important, such attitudes did not arise solely from cramped spirits or blighted lives. In much of the United States a concern over the decline of agrarian and religious values, fears about the emergence of the city, and suspicions of the effects of liquor represented a comprehensible response to existing circumstances.

Many Democrats who supported the tenets of rural, old-stock Americans did not see themselves as agents of reaction. Veterans of protracted local contests before 1920, they regarded their cause as progressive and believed their programs served the interest of reform. These men worked for the nomination of Woodrow Wilson, endorsed the measures of his presidency, and looked to William G. McAdoo as the heir of the Wilsonian legacy. What represented social change in a state or regional context, however, appeared parochial when transferred to the counsels of the national party. This seeming paradox left some Democrats from the South and West bitter and confused, and does much to explain their frustration and rancor in the 1920s.

Few states offer a better opportunity for an examination of this wing of the Democrats than Texas. In the decade after 1911 the state enjoyed a deserved reputation as a bastion of reform. Nationally, it contributed heavily to Wilson's nomination in 1912, and supplied three cabinet officers, an influential advisor in Colonel Edward M. House, and several important bureaucrats to the Wilson administration. Texas congressmen gave vital votes for Democratic legislation, and Senator Morris Sheppard sponsored the prohibition amendment to the Constitution. On the state level the tradition of change associated with Governor James S. Hogg broadened out to embrace regulation of insurance companies, woman suffrage, and electoral reform. These local reformers included Thomas M. Campbell, progressive governor from 1907 to 1911, Cone Johnson, who served in the State Department under Wilson, and Thomas B. Love, a Dallas attorney and leader of the Woodrow Wilson movement in 1911-1912.

These achievements did not come without a struggle. In the years before 1920 Texas Democrats, like their counterparts in other states, debated vigorously the direction that the party should follow. Most of the progressives accepted the traditional dogma of states' rights, but wished to make local government more effective. "I believe that the best vindication of State's rights," said Thomas B. Love in 1908, "will be brought about by the State's governments doing as thoroughly and wholesomely and effectively the things lawfully within their spheres as the National Government does those things lawfully within its sphere to do." Other Democrats proved receptive to federal action when state solutions failed. Congressman Rufus Hardy favored the Federal Reserve bill in 1913 because "the refinements and developments of modern civilization have taught us that our former narrow conceptions of the scope and functions of government must give way to broader views and high estimates of the duties and powers of the State."

Conservatives would have no part of a stronger government or increased popular participation. "The initiative and referendum as a substitute for representative government found its birth in the ranks of the Socialist party," charged Jacob F. Wolters in 1912. Retiring from the Senate a year later, Joseph Weldon Bailey assured his colleagues: "I believe in the rule of the people, but I do not believe that vice or ignorance should govern this country. I believe in the rule of those who possess intelligence and virtue, because I know that they alone can save this Republic." Beneath warnings of mob rule and federal tyranny lurked, of course, the omnipresent menace of the black man. Pass a national prohibition amendment, Bailey warned, and "there will not be a square foot of territory in the United States where it will be unlawful for negroes and white people to intermarry."

The particularly divisive issue between the two wings of the Democratic party was prohibition. "The great majority of progressive Democrats are Prohibitionists, and the great majority of reactionaries are anti-Prohibitionists," Thomas B. Love informed Woodrow Wilson in late 1912. Governor Oscar B. Colquitt summarized the wet view of attempts to use the power of government to regulate personal morality and behavior: "Is the crime of taking a drink as a beverage so bad as to justify such tyranny? Is [*sic*] all civil liberty and human rights to fall prostrate and be trampled under foot in this way?" Drys replied that alcohol was "the greatest menace of the Twentieth Century to civic righteousness, clean politics, pure elections, and the sanctity of the ballot box, upon which depends the value and success of popular government."

Reform Democrats emphasized prohibition because it seemed to them the state's most pressing social problem. Sharing the evangelical Protestantism of the majority of the white population, they agreed with a clergyman who called the saloon "the most malignant product that our civilization can ever evolve." Progressives also regarded the sizeable black, Mexican, and German elements in the state as corrupt and dangerous influences on politics. "The negro ought not to be permitted to vote on the question of whether or not liquor shall be sold in Texas," concluded Love in 1915, "any more than the Indian should be permitted to vote on the question of whether or not liquor shall be sold in Indian country." Finally, progressives watched the growing urbanization of Texas apprehensively and concurred with drys who, according to the *Baptist Standard,* saw prohibition as "a struggle for a higher Anglo-Saxon civilization against the slum civilization of the great cities."

Progressives devoted special attention to the liquor industry because it appeared to be "the only dangerous special interest left with any potency in the State." In view of the present condition of Texas politics, this statement seems fanciful, but in 1911 it had a great measure of accuracy. The Texas Railroad Commission had brought the railroads to heel between 1895 and 1910. The Robertson insurance law of 1907 had purged the state of most "foreign," or non-Texan, insurance companies. The lumber industry was confined to the extreme eastern portion of Texas, while oil was still experiencing growing pains, and lacked the political clout it would later acquire.

The liquor industry, on the other hand, was highly visible. It worked to repeal local option laws in dry counties and towns, and used cash and persuasion in legislative sessions and primary elections. Actually divided and faction-ridden, the brewers and distillers appeared formidable opponents to the zealous drys. As prohibitionist D. E. Simmons explained:

The liquor power is so strong, its organization so perfect and its resources so unlimited that it maintains bureaus of information, employs expert legal counsel to try every issue before the courts, largely controls the daily press, employs men of the lowest moral character to break down the laws which attempt to regulate it or drive it out of a county or State.

Putting "Rum on the Run in Texas" was a difficult assignment. Effective use of the local option provisions of the Constitution of 1876 dried up North Texas, outside of Dallas and Fort Worth, by 1903. In the central and southern portions of the state, including Houston and San Antonio, the Mexican, German, and black minorities joined with wet, conservative Democrats to repulse the dry offensive between

1904 and 1911. Supporters of liquor plausibly contended that a majority of the party did not endorse prohibition, and the narrow defeat of a prohibition amendment to the state constitution in July, 1911, added weight to these claims.

Divided goals also hampered the cause of temperance. While Democrats like Love, Sheppard, and Cone Johnson viewed prohibition as part of a general effort to reform Texas and purify its politics, some of their dry allies took a more limited position. The ministerial spokesmen of the Baptists and Methodists, the members of the Anti-Saloon League, and such splinter groups as the Prohibition party and the Women's Christian Temperance Union tended to emphasize doctrinal purity instead of electoral success. Ambitious leaders insisted upon fine ideological distinctions among degrees of allegiance to the cause and occasionally tried to read faltering members out of the coalition.

The peculiar nature of the one-party system further complicated the task of the prohibition Democrats. Fluid and unstable, Texas politics resisted attempts to make a single issue the key to party loyalty. Strong personalities, like Joseph Weldon Bailey, Oscar B. Colquitt, and James E. Ferguson, caused factional divisions that cut across wet and dry alignments. The severe limitations on governmental power in the state constitution circumscribed the influence of office holders and prevented the growth of effective political organizations. The resulting complexity made creation of a rational public policy difficult and produced a situation of constant turmoil. "Whatever else may be said of us," sighed a female politician in the midst of a hard campaign, "we never politically speaking reach a state of 'innocuous desuetude.' "

Between 1912 and 1920 progressives and prohibitionists sought to overcome these obstacles and to use the Democratic party as a vehicle for moral reform. Following the defeat of the amendment in 1911, they challenged the wet, incumbent governor, Oscar B. Colquitt, in 1912. Flouting the informal tradition of a nearly automatic second term for a governor, the drys selected a state judge to oppose Colquitt. The jurist was an inept campaigner, and Colquitt won the primary easily. Prohibition Democrats prepared to make another effort in 1914 when Colquitt would step down.

The prohibitionists lost the governor's race in part because the major focus of progressive work in 1912 was the presidential candidacy of Woodrow Wilson. As a reformer and a southerner, Wilson won the early endorsement of men like Thomas B. Love and Thomas Watt Gregory. Only after the Wilson movement was well launched did Colonel House enter the picture. Love and his allies organized the state, defeated conservatives in the primaries, and sent forty dedicated delegates to the Democratic convention at Baltimore. Though Wilson equivocated on prohibition, his Texas reformist friends felt confident that he would assist them in making the state party both dry and progressive.

The Wilson administration disappointed these hopes during its first year in office. Under the guidance of Postmaster General Albert S. Burleson, the president rebuffed attempts to make progressivism a criterion for federal office. Wilson gave the congressional delegation a larger patronage voice than his reform supporters in an attempt to insure votes for his legislative program. Burleson and House—both wet, inclined toward conservatism, and long-time residents of Austin—also allocated some of the best positions to friends and associates in the Texas capital. "If this thing continues," complained a Fort Worth paper, "all prominent citizens of Austin who dwell in the Burleson zone will be holding fat offices under President Wilson." Only in a bitter dispute over the collector of customs at Brownsville did the progressives win a patronage triumph. In Texas, as in other states, the demands of national policy limited Wilson's commitment to fostering reform factions within a local Democratic party.

The progressives and their dry allies looked to the 1914 gubernatorial primary with more optimism. Between July, 1913, and February, 1914, they rallied behind a single candidate, a Houston attorney named Thomas H. Ball, and prepared to defeat the apparently disorganized wets. "Every day reveals something that gives more definite assurance of the election of Mr. Ball," wrote Samuel P. Brooks, the president of Baylor University, in late March. Ball had much surface strength, but he was more of a prohibitionist than a progressive. A lawyer for railroads and corporations, he had an erratic personal background, and lacked the ardor of some of his more intense supporters. The prohibitionist standard-bearer was the best candidate his faction could offer, but he was also a vulnerable target for an opponent with stamina and a taste for demagogy.

The wets found such a man in James E. Ferguson. A Central Texas banker who had moved on the fringes of state politics for five years, Ferguson announced his candidacy in November, 1913, on a platform that emphasized the evils of farm tenancy and promised regulation of the rents the tenants had to pay. Tenants operated nearly 52 percent of all farms by 1911, and Ferguson had found an issue that, combined with his own antiprohibition sentiments, could carry him to victory. He drove the other wet candidates from the field by April, 1914, and brought his unique campaign style to bear on the hapless Ball. Worried drys reported that the farmers were "taking to [Ferguson's] land proposal like a hungry cat to a piece of fresh beef liver."

Ferguson gave Ball no rest. On the stump, "Farmer Jim" used agrarian props like a gourd and wooden dipper to underscore his rural allegiance. He assailed Ball for belonging to a Houston club that sold liquor, and promised that his opponent would "go down in history as the biggest political straddler that ever lived." By mid-June a prohibitionist worker concluded: "unless some very aggressive and active efforts are made, we stand to lose." Shortly thereafter a vicious whispering campaign labeled Ball a drunk, a philanderer, and the victim of "a very loathsome disease which he contracted while leading a double life."

Ball's progressive advisors turned to the Wilson administration to stave off defeat. They sought an endorsement of the dry cause and told the president that Ferguson was an agent of reaction. "Silence by the administration here as to Ball," said Senator Morris Sheppard, "will be disastrous to progressive Democracy." Wilson, Secretary of State William Jennings Bryan, and Burleson issued public statements for Ball in mid-July, a tactic that moved Ferguson to denounce federal interference in state affairs. Despite the presidential action, Ferguson combined the wet vote with the ballots of North Texas farmers disturbed over tenancy and carved out a 45,000 vote majority.

Ferguson's nomination inflicted a serious setback on the progressive Democrats. The new governor was a master campaigner, a deft manipulator of the wet faction, and a clever opportunist with an eye on the state treasury and other sources of personal profit. His ability to blur differences over prohibition and the land question meant that state politics would continue to be internecine, convoluted, and nonideological. Drys and progressives again faced the prospect of four years of antiprohibitionist leadership in Austin. In addition, what Wilson's secretary later called the "disastrous results" of the president's intervention meant that the administration would be slow to interfere again in a local "wet and dry fight."

A rapport between Ferguson and Wilson emerged during the aftermath of the primary and lasted through the spring of 1917. In contrast to Colquitt, who bickered openly with the president over Mexican policy, Ferguson deferred to Washington in his public statements and confined disagreement to private correspondence. A similarly cooperative attitude marked the governor's actions on neutrality. In 1916, after Ferguson supported the Wilson campaign for preparedness, the administration acquiesced in the governor's domination of the state convention at San Antonio and tacitly endorsed his leadership of the delegation to the national convention. The progressives, said Love, wanted to keep "men who wear the political collar of the liquor traffic" off the slate, but they were no match for a coalition of Ferguson backers, friends of former Senator Bailey, and moderates who thought the governor was doing Wilson's bidding. "There seems to be some fate that prevents our folks from hanging together," sighed Cone Johnson.

Progressives took some comfort in the defeat of Colquitt in the 1916 senatorial race. Long a wet stalwart, he moved away from the mild progressivism of his first gubernatorial term, and broke with Wilson in 1914 over patronage, cotton legislation, and Mexico. In a New York *Times* interview Colquitt described the administration as "the greatest failure in the history of the Presidency." After leaving office, he supported Germany in the quarrels over neutrality, in part to preserve his base of support among the German-Americans in South-Central Texas, and continued to scold the president. He ran first in the six-man senatorial primary in July, and went into a runoff with the incumbent, Charles A. Culberson. This development caused dismay in the White House. "It would be disastrous to have him up here disgracing the State and the Senate of the United States," Thomas Watt Gregory, now Wilson's attorney general, told Love.

To defeat Colquitt, the Democrats had to opt for a politician whose loyalty to dry progressivism was doubtful. As state attorney general, governor, and senator, Charles Culberson turned silence into a settled habit and rarely revealed his convictions. Ben Tillman and Theodore

Roosevelt called him more of a detective than a senator. A taste for alcohol and the infirmities that flowed from its excessive use made Culberson a semi-invalid who lacked the endurance to campaign personally. Never setting foot in the state during the canvass, Culberson rode to a runoff victory behind the votes of conservative and progressive Democrats, joined together temporarily to defeat the open enemy of a Democratic president. This kind of negative victory did not mean that the prohibitionist-progressive wing had rebounded from the effects of 1914. With Ferguson a potential candidate in 1918 against the arch-dry senator, Morris Sheppard, and no strong gubernatorial hopefuls on the horizon, prohibition Democrats still displayed their "inherent inability . . . to 'hang together,' " as 1917 began.

American entry into World War I removed some of the obstacles in the path of temperance. Prohibition became a patriotic cause to conserve foodstuffs, protect the soldiers in training camps, and injure the German-dominated brewing industry. The Wilson administration abandoned its previous coolness on the subject and endorsed wartime restraints on alcohol. Within Texas itself, reformers marched on such wet bastions as Dallas, Waco, and Austin in the fall of 1917. A dry leader, Cullen F. Thomas, noting the progress, remarked: "Reform seems awfully slow but wrong will not always be on the throne."

Even more effective in promoting the antiliquor movement was the impeachment of Ferguson over his personal finances and protracted controversy with the University of Texas. The political repercussions of this dispute, which raged from mid-1915 until Ferguson's ouster by the state senate in September, 1917, devastated the wets. By attacking the university, the governor united its alumni, the drys, the woman suffragists, and the press against him. As a result, the forces of moral reform acquired a cohesion that contrasted sharply with their earlier disunity. The revelation in Ferguson's trial of his misuse of state funds and shady financial relations with the brewers left the antiprohibitionists "practically wrecked."

Over the next year the drys remained on the offensive. The acting governor, William P. Hobby, renounced his wet past, and called the legislature into special session to deal with the sale of liquor near military training camps. The lawmakers went far beyond this topic, and passed a statewide prohibition law, ratified the national prohibition amendment, and gave the women the vote in the Democratic primary. Thomas H. Ball told the state senate that the "destruction of the liquor business" and the other achievements of the winter of 1918 "record a new high water mark in patriotism and progressive Democracy."

"Progressive Democracy" also prevailed in the gubernatorial election as Hobby turned back Ferguson's bid for vindication. The same coalition of progressives, drys, and organized women gave the Hobby campaign its thrust. Labeling Ferguson as an agent of the Kaiser because of his brewery connections, the Hobby camp made patriotism the keynote. "From a political campaign" boasted the Houston *Post*, "this has become an impetuous, patriotic impulse to 'slay the beast' at home." Hobby won a smashing 244,000 vote majority, and the drys took over the party. "Politically our situation is a most happy one," wrote clergyman J. B. Cranfill: "The prohibitionists swept the State, thrust the Ferguson gang out, and will save the State by adopting next year a prohibition amendment that will clean up the liquor dens for all time."

A final challenge to dry supremacy appeared in 1919. Joseph Weldon Bailey decided to reshape the Democratic party in accord with his conservative, states' rights views. Suspect among progressives because of his financial dealings between 1900 and 1906, Bailey opposed Wilson's candidacy in 1912, criticized the president after 1913, and was an open foe of prohibition and woman suffrage. He urged party members to repudiate Wilsonian "Socialism" and sponsored a statewide convention of conservative Democrats in August, 1919. To assist in the selection of an anti-Wilson delegation to the national convention, he became a candidate for governor early in 1920, and began a campaign that accused the Wilson administration of extravagance, softness on the race question, and usurpation of states' rights.

The progressives, under the leadership of Hobby, Love, and Gregory, responded vigorously to Bailey's assault. Proadministration Democrats forged a campaign organization, called Bailey a traitor to the party, and soundly trounced him over the selection of delegates in May, 1920. In the gubernatorial race Bailey led in the first primary, but lost decisively to the prohibitionist Pat M. Neff in a singularly dirty runoff campaign. When Bailey's defeat was final, his enemies called the outcome an endorsement of "the achievements of the Wilson administration, prohibition and equal suffrage, the rule of right in this land of ours and for honest and progressive government conducted by honest and progressive men."

This judgment accurately caught the spirit of the prohibitionist faction of the Texas Democracy between 1911 and 1921. Far from being parochial advocates of cultural reaction, these politicians campaigned for what seemed to them progressive changes in the state's public policy. Prohibition was, within the Texas context, an attempt to purify politics, improve the moral quality of life, and adapt the traditional values of a rural society to a rapidly changing situation. It supplied an outlet for ethnic hostility and appeared to accord with the goals of the national party. Some dry progressives, like Love and Morris Sheppard, even made the transition to the New Deal without losing their reform credentials.

The record of Texas politics in this period suggests the need for a fresh look at the internal history of the Democrats in the Wilson era. A recent student of the 1920s argues that southern and western party members had developed "a complex of political, social, and moral attitudes" by 1920 that was a compound "of nativism, fundamentalism, prohibitionism, and a conviction that the American character resided in the farm and hinterland town." These diverse elements were fused into a tangible public philosophy in Texas during the contests over alcohol before 1920, and Democrats carried memories of these local struggles into the following decade. Dry progressives who had prevailed in the battles with Bailey, Colquitt, and Ferguson were hardly likely to defer meekly to the divergent cultural views of Al Smith. The position of these Democrats may have reflected "cultural provincialism," but it was not carelessly adopted nor lightly held. Historians of the Democratic party will have to give it intensive scrutiny to comprehend fully the fascinating history of the party in the years before the New Deal.

President Wilson's Politician:
Albert Sidney Burleson of Texas

ADRIAN ANDERSON[*]

The ascension of Woodrow Wilson to the presidency in 1913 signaled the return of the South to political power. Southern statesmen had played major political roles before the Civil War, but their influence diminished after Appomatox. They began to reclaim important positions in the Democratic party in the 1890s. William Jennings Bryan, with his emphasis on the agrarian way of life, had special affection for southerners. They returned it in kind. Bryan, however, won no presidential elections. But as Professor Adrian Anderson's account of Albert Sidney Burleson points out, southerners did win important legislative posts in the early twentieth century, and, with Wilson's triumph, executive influence as well.

Burleson's friends Thomas Watt Gregory and Edward M. House served Wilson, too. Gregory became attorney general, and House was, for some time, the president's closest confidant. Texans in 1913 thus achieved their first actual national power since Sam Houston. Texans held such power through 1968—a point that Anderson alludes to in his citation of Lyndon Johnson's delivery of Burleson's funeral oration. Also worthy of examination is the way in which Burleson represented

[*]Adrian Anderson, "President Wilson's Politician: Albert Sidney Burleson of Texas," *Southwestern Historical Quarterly*, LXXVII (January, 1974), 339–354.

southern ideology in the Wilson cabinet. The conflicts between rural and urban progressive ideas divide the Democratic party throughout the 1920s. As Anderson implies, Burleson also represented that clash.

Traditionally presidents of the United States have appointed postmasters general who were known more for their political skill than for their administrative talent. In 1913 President-elect Woodrow Wilson, though a progressive and an idealist, was no exception. After long deliberation he offered the position in late February to a veteran congressman from Texas, Albert Sidney Burleson. Burleson, who had discreetly but anxiously sought a cabinet post, accepted eagerly.

The first of his family to achieve national recognition, Albert Burleson was descended from a long line of Texas soldiers and statesmen. His grandfather, General Edward Burleson, commanded toops at San Antonio and San Jacinto in the Texas Revolution, served in the Congress of the Republic of Texas, and won a term as vice-president of the Republic in 1841, but lost his bid for the presidency three years later. Major Edward Burleson, Jr., the father of Albert, fought in the Mexican War, took part in a number of Indian campaigns, and performed the duties of enrolling officer in charge of military conscription for the Confederacy in the San Marcos area. After the Civil War the major retired to private life, but turned to the political scene a few months before his death when he was chosen a delegate to the Texas constitutional convention of 1875.

While Major Burleson was serving the Confederate cause, his wife, Emma Kyle, gave birth to her fifth child, Albert Sidney, in a farm home near San Marcos. Albert was orphaned at an early age, but a comfortable inheritance assured him an education. After graduating in the first class of the University of Texas Law School, he settled in Austin, where he joined a firm of locally prominent attorneys, married, and acquired investments, eventually including a large cotton plantation near Waco.

Although Burleson was a successful lawyer, he soon became interested in politics. The Democratic party of Travis County in the late nineteenth century was in a process of transition and reorganization, thus providing opportunity for the ambitious ones who would attend caucuses and conventions and minister faithfully to the dozens of petty organizational chores. While serving as assistant city attorney of Austin and, after 1891, as district attorney, Burleson worked his way up in the local ranks to a position of some power, acquiring at the same time considerable experience and developing a value system that would guide him in the future. Early in his career he concluded that party organization was the key to political success; hence party identification, discipline, and loyalty held precedence over other virtues.

Burleson's entry into politics coincided with a rising tide of agrarian protest in Texas and throughout much of the nation. The Populist agrarian reformers, who by 1892 were winning much of the traditional support of the Democratic party, did not attract the young politician. His affluent background, cautious business attitudes, political associations, and, above all, his belief in party solidarity precluded that. But he was sympathetic to some of the demands of agrarian reformers. He was a staunch advocate of free silver. When the Democratic party of Texas split in 1892 between conservative forces led by railroad attorney George Clark and Progressive followers of Governor James Hogg, Burleson, in the words of a Clark man, made himself "obnoxious" in his campaigning for Hogg and free silver. In 1896 he was an exuberant member of the Texas silver delegation to the Democratic National Convention; he was still talking silver as late as 1900. His stand was not a matter of political expediency. Two of his closest friends throughout his life were Thomas Watt Gregory, an Austin attorney, and Colonel Edward M. House, a powerful figure in Texas politics around the turn of the century. Gregory supported Clark in 1892 and continued thereafter to oppose free silver. Colonel House, though a Hogg man in the early nineties, avoided a stand but obviously cared little for the silver cause. Moreover, Travis County, which made up the bulk of Burelson's constituency, was conservative on the money question, giving its vote to the Republican William McKinley and the gold standard in the election of 1896.

The young politician's first campaign for Congress, in 1898, reflected additional evidences of agrarian liberalism. He called for a reduction in the tariff, prison terms for violators of antitrust laws, restriction of immigration, limitations on the use of injunctions against labor unions, and a constitutional amendment allowing the enactment of an income tax. He denounced national banks and repeated his plea for free coinage of silver. But he also emphasized that he would "at all times oppose communism, paternalism and socialism."

Victory in the election of 1898 opened the way to fourteen years of congressional service. The list of legislation sponsored by Burleson during these years reveals little except a readiness to seek government assistance for agriculture. Preoccupied with rural problems, he introduced bills dealing with such matters as boll weevils, Johnson grass, cotton, oleomargarine, and mistletoe.

More significant were Burleson's activities within the Democratic party in Congress. He first called attention to his obsession with party discipline in 1901 by demanding that the Democratic caucus of the House be bound by the national party platform. Soon he secured recognition in House Democratic councils, and by 1907 speculation suggested that he might replace the embattled Democrat, House Minority Leader John Sharp Williams.

The rumors were unfounded, but in 1909 he did promote an abortive revolt against the autocratic House rules and still more autocratic House Speaker Joe Cannon, one of the Republican Old Guard. Later, when a Democratic-Republican insurgent coalition succeeded in revising the rules in 1910, Burleson demonstrated his political partisanship. By offering a resolution removing Cannon from office, he forced the unfortunate Republican insurgents to choose between an endorsement of Cannon or party oblivion. A few months later, and probably in recognition of his role in the House rules fight, Burleson was elected chairman of the House Democratic caucus.

By early 1912 Burleson was deeply involved in the contest for the Democratic presidential nomination. Thomas Watt Gregory, already Burleson's close friend, had joined with Thomas Love, of Dallas, and others in lining up support for the cause of Woodrow Wilson in Texas. Burleson joined the fray publicly in January, 1912, with a blast at the critics of Wilson. Thereafter he was involved in the preconvention maneuvers of the candidate. One of four Texas congressmen who supported the New Jersey governor, his efforts were welcome. In the Democratic Convention at Baltimore, in June, he served with A. Mitchell Palmer as floor leader, and in the following campaign he directed the Speaker's Bureau.

While newspapers were still featuring stories of the election results, speculation appeared that Burleson might enter the presidential cabinet. The Texan undoubtedly wanted a cabinet post, but his statements and actions concerning such an appointment were inconsistent to the point of duplicity. He repeatedly asserted that he was not an applicant, that he did not want any endorsements, and that he would not make any effort to secure a position. Actually, behind the scenes he was busily at work.

During the campaign Burleson's long-time friend and political ally, Colonal House, had won Wilson's friendship and the role of confidential advisor. Before the election Burleson asked the Colonel to suggest his name to Wilson for the position of postmaster general, and less than a week after the election he sent House a list of congressmen who had assured him their support. Accordingly, when the Colonel and Wilson discussed the cabinet in mid-November, House proposed Burleson for postmaster general. Wilson preferred Joseph Daniels, newspaper editor and national committeeman from North Carolina, but House argued that Daniels was not sufficiently aggressive and that the position demanded a man with congressional experience. No decision was made and further discussions were delayed until early January, 1913.

When conferences regarding the cabinet were resumed Wilson advised House that he had eliminated Burleson from consideration; he did not want to take him away from Congress. Furthermore, Joseph Tumulty, his private secretary, had told him that Senator-elect William Hughes of New Jersey had confided that members of the House considered Burleson a "scheming and uncertain quality." When House sent Wilson a "slate to ponder over" a few days later, Burleson's name was not included, and during subsequent conferences Wilson reiterated his desire to keep Burleson as an active lieutenant in Congress. Thus when Burleson on January 18 or 19 inquired about his prospects, House gave him little encouragement. A few days later, however, Tumulty decided to support Burleson, and near the end of the month House and Wilson talked of a cabinet with Burleson as secretary of war.

Meanwhile others were advocating the Texan's selection. Senators Thomas Gore and Hoke Smith and Senator-elect Ollie James solicited his appointment. More valuable was the support of Congressman Oscar Underwood, of Alabama, who on January 13 wrote a lengthy letter to Wilson. Since maintenance of cordial relations between the executive and the majority members of the legislative branch was imperative, Underwood felt that the cabinet should contain one or two members who had the "confidence and esteem of the Democratic members of the House and Senate." Burleson, he declared, met this requirement admirably.

Wilson remained unconvinced. When House again suggested Burleson for postmaster general in mid-February, Wilson replied that the congressman might build a political machine and might not be "able to hold down the place." House countered with the argument that such a machine, if built, would be Wilson's. Apparently Wilson was receptive. After another session with the president-elect, House confided to his diary on February 14 that the cabinet was "fairly well determined" with Burleson as postmaster general. Burleson wrote Gregory on February 23 that "I think, now, I will be in the cabinet." That same day Wilson offered him the post.

Credit for Burleson's appointment belongs to several persons. Burleson and his wife believed that Mrs. Wilson influenced the decision. James Kerney, publisher of the Trenton *Times*, claimed that Thomas Pence, a newsman prominent in the campaign, and Tumulty deserved much of the credit. Obviously the support of Underwood and other powerful legislative figures who wanted a sympathetic voice in the administration was significant. Accurate determination of House's influence is impossible, but it seems fair and logical to conclude that his help alone would not have been sufficient and that without it the appointment would have been unlikely.

The contrasting personalities and value systems of Burleson and Wilson make understandable the president's reluctance to appoint the congressman. Wilson was an austere and scholarly idealist, who, according to Burleson, used and knew that he needed politicians but who "never appreciated them." Burleson, though educated, surely was neither a scholar nor an idealist. Proud of his profession, he was a politician who understood the intricacies of the political process and accepted them as legitimate realities.

Moreover, while Wilson in most respects was a Progressive, Burleson's status as a reformer was at least debatable. To be sure, he considered himself a Progressive, and his congressional record, except on matters of conservation, was in keeping with the tradition. Furthermore the Progressive spokesman, Robert La Follette of

Wisconsin, praised the Texan's appointment, writing that Burleson was "honest and fearless" and a "pronounced progressive." But Burleson's colleague and close friend, William Jennings Bryan, thought otherwise, arguing that the congressman was a "conservative, if not a reactionary."

Viewed in terms of the dichotomy of progressive versus conservative, Burleson's record as postmaster general would prove a mixed one. He bore much of the responsibility for the extension of Negro segregation to government employment during the Wilson administration; he was less than sympathetic to the cause of organized labor in his dealings with government employees; and his censorship policies during World War I were considered by many to be serious transgressions on the traditional values of freedom of the press. On the other hand, he extended parcel-post service in the postal system and introduced air-mail delivery. Moreover, he fought determinedly throughout his eight years in office for a goal that was really a little too radical even for most Progressives, government ownership of the telephone and telegraph systems.

Certainly Burleson, guided by his agrarian heritage, had little sympathy with the demands of the evolving urban society. Wilson, he complained, in supporting child-labor laws, woman's suffrage, the initiative and referendum, and other legislation favoring particular interest groups, departed from the "sound old principles" of the Democracy. By 1914 the Texan was demanding that the president listen more attentively to the advice of the nation's businessmen.

In many ways very different in personality and sense of values, Wilson and Burleson were quite similar in one respect; both were stubborn and slow to compromise. Yet the two worked together for eight years with surprisingly few difficulties. A number of reasons explain the anomaly. Burleson's devotion to, admiration for, and loyalty to Wilson approached dedication to a charismatic figure. Wilson, he asserted in retrospect, had "incomparably the greatest mind" of all; he was "an intellectual miracle" who with "great conviction...[and] courage...never permitted expediency to control his actions." The president, he believed, was not an originator but an organizer who assimilated ideas into workable form, a "very peculiar man ... who didn't care for individuals" but who had a "passion" for the masses.

Furthermore, Wilson seldom interfered with Burleson's man-

agement of the Post Office. Even when not in complete sympathy with
a policy, he only delivered a mild and courteous rebuke or a request
for an explanation. Whenever the postmaster general was criticized,
which was not infrequently, the president steadfastly supported him.
Considering Burleson's emphasis on loyalty, tenacity, and courage,
this characteristic of Wilson did much to ensure the postmaster
general's devotion. In later years Burleson remarked that he was
probably more "bitterly attacked" than any other in the administration but that "no man could have stood by another better than
Wilson." "Wilson," said Burleson, "was a man one could go into a
panther fight with."

The president also respected the postmaster general's ability.
Wilson was not close to Burleson personally, but he valued the Texan's
utility and advice, especially on political and legislative issues, and
perhaps discussed politics with him more than with any other cabinet
member. Burleson shrewdly understood his role. Wilson, he realized,
would make his own policy decisions; Burleson was an advisor. When
consulted Burleson bluntly stated his own opinion. Indeed, according
to Secretary of the Treasury William McAdoo, he was the most
outspoken "conspicuous fighter" in the cabinet. "About nine out of
ten times I myself was wrong," recalled Burleson, "but at least I told
him my opinion." Wilson always listened attentively, but never
revealed his intentions. Whatever the president's decision, Burleson
supported the policy. As a matter of fact, he sometimes compromised
his own principles. Once Wilson asked him for assistance in securing
a child-labor law. "I'll tell you," replied Burleson, "but if I were in
Congress, I should vote against it." Thus Burleson accepted his role as
an influential advisor, rather than as a policymaker. Wilson's policies,
he consistently maintained, were the result of Wilson's decisions.

As Albert Burleson moved from the House of Representatives to the
Post Office Building in the spring of 1913, he was already one of the
more familiar figures around the Capitol area. Although balding
rapidly, he retained the erect figure and ruddy countenance of his
youth. He had a round, almost chubby face, a hook nose, gray and
rather cold eyes, and short side whiskers. With his conservative black
suit and eccentric round-brim hat, he closely resembled an English
cleric. Rain or shine, night or day, winter or summer, he carried a black
umbrella. According to a fellow cabinet officer, he deliberately

played the role of a "homely, uncouth politician" in rumpled clothing to create the impression that he was no better than the humblest citizen. Of the cabinet members his appearance was the most distinctive, winning him the sobriquet of "the Cardinal."

His personal habits while in the Post Office were similar to those of earlier years when he served in Congress. Away from his office he spent most of his time with two younger daughters, Lucy Kyle and Adele Sidney, and Mrs. Burleson, an alert and intelligent woman who devoted much of her energy to writing. For the most part, the Burlesons led a quiet life. In his own inimitable fashion, however, Burleson doggedly maintained his personal values even in his social activities. When the ardent prohibitionist William Jennings Bryan came to dine, the Burlesons, ignoring the practice of many colleagues, served wine.

At work Burleson gave many hours a week to the routine of Post Office administration, but a large part of his time was devoted to political affairs. Most observers quite accurately regarded him as the president's politician, an advisor primarily on matters of appointments, patronage, and legislation.

Although President Wilson depended largely upon his own judgment when making major appointments, Burleson exerted some influence, not always in a predictable pattern. Burleson tended, as the irate Tumulty charged, to favor southerners, including the appointment of Gregory as attorney general and Carter Glass of Virginia as secretary of the treasury. He was too politically conscious, however, to be completely sectional. He vigorously supported Pennsylvanian A. Mitchell Palmer for several offices, and after Gregory resigned worked for Palmer's appointment as attorney general. Likewise, ideology was not always a consideration. For Supreme Court positions he backed James McReynolds, a conservative at heart and in practice, and Louis Brandeis, the epitome of the progressive reformer. In some instances his position was based on pragmatic politics. During the campaign of 1912 Wilson asked: "If I am elected, what am I to do with Bryan?" Burleson immediately replied: "Make him secretary of state." Bryan, he argued, had been a loyal party leader and had a large personal following. The advice, consistent with Burleson's views on party loyalty, only reinforced what others had and would tell Wilson. Though reluctant, Wilson made the appointment.

Appointments to lesser positions absorbed more of Burleson's attention. For everyone in the Wilson administration the thousands of minor jobs, patronage vital to congressmen and state politicians, were a troublesome and complicated problem. Having been out of power for sixteen years, the Democrats found most offices filled with Republicans. Republican howls when replaced by Democrats were to be expected, but the appointments often produced nearly as much turmoil among the Democrats. Further complicating the situation were the aggressive demands of civil-service reformers who wanted to take all consideration of politics out of governmental service. Many in the administration shared in the decisions; Joe Tumulty and Secretary of the Treasury William McAdoo were especially influential. But the voice most often heard on patronage was Burleson's.

Power, not ideology, was the essence of the veteran politician's patronage policies. In Texas, where his own power was at stake and where "original Wilson men" were in a minority in the congressional delegation, Burleson distributed favors among his own camp, ignoring the squalls of anguish emitted by most Texas congressmen. Since Burleson's friends were Wilson people, most appointments went to "original Wilson men," but those "original Wilson men" in the state who were at odds with Burleson had scant hope for any federal patronage.

Elsewhere Burleson generally favored the factions already controlling state politics and congressional delegations. In practice this sometimes meant awarding favors to interests that had traditionally opposed reform. In Kentucky, Virginia, and Alabama, Burleson listened to organization men, nearly all of whom had opposed Wilson's nomination. In New York, where disorganized Progressives led by Franklin D. Roosevelt, William McAdoo, and Colonel House were attempting to seize control of the party from Tammany, he was obstinately determined that Tammany must be given a share of the patronage. Ignoring Wilson's frigid frown, he campaigned in Illinois for the senatorial candidacy of Roger Sullivan, a man who had played a vital role in Wilson's nomination but who possessed an unsavory reputation as a machine politician.

Wilson accepted Burleson's patronage policies only with reluctance. Early in the administration the idealism of the reformer clashed with the realism of the politician when Wilson declared his intention of appointing only Progressives and ignoring the wishes of "reactionary or standpat" congressmen. Convinced that the policy spelled "ruination" for Wilson, Burleson argued that the offices were inconsequential but meant much to the legislators, who depended on patronage and who would turn their backs on Wilson if denied. After several conferences Wilson reluctantly agreed. Although he did not completely remove himself from matters of patronage, he paid less attention to them. Later he reportedly observed that his head was with the Progressives of the party but that his heart was with the "so-called Old Guard" because of their loyal support.

Wilson likewise endorsed Burleson's civil-service policies. Implicit in Burleson's actions, which included a campaign to extend civil service to all classes of postmasters, was a conflict between an evidently sincere desire to expand the merit system and the conviction that partisan patronage was politically necessary. He was not the most ardent spoilsman in the party; House Democratic Speaker Champ Clark denounced him for his concern for merit in postal appointments. On the other hand, he asked congressmen recommending postmasters to furnish affidavits of the applicants' Democracy. In consequence, while party faithful were angrily complaining that appointment policies were alienating Democratic support, the National Civil Service Reform League was maintaining just as angrily that Burleson was debauching the ideals of the merit system. Wilson, avoiding the clamor whenever possible, steadfastly backed his subordinate, even to the point of removing some members of the Civil Service Commission who were critical of the postmaster general.

When not occupied with postal affairs and patronage, Burleson acted as Wilson's liaison agent, expediting legislation and maintaining communication between the White House and the "Hill." The president and the postmaster general conferred frequently over legislation, often over the telephone. At the beginning of each session of Congress, Wilson asked him for a "memorandum of what you think we ought to do." Burleson, after considering the disposition of the country and the feeling in Congress and talking to House and Senate leaders, presented his conclusions and recommendations to the president. Wilson did not always concur. Feeling that currency reform would split the party, Burleson vigorously opposed it, but Wilson went ahead. "I was wrong," Burleson afterwards recalled. Whatever the decision, Burleson loyally went to work.

Although most of the discussions relative to legislative matters took place in person or by telephone, the reliance of the administration on Burleson is often reflected in his correspondence. Wanting to aid hurricane-stricken Japan, Wilson wrote Burleson that "you know to whom in Congress such a thing might be suggested. . . . Would you . . . [bring] the matter to their attention?" On another occasion he wrote: "I am very anxious indeed to get the appropriation . . . enacted. Will you . . . call the matter to the attention of the House conferees?" Disgruntled when his first request directed to Champ Clark was ignored, he asked Burleson to intercede on behalf of the bill purchasing Monticello. Again he wrote, sending copies of two bills and saying: "My trouble is that I do not know what committee chairman and chairmen should be consulted. Won't you give me the right tip?" On another matter he asked "what sort of a man" was a certain New York representative. "I have some important questions [that] I would like to discuss with him if he is entirely the right sort."

Other administration officials also relied on the legislative experience of the veteran former congressman. Secretary of Labor William B. Wilson asked him to arrange for the submittal of a child-labor law; Secretary of Commerce William C. Redfield asked for his assistance in putting through several bills affecting his department; and a southern senator called on Burleson for help when a cotton-marketing bill came up for consideration. Secretary of War Newton Baker inquired: "I enclose two letters [to the chairman of the Committee on Military Affairs.] Which had I better send?"

An analysis of Burleson's relations with Congress, which were seldom committed to writing, obviously must be to some degree conjectural. The postmaster general, however, maintained that he essentially relied on knowledge of the legislative machinery, persuasion, and patronage. From his long experience as a congressman he understood the committees, the method of moving bills through the houses, and, perhaps most important, the peculiarities of the congressmen. An organization man and a native of the South, he understood and accepted two main elements of his party, the urban machine politicians and the large block of southerners. He praised those who fought for the administration's cause, and, more significantly, from time to time persuaded Wilson to do likewise. His acknowledged position as Wilson's spokesman on Capitol Hill was valuable, and he did not hesitate to wield the stick of patronage. Once when passage of tariff legislation was before Congress, one of the Kansas senators received five postmasterships, long overdue, after indicating that he would back the administration. The two events were not unrelated. The Texan succinctly summed up his power: "I had the bait gourd. They had to come to me."

Burleson participated in the passage of most of the Wilson administration reforms. The Underwood-Simmons Act, Federal Reserve Act, Adamson Railway Act, Panama Tolls Act, Alaskan Railroad Act, and many others brought the postmaster general to Capitol Hill, or at least to his telephone. When the Federal Reserve Act was pending, Burleson told House that "every day I find many things to do to further the passage of this bill in accordance with the wishes of the administration." As the vote on the administration's controversial Panama Tolls Act drew near, Burleson sat at his desk and called senators and representatives, "bringing to bear every possible kind of pressure."

If the administration objected to a measure Burleson entered the fight. When southern lawmakers demanded cotton-relief measures in 1914, Burleson abandoned his agrarian loyalties to assist the administration's fight against the bills. In 1916 fellow Texan Jeff McLemore introduced a resolution in the House of Representatives which seriously challenged the president's leadership in foreign affairs. Burleson, joined by Secretary of the Treasury McAdoo and Attorney General Gregory, urged Wilson to make an open fight. A few days later Burleson and McAdoo, armed with handwritten notes from Wilson, went to Capitol Hill and pressured the House leaders for a vote. In truth, many Democrats, probably most of those from the South, favored the resolution, but the pressure of party discipline exerted by the White House spokesmen was sufficient; by a count of 276 to 142 the measure went down to defeat.

Ample evidence indicates that Burleson was an effective advocate with Congress. Carter Glass, the father of the Federal Reserve, wrote Burleson that "at many strategical points your timely aid and influence helped to save the day. . . . The President will never know ...in how great a degree you contributed to the passage." Congressman W. C. Houston congratulated Burleson for the "very great aid" rendered in the passage of the Alaska Railroad Bill. In the Panama Canal Tolls controversy Wilson, House, and Representative W. C.

Adamson, who sponsored the bill, praised the postmaster general for his role in the action. After the bill had passed, Wilson remarked, "Burleson, it was a great fight," "It was a great victory for you," replied the Texan. "No," answered the president, "it was a great victory for you." The historian and contemporary observer Ray Stannard Baker concluded that Burleson was one of Wilson's most useful officers. These favorable comments came from friends, but even foes testified to Burleson's influence. The New York *World*, an administration ally but no friend of Burleson, complained that he had blocked some favorite measures.

Burleson's final years in the Wilson cabinet were difficult ones. His effectiveness with Congress unquestionably declined during Wilson's second term. Controversy generated by his management of the Post Office alienated many congressmen and other powerful forces. Quarrelsome and demoralized factions of northern and southern Democrats drifted farther and farther apart as Wilson, preoccupied with details of war and plans for peace, paid less attention to party and legislative matters. The Republican victory in the congressional election of 1918 and Wilson's illness the following year rendered Burleson almost powerless. Congress adopted major legislation over his strenuous opposition, and his efforts on behalf of the ratification of the Treaty of Versailles failed. Shortly thereafter defeat of his candidate, William Gibbs McAdoo, in the Democratic National Convention of 1920 was followed by the unmistakable repudiation of his party in the general election. By 1921 Burleson was ready to retire.

In retirement Burleson lived quietly in Austin, observing politics closely but seldom assuming an active role. In 1928 he broke his silence in support of the presidential ambitions of Alfred Smith, the antiprohibition Catholic governor of New York, denouncing the critics of Smith in terms of "bigotry, intolerance, and fanaticism." In 1932 and the years which followed he supported Franklin Delano Roosevelt, although he found little in the New Deal to his liking. At dawn, on the morning of November 24, 1937, victim of a heart attack at the age of seventy-four, he died. The traditional eulogy in the House of Representatives was delivered a few days later by a rising young Texas politician, Lyndon Baines Johnson.

The eight years between 1913 and 1921, in which Woodrow Wilson and Albert Sidney Burleson shared a relationship, yield at least two inferences. In the first place, although his own prowess as a politician varied from one extreme to another, Wilson had more of a pragmatic appreciation for the value of a professional politician than is generally realized. In view of Burleson's habitually blunt, outspoken pronouncements of his position, Wilson surely knew that the Texan often supported his policies out of loyalty, not conviction. Yet the two had only one serious difference, and this over politics, not principle. Burleson's effort in 1920 to straddle the fence and support both Wilson and McAdoo for the Democratic nomination provoked the president's wrath, Burleson narrowly escaping summary dismissal.

An understanding of Burleson's role in the Wilson administration underscores another perspective on the Progressive era. The Texan, undoubtedly conservative in many respects, cannot be placed with precision either in or out of the Progressive tradition. In his case, actually, the distinction is virtually meaningless. Though he had strong convictions on most questions, the demands of power politics, not reform, were the primary guide for his activities. Nevertheless, working within the framework of a Progressive administration, he did contribute to the accomplishment of reform. Others, no doubt, were of Burleson's breed. Perhaps studies of progressivism, already frustrating in their breadth and complexity, should place more emphasis on the organizational values of politics.

The Houston Mutiny and Riot of 1917

Robert V. Haynes[*]

*Progressivism touched the lives of all Texans. Because it was a reform
movement born in prosperity and aimed at correcting the excesses of
corporate capitalism, it was concerned more with the regulation of
business and the creation of economic opportunities than with the
elimination of segregation. Consequently recent historians have
criticized progressives for being shortsighted in their attitudes towards
the aspirations of black Americans. These scholars have conceded that,
by fighting economic abuses, progressivism bettered the lot of the
common folk. They have maintained, however, that the reformers
stopped short by not translating their rhetoric of equal opportunity into
the fight for social justice.*

*Progressive prose spoke of the equality of man, and its words were
refined by World War I into the promise of democracy for all the
nations of the world. Black Americans took these words seriously.
Hence racial clashes occurred in six major northern cities in 1917, and
twenty-five riots would flare in 1919, as black Americans demanded a
lessening of Jim Crow. Black aspirations, stirred by progressive
rhetoric, thus met with fierce, white resistance.*

*Robert V. Haynes, in this perceptive article, describes the reaction of
whites to black soldiers' demands for dignity in Houston, Texas, in the*

*Robert V. Haynes, "The Houston Mutiny and Riot of 1917," *Southwestern Historical
Quarterly,* LXXVI (April, 1973), 418–439.

summer of 1917. He points out two themes that should interest a student of Texas history: first, black Americans truly believed the propaganda of World War I, and second, they were unwilling to accept violence without retaliation. In that sense the Houston riot was an omen.

Haynes has published a longer work on the riot, A NIGHT OF VIOLENCE: THE HOUSTON RIOT OF 1917 *(Baton Rouge, 1976), which amplifies the themes stated in this article.*

On the morning of August 25, 1917, two heavily guarded trains carrying the disarmed men of the Third Battalion, Twenty-fourth United States Infantry, left Houston, Texas, for Columbus, New Mexico. After the trains had passed through Schulenburg, Texas, a resident of that town picked up a small piece of paper on the railroad right-of-way near his icehouse. He discovered scribbled on the back of a soldier's unused pass a hand-written message: "Take Tex. and go to hell, I don't want to go there anymore in my life. Lets go East and be treated as people."

Less than four weeks earlier, 654 black soldiers and 8 white officers of this battalion had arrived in Houston to assume guard duties at Camp Logan, a new training cantonment then under construction and located approximately three and a half miles from the center of town. On the evening of August 23, a sizeable group of enlisted men participated in a mutiny and in a march on the city which left twenty persons dead or dying on the streets of Houston.

As acting Mayor Dan M. Moody later stated, the "feeling that something was going to happen [was] in the air" from the moment the Twenty-fourth Infantry arrived on Saturday, July 28, 1917. The white citizens were apprehensive about the presence in their city of armed blacks wearing the uniform of the United States army, especially since as military guards the soldiers would be in a position to exercise authority over them. The Houston Chamber of Commerce carefully debated whether or not to allow these soldiers in the city and acquiesced only after the War Department had informed its president that black troops alone were available for such duty and that they would remain in Houston no longer than seven weeks. Anxious not to jeopardize the city's chances to gain lucrative federal contracts, the chamber promised "that, in a spirit of patriotism, the colored soldiers would be treated all right."

The city authorities made no more mention of their coming than was necessary. As soon as the Third Battalion arrived, however, the local newspapers began a campaign to educate the white citizens about the exceptional talents, the good moral character, and the strict discipline characteristic of black soldiers in the regular army. In an interview with a reporter for the Houston *Post*, Major W. A. Trumbull, quartermaster at Camp Logan, maintained that the Negro soldier was "a 'bear-cat' as a fighter," that discipline in the ranks was "almost perfect," and that the soldiers were recruited from the "best and most intelligent negroes in the country." Even more capable, he asserted, were the black noncommissioned officers, who were "among the most efficient in the army." Trumbull explained that it was "harder to get to be a noncommissioned officer in a negro regiment than it [was] to get a commission as an officer in a white regiment." Although the more prejudiced whites were hardly convinced by these pronouncements from an army officer, they were at least silenced for the moment.

On the other hand, the soldiers' apprehensions were not so easily relieved. Prior to coming to Houston, the Twenty-fourth Infantry had fought in the Indian conflicts of the late nineteenth century as well as in the Spanish-American War, had served in the Philippine Islands and in Alaska, and had recently returned to New Mexico after participating in the Punitive Expedition of 1916–1917 into Mexico. Most of the soldiers were not elated over being suddenly reduced from the position of a fighting force to that of a guard detail.

For the Third Battalion, consisting of companies J, K, L, and M, the prospect of service in Texas was grim if not frightening, since the experiences of black soldiers in the Lone Star State had been anything but pleasant. In 1906, three companies of the Twenty-fifth Infantry were discharged without honor by President Theodore Roosevelt for allegedly shooting up the border town of Brownsville. In 1911 and again in 1916 black soldiers nearly came to blows with white citizens of San Antonio over disagreements involving racial insults and unequal access to places of public accommodation. In 1916, black troopers of the Twenty-fourth's First Battalion, enraged by the refusal of white prostitutes in Del Rio to accommodate them, pelted the brothel with rocks until the local police and a small detachment of Texas Rangers arrived to stop the bombardment. In the process a Texas Ranger killed one of the soldiers, supposedly in "self-defense," and the army court-martialed two others for inciting the brawl.

The men of the Twenty-fourth Infantry were also aware that Texas was a rigidly segregated state and that it had a reputation for violence against nonwhite citizens. Two brutal lynchings of Negroes, one at Temple in 1915 and another at Waco in 1916, had been well publicized by black newspapers and journals. Only a month before the Third Battalion's arrival in Houston, a mob of two hundred whites had hanged a Negro in nearby Galveston. Finally, the East St. Louis Massacre, which had occurred in early July, 1917, was still vividly in their minds, and men of the Third Battalion contributed nearly $150 to a relief fund for the displaced and homeless blacks of that city.

With both white civilians and black troopers anticipating trouble, it was not slow in developing. On Saturday evening, July 28, most of the newly arrived soldiers went into town to acquaint themselves with Houston and to locate the most suitable places of entertainment. Several incidents occurred on streetcars over the segregated seating arrangements required by city ordinance. In most cases the soldiers obeyed the law or the white conductors disregarded minor violations, but a few black troopers openly defied the system of discrimination by removing the Jim Crow screens, which they either kept as "souvenirs" or tossed out the windows.

The most serious confrontation happened the next evening. Two platoons of the Twenty-fourth, fearful about missing the eleven o'clock check, piled onto a streetcar only to have the annoyed conductor order them off for violating the segregation ordinance. While a handful of angry soldiers were threatening to "throw the goddamn thing off the track," others spotted another trolley. As the fifty-eight men swarmed aboard it, one of the soldiers firmly told the conductor that "they would just like to see the first son of a bitch that tried to put them off," while a few others enlarged the "colored" section by ordering six white passengers to move up front.

By Monday morning, news of the weekend altercations was all over town. Anxious to cool racial tensions before they erupted into serious violence, Houston's chief of police, Clarence Brock, met with the traffic manager of the Houston Electric Company and Colonel William Newman to work out a compromise arrangement. Brock agreed to leave punishment of soldiers who violated the segregation ordinances to the army and to allow sixteen specially chosen provost guards to assist police in patrolling black neighborhoods frequented most often by the soldiers. In return, Colonel Newman consented to withhold sidearms from the military police and to equip them only with billy clubs furnished by the Houston Police Department. He also promised to inform the soldiers that they were not to congregate outside the camp in groups of more than three. While these "unprecedented" arrangements assuaged most of the fears of white Houstonians, they multiplied those of the black soldiers, who believed that, by depriving them of effective military protection, Newman had left them almost defenseless in a hostile southern community. In time, they would come to feel that justice could not be obtained through normal channels.

The friction that first began on the streetcars soon spread to other areas of contact between soldiers and civilians. The most frequent point of conflict was Camp Logan, where 148 men were daily assigned to mount seven guard posts. Although the guards were issued five rounds of ammunition, they were instructed to load their rifles only in case of an emergency and to treat all authorized personnel with respect. While they generally followed these orders explicitly, most white employees at Camp Logan resented having to show their credentials to black soldiers and treated the guards accordingly. In fact, a few even made sport of the situation. One reported story that a city engineer had been admitted after flashing a baseball pass became a standing joke among white workers. Sergeant William C. Nesbit of Company I, later convicted of participating in the mutiny and riot, reported that "those [white] people out there wouldn't obey and said they weren't taking orders from niggers."

On the other hand, the slightest sign of discourtesy or evidence of misbehavior on the part of the black guards was immediately reported to one of the foremen or to a white officer. As the number of complaints increased, Newman detailed an officer of the day to remain at Camp Logan in order to resolve matters of friction before they became serious. In cases where the soldiers were judged at fault, they were appropriately and swiftly disciplined. As long as he was in command, Newman "habitually" made daily inspections of the guard posts at Camp Logan to see that the soldiers were performing their duties in an efficient and military manner. From all indications, the soldiers were, if anything, too conscientious. Workmen coming to and from the camp demonstrated their resentment by making snide comments as they passed or by blatantly addressing the guards as "niggers." Like other white Houstonians, they made no distinctions between black soldiers and black civilians and treated both groups as inferior persons.

In response to these daily reminders of their degraded position in Houston, black soldiers grew increasingly irritable. By mid-August they were making their annoyance at this treatment obvious to those whites who made frequent use of this type of opprobrium. On several occasions, they firmly declared that they were not "niggers" and that they expected to be addressed as "colored men." "Look here," one guard told the paymaster of the Houston Lighting and Power Company, "I want you to understand that we ain't no niggers. I am no nigger."

Two incidents in mid-August nearly escalated into serious violence. The first involved the refusal of several guards to drink from the water barrels labeled "colored." Instead they insisted upon using the cans labeled "white." Recognizing the explosive nature of this situation, the contractors hastily added another receptacle and marked it "guards." The second episode occurred on Saturday, August 18, when a white tradesman knifed Sam Blair, a black worker, for allegedly butting ahead of him in the pay line. In the ensuing "payroll riot" forty black and white workers engaged in a free-for-all, while the only guard present disregarded the exhortation of one worker who urged his black brothers to "clean up the white laborers."

In contrast to the rather tense situation at Camp Logan, most white Houstonians were unaware of the black soldiers' presence. At least two factors were responsible for this situation. In the first place, the white officers made a conscious effort to discourage the soldiers from going into town. Instead they tried to attract the Negro community to the Twenty-fourth's camp by adopting a lax policy of visitation, whereby civilians could visit the camp each day between 1 P.M. and 10:45 P.M. The black townspeople, curious about military life and proud of the soldiers, flocked to the Twenty-fourth's camp, located on the western outskirts of the city about one mile east of Camp Logan. Civic groups prepared special entertainment; ladies' auxiliaries kept the soldiers well supplied with reading material and culinary delicacies; black ministers frequently held worship services on Sundays; and young ladies came to renew old acquaintances or to make new ones. In the process, a few prostitutes came in search of additional clients, but they were the exception rather than the rule. In general these visits were both pleasant and rewarding for civilians and soldiers alike, and a few of the men established lasting relationships with black Houstonians. On weekends the numerous visitors from the city's most respected black families gave the camp, according to one curious white officer, the appearance of a "very orderly ... big picnic."

In the second place, most soldiers preferred to avoid unpleasant contact with whites whenever possible, since the troops hardly enjoyed these humiliating encounters. Furthermore, they felt more comfortable and secure when racial conflicts occurred on federal property than in the city. Almost invariably, the soldiers avoided white neighborhoods and business establishments; instead they frequented "the lower end of Milam Street" and the San Felipe district in search of pleasure and fellowship.

Although racial contacts were kept to a minimum in the city, nevertheless a few black soldiers and one or two white officers received verbal abuse from white Houstonians. One of the latter proudly informed First Lieutenant William L. Chaffin, the battalion's medical officer, "that in Texas it costs 25 dollars to kill a buzzard and five dollars to kill a nigger. . . ." Following the streetcar incidents of July 28 and 29, several of the more prejudiced citizens circulated a wild rumor that the soldiers had assaulted one white conductor so severely that he was not expected to live. In passing black soldiers on the streets, white Houstonians sometimes muttered obscenities or hurled racist epithets at them. Some men in the Fifth Infantry of the Texas National Guard, which was temporarily stationed in several downtown buildings, also made derogatory remarks whenever they met black soldiers in the city. In at least two incidents where misunderstandings over saluting occurred, serious trouble was barely averted.

Of all the prejudiced groups which they encountered in Houston, black soldiers as well as black Houstonians resented most the condescending manners and the strong-armed tactics of the city police. Although both Colonel Newman and Chief of Police Clarence Brock had arranged for cooperation, members of the police force either had not been properly informed of the agreements or chose to ignore them. Consequently there was never any real communication between the military and civil police. Despite the fact that the soldiers were "kicking about their side arms," Newman followed Brock's advice and kept the provost guards unarmed whenever they patrolled the streets of Houston. Even in situations where blacks were denied adequate protection or where discrimination against them was obvious, the military policemen were helpless to intervene.

The principal cause of racial bitterness between soldiers and police did not stem from these confused arrangements but from a series of physical assaults on blacks by law officers. On August 18, two policemen arrested a black youth for allegedly "throwing bricks promiscuously." After two soldiers who were passing by in a streetcar protested what they regarded as unwarranted harrassment, the two patrolmen stopped the trolley and tried to apprehend the two "uppity" soldiers. When the latter "showed fight," the two officers slugged them with their pistols and escorted them to the police station.

Later the same day, two other soldiers complained to the desk sergeant that two policemen had severely beaten them for objecting to being called "niggers." The next day a deputy sheriff of Harris County arrested another soldier for sitting in the "white only" section of a streetcar. When the private allegedly drew a "penknife" the sheriff pistolwhipped him and took him to the county jail, where he remained until after the disturbance of August 23.

By late August, as the list of grievances mounted, the situation was becoming intolerable for several black soldiers. On Thursday, August 23, when the temperature soared to 102 degrees, there occurred a series of incidents which channeled the frustrations of this small but influential group of black soldiers into armed revolt. During the morning, Rufus Daniels and Lee Sparks, two mounted police officers, assaulted Private Alonzo Edwards of Company L for interfering in the arrest of a black housewife. Early that same afternoon Corporal Charles Baltimore, a provost guard from I Company, tried to obtain information from the two mounted policemen about the circumstances which had led to Edwards's arrest. Annoyed by this inquiry from a Negro, Sparks, generally regarded as one of the more vociferous racists on the police force, struck Baltimore with his pistol and fired at him three times. Baltimore fled with Sparks in close pursuit. The policeman cornered the bloodied solider underneath a bed in an unoccupied house on Bailey Street, arrested him, and sent him to jail in a patrol wagon.

Immediately news of the beatings of Private Edwards and Corporal Baltimore reached the Twenty-fourth's camp. The report that Baltimore was "shot at" soon grew into the rumor that he was "shot." Incensed by what they regarded as the unwarranted shooting of one of their most respected noncommissioned officers, several soldiers vowed to avenge Baltimore's death by getting the policeman who had killed him. Concerned but unaware of the seriousness of the situation, Major Kneeland S. Snow, former commander of I Company, who had only two days before replaced Colonel Newman as battalion commander, dispatched his adjutant, Captain Haig Shekerjian, to the police station to investigate the circumstances surrounding the arrests of both soldiers.

After Shekerjian had returned to camp with Baltimore, white officers mistakenly believed that the trouble had ended. Lest some individuals become too agitated and foment trouble, however, Snow canceled the "watermelon party" scheduled that night at Emancipation Park, revoked all passes, increased the number of sentries on guard duty at the Twenty-fourth's camp, and ordered all sixteen military police to patrol the black neighborhoods that evening.

Not satisfied with Snow's assurance that Sparks would be suspended, several black soldiers were determined to avenge the assaults on Baltimore and Edwards and, if possible, to guarantee that no further incidents of this sort would occur. A few of the more dissatisfied men, however, threatened to "burn down the town," and one promised to "shoot every white face he saw."

Shortly after eight o'clock that evening, Vida Henry, acting first sergeant of Company I, informed Major Snow, who was at the moment preparing to ride into town with a civilian friend, that he was afraid there might be trouble in the company. In the process of investigating this report, Snow caught a few men stealing ammunition from one of the company supply tents. He instantly ordered the first sergeants to collect all rifles and to search the men's tents for loose ammunition.

While Snow's orders were being carried out, Private Frank Johnson of Company I slipped to the rear of the company street and yelled: "Get your guns men! The white mob is coming!" This cry stampeded the frightened men into rushing the four company supply tents where they grabbed arms and ammunition. After approximately thirty minutes of confused and indiscriminate firing, Sergeant Henry ordered the men of Company I to "fall in" and to fill their canteens. Rallying the soldiers with cries of "stick by your own race" and "To hell with going to France... Get to work right here," and with threats to shoot anyone who refused to join them, ringleaders of the mutiny were able to attract the support of the bulk of Company I and a small contingent from Company M, together with a scattering of men from the other two companies. In all, some 75 to 100 men moved out of camp and, about nine o'clock, began a determined march on the city.

Circuitously approaching the city through the friendly confines of the San Felipe district, where they hoped to find Lee Sparks and Rufus Daniels, the black soldiers encountered the police first at Washington Avenue and Brunner Street and later at Wilson and San Felipe streets, and easily repulsed them each time. After killing Daniels and three additional policemen and wounding three others, one of whom subsequently died, the black rebels, weakened by numerous desertions, fell into disagreement over what course of action to pursue next. The vast majority balked at Sergeant Henry's proposal to continue the march to the police station. They left and circled back to camp. The remainder, too small to accomplish Henry's objective, sought refuge in the homes of black Houstonians, where they were captured the following day by city police and soldiers. Sergeant Henry, one of the few to realize the true seriousness of their actions, refused either to return to camp or to implicate others by hiding in their homes. Instead he shook hands, one by one, with his fellow soldiers as they departed for the Twenty-fourth's camp. Supposedly he later placed the barrel of his rifle against the roof of his mouth and pulled the trigger. The next morning, some boys discovered his body, with the back of his head blown out, lying across the railroad track in the city's Fourth Ward. [There is good evidence in the trial records that some of the whites killed that night were not victims of Henry's group. Instead they were shot by soldiers who left camp individually or in small groups during the firing and returned before Henry's column of men could have reached the San Felipe district. Since it is the contention of this paper that the soldiers were interested in wreaking vengeance only against the police, the author has avoided any prolonged discussion of the others killed in the riot. In addition to the four policemen mentioned above, eight white civilians, one Mexican-American, and two national guardsmen were also killed. A fifth policeman, who had been shot during the riot, later died of tetanus.]

In evaluating the tragic disturbances of August 23, 1917, several groups must share responsibility for the Houston mutiny and riot. In many ways, city officials were the most culpable. Having decided against jeopardizing the economic opportunities associated with a new training camp and in favor of allowing black troops temporarily in Houston, they were unwilling to endanger their political popularity by guaranteeing that the soldiers receive fair and impartial treatment within the confines of the city's segregation system. Although the men of the Twenty-fourth were willing to accept proscription as long as it was courteously applied, they absolutely refused to tolerate the unrestricted police brutality against Negroes which city officials were unwilling to stop. The acting mayor of Houston, who took over the reins of city government in early July following the sudden death of Mayor Joseph Jay Pastoriza, felt insecure in his new position. He pursued a hands-off policy toward the police department, even though he realized that Chief of Police Brock was incapable of controlling the actions of individual policemen who delighted in making life miserable for black Houstonians. As the former superintendent of city parks, Brock was unfamiliar with police practices and never able to win the respect of a majority of his men. Most policemen disregarded his instructions as frequently as they obeyed them, and several looked to former Chief of Police Ben Davison for advice and counsel. Consequently, mounted police officers like Sparks and Daniels felt free to use any tactic they desired against Negroes without fear of permanent suspension from the force.

Brock also abdicated his responsibilities on the evening of the riot. Although he urged Major Snow and Captain Shekerjian to take strong precautionary measures against a possible raid on the city, Brock refused to do likewise, insisting that he lacked jurisdiction over the military. Consequently, he failed even to alert the police department of any potential danger to the safety of the city. Either Brock was immobilized by loss of nerve or he really did not believe the threat was as great as he intimated to Snow.

The War Department was also guilty of misjudgment. In ordering the Twenty-fourth Infantry to Texas, the army ignored the objections of southern whites to the training of Negro troops in the South and the advice of Newman, who strongly disapproved of again sending black troops into Texas. By deciding to throw proud black soliders of the regular army into the maelstrom of southern racism, the War Department must bear some of the blame for the Houston tragedy.

In the final analysis, however, the men of the Third Battalion had to decide whether to accept the oppressive conditions of Houston or to fight back. A sizeable number chose the latter course. By retaliating against the police, they resorted to what they regarded as the only system of justice available to them, an option open to them but not to black Houstonians since as soldiers they had better access to firearms and were more proficient in their use. In addition, a few of the troopers acted as self-appointed protectors of Negro rights. Enraged by the treatment given black civilians, the soldiers at first berated them for enduring it, but they came to realize that the local citizens had no other choice. Once they were aware of this fact they decided upon retaliation in order to restore their own dignity, as well as to advertise the sufferings of black Houstonians.

Infuriated by the assaults on Edwards and Baltimore, they reacted out of hostility and in a fit of rage but not without planning. By convincing most of the men that a white mob was approaching the camp, the organizers of the mutiny stampeded them into rushing the supply tents and indiscriminately grabbing rifles. In this way they precluded the possibility that the army could later connect participants in the mutiny with rifles discovered on the city streets. By frightening the men into discharging their pieces in camp, they also prevented the army from using the evidence of their rifles having been fired as proof that they were involved in the riot. By creating panic and confusion, they hoped to clear the camp of all men by forcing those uninformed about the plans either to join them in the march to town or to flee into the adjoining woods for safety. Finally the leaders of the mutiny pledged themselves to secrecy and swore not "to snitch" on each other.

If these fairly elaborate preparations had proven successful, the army would have been hard pressed to discover the guilty persons. Since the majority of those involved had to believe in the success of this venture, they fully expected to escape severe punishment and calculated that the worst that could happen to them would be dishonorable discharge from the army—the fate of the Brownsville soldiers in 1906. Military investigators successfully persuaded eight participants, four of whom were new recruits and one a twenty-year veteran, to testify against the others in return for promises of immunity. In this way the military authorities broke the case and saved the United States army from the embarrassment of another Brownsville.

The Houston riot of 1917 was in several respects a prelude to what James Weldon Johnson later described as the "Red Summer of 1919," when the ostensible racial harmony of at least twenty-five American communities was suddenly disrupted by rioting and serious bloodshed. In rather marked contrast to their behavior in riots before World War I, black Americans in the immediate postwar period were no longer disposed to endure violence against themselves without some type of retaliation. When whites in the summer of 1919 invaded their neighborhoods intent upon murder, plunder, and wanton destruction of property, they usually fought back. For black Americans, the period during and after World War I was one of rising expectations, combined with a determination to claim those lawful rights which had been deferred for too long. One of the earliest manifestations of this spirit of militant self-defense occurred in Houston, when approximately one hundred black soldiers protested against police harassment and streetcar proscription by seizing arms and marching on the city.

Except for the Houston affair, however, the other racial outbreaks during the summer of 1917 followed the more traditional pattern of white aggressiveness and black passivity. The most serious of these took place at East St. Louis on July 2, 1917, when white mobs invaded Negro neighborhoods, inflicted thousands of dollars worth of property damage, and killed at least thirty-nine blacks and wounded scores of others. Most Negroes in East St. Louis preferred to flee the city rather than to risk further physical violence by striking back. Smaller racial disturbances also broke out in Chester and Philadelphia, Pennsylvania; Lexington, Kentucky; Newark, New Jersey; and New York

City. In all but one of these racial clashes, more blacks were killed and wounded than whites. The lone exception was the Houston riot, where sixteen whites and four blacks died. None of the four Negro soldiers, however, lost his life at the hands of a white assailant. [Henry, the recognized leader of the riot, committed suicide; two other black soldiers were accidentally shot by their own men; and a fourth subsequently died of gangrene resulting from medical neglect of wounds he received after the riot.]

The one ingredient which separated the Houston affray from the other racial disturbances of 1917 was the involvement of black soldiers of the regular army. Although the vast majority of the men in the Third Battalion were born and raised in the South, the years of rigorous military training had liberated many of them from the psychological trauma of the southern caste system. While their parents remained faithful to Booker T. Washington's philosophy of accommodation and forbearance, black troopers found the concepts of racial pride and equality as expressed by William E. B. DuBois more germane to their experiences and more in tune with their aspirations. Several men in the Twenty-fourth Infantry were avid readers of DuBois's *Crisis,* the influential organ of the National Association for the Advancement of Colored People, and Robert S. Abbott's Chicago *Defender,* a militant black newspaper with a decidedly antisouthern posture. The regimental chaplain expressed the views of more than one member of the Third Battalion when he praised DuBois for his "noble fight for manhood rights for our people" and asserted that "the entire enlisted command" of the Twenty-fourth Infantry was ready "to aid you in any way...."

Proud to be participants in a military crusade "to make the world safe for democracy," black troopers nevertheless expected to be accorded the same privileges and to be shown the same respect as other men in uniform, and they were also intent upon achieving those same rights at home that they were fighting to uphold in Europe. The historical record of black involvement in American wars, however, should have provided little encouragement for this hope, and the experiences of the Second and Third Battalions in Texas in 1917 were hardly reassuring. Their intense resentment of the humiliations and injustices they encountered was one early indication of this disappointment, and the resort to armed retaliation in Houston was another.

Although Negro troopers had demonstrated remarkable restraint in most situations of discrimination, they were nevertheless in the best position of any black Americans to insist upon respect and equitable treatment. In the past they had employed more than militant rhetoric in protesting various forms of offensive insults. The Houston affray was only the latest as well as the largest, in terms of the number of men involved and of persons killed, of a long line of militant protests by black soldiers who had always insisted upon fairer treatment than most southern whites were accustomed to give Negroes. The fact that black troopers were both young and single also made them less inclined to brook unprovoked racial insults from prejudiced whites.

On the other hand, the mere presence of black soldiers was sufficient in most areas of the South to activate anti-Negro prejudice. White Houstonians would tolerate no breach of existing racial customs by soldiers for fear it would set off a chain of black civilian reaction. Lee Sparks was representative of southern policemen who saw themselves as self-proclaimed defenders of the "southern way of life," and few prominent Houstonians were bold enough to criticize their methods of enforcing racial segregation.

The results of this Houston encounter were tragically predictable. The Houston mutiny and riot of 1917 was closely followed by the largest court-martial in American military history, by the mass execution of thirteen soldiers at Camp Travis at dawn on December 11, 1917, and by the sentencing of forty-one others to life in prison. Not satisfied with this impressive retribution, the army tried fifty-five more soldiers in two additional courts-martial, which sentenced sixteen to hang and twelve to life terms. Under extreme pressure from enraged Afro-Americans, President Woodrow Wilson saved ten of the latter sixteen men from the gallows by commuting their sentences to life in prison. The rendering and execution of these verdicts closed one of the most tragic chapters in American race relations and one of the darkest hours in the annals of the United States army.

The Oil Industry in Texas
Since Pearl Harbor

C. A. WARNER[*]

World War II forced Americans to organize, to direct and to utilize their nation's resources more efficiently. In particular, an economy to wage a war demanded governmental organization. No industry was more vital to the war effort than that of petroleum. Consequently the Office of Production Management began in 1941 to create a bureaucratic network that would guide production and distribution of oil during the war years and that would teach practices of conservation and efficiency that would continue thereafter.

In this article C. A. Warner describes the process of mobilization and the impact of V-J Day on the petroleum industry. The article is an optimistic one, possibly more so than events twenty years later have found altogether warranted. Nevertheless it is not only a good historical description of the development of the oil industry during the fifteen years after Pearl Harbor, but it demonstrates that the issues of conservation and regulation of natural resources long preceded the gas lines of 1973 and 1979.

Students of the petroleum industry in Texas will find a surprising lack of concise information concerning that major economic force. OIL!

°C. A. Warner, "The Oil Industry in Texas Since Pearl Harbor," *Southwestern Historical Quarterly*, LXI (January, 1958), 327–340.

TITAN OF THE SOUTHWEST *(Norman, 1949), by Carl C. Rister, remains the best source for the general reader, but Henrietta Larson and Kenneth W. Porter's* HISTORY OF HUMBLE OIL AND REFINING COMPANY *(New York, 1959) and Warner's* TEXAS OIL AND GAS SINCE 1543 *(Houston, 1939) will be valuable supplements for most students.*

The impact of Pearl Harbor on the oil industry of Texas was as pronounced and as far-reaching as the outbreak of hostilities was on the youth of the state. The change from a nation at peace to one at war was instantaneous, and it brought with it a necessity for the immediate revamping of all branches of the oil industry. Maximum production had to be established and maintained with the minimum expenditure of steel and highly skilled manpower. Such production had to be moved efficiently and with the least possibility of loss to refining centers. Refinery output had to be adjusted radically, and the production of aviation gasoline, of aviation lubricants capable of successful use in any climate, and of tolulene, butadiene, and other highly specialized products took priority over the then less essential products normally required more in peace time.

On December 23, 1941, the Office of Production Management, on the specific recommendation of the Office of the Petroleum Coordinator, issued General Preference Order M-68. This order was the first of many which affected directly the entire oil industry, but all were calculated to assure an ample supply of petroleum products to the armed forces of the government and to industry behind those forces.

Immediate plans were developed for the rapid and safe transportation of more oil and products by pipeline to mid-continent and eastern refining centers, and construction work was started under the supervision of the most skilled pipeline men. The first project completed permitted the movement in December, 1942, of approximately twenty-five thousand barrels of gasoline per day from the Port Arthur area to Mississippi River terminal facilities at Helena, Arkansas. This project involved the construction of a ten-inch line from El Dorado, Arkansas, to Helena, and the reversal of existing lines from the El Dorado-Shreveport area to the Port Arthur area.

Construction proceeded rapidly on the "Big Inch," the "Little Big Inch," and other projects, and within seventeen months from Pearl Harbor Day facilities had been completed for the movement north and east from Texas of approximately 150,000 barrels of products and approximately 350,000 barrels of crude oil daily. Before the end of the war these facilities had been expanded until approximately 800,000 barrels of oil and products were being moved inland or to the Atlantic Coast from Texas daily. Interconnecting or enlarged facilities in Texas, such as those from the Corpus Christi area to the Houston area and from West Texas fields to the Corsicana and East Texas area, permitted the movement of approximately 200,000 barrels more than at the beginning of 1942.

The increasing need for a convenient and efficient fuel in more ample quantities along the eastern seaboard was reflected in the granting of a permit to the Tennessee Gas Transmission Company for the construction of a gas transmission line from Texas to West Virginia in September, 1943. Construction commenced in December, and the first gas was delivered through the line eleven months later.

Exploratory activity in Texas during 1941 had resulted in significant discoveries along the newly established Wilcox trend of the Gulf Coast region, in deeper production on the flanks of salt domes, in excellent production from Mississippian horizons in North Texas, and in the discovery of deep pay horizons in the Ellenberger and Simpson horizons of West Texas. These proved a sound formation from which to carry on development and further exploration during the years of war need. The problem of establishing and maintaining an efficient high rate of daily production was increased during 1942 and the years immediately following by difficulty in securing pumping equipment and replacement material for stripper wells, which resulted in an increased rate of abandonment of such wells. The problem was further complicated by the large decline in drilling activity caused by the shortage of steel and the fact that many highly skilled technical men and lease employees left the industry to serve in the armed forces, agencies of the government, and defense plants. That the industry was able to cope with the situation, however, is demonstrated by the fact that productive capacity was not only maintained but was increased, and by the further fact that while the total number of wells completed in the state dropped 50 percent from 1941 to 1942, the number of new fields discovered in 1942 was 12 percent greater than in 1941. Significant discoveries during the first year of all-out effort included first commercial production of oil in Coke, Hunt, San Jacinto, Wilson, and Wise counties, first production in North Texas from the Simpson formation, and the first production in the state from the Viola lime. In the years immediately following were such discoveries as the TXL and Block 31 fields and commercial production from the Devonian in West Texas. At the same time the recovery of liquid hydrocarbons by cycling moved ahead rapidly with the completion of such plants as La Gloria, Katy, and Sheridan, all in the coastal area.

As a result of restricted but most effective exploration and development during the war years, Texas was able to supply necessary production, not only without waste, but also while maintaining excess productive capacity, as shown by the fact that shutdown days were continued throughout the period. Development in the Panhandle was greatly restricted in 1942 following a ruling by the Petroleum Administration for War that exploration for gas in that area should be discontinued.

The need for rubber and other highly specialized products caused a tremendous expansion in the petrochemical industry, the foundations for which had been laid along the Gulf Coast in 1941. By the end of 1943 there were eight completed plants for producing butadiene, eight completed plants for producing 100-octane gasoline, and plants for producing tolulene and other products, with additional plants under construction.

With the close of the war in 1945, there came another period of radical adjustment. The end of hostilities in August was almost immediately reflected in a reduction by the Railroad Commission of some 370,000 barrels daily in the state's allowable production for the month of September. Prior to V-J Day the industry had been straining to attain higher peaks of activity, but after that there was an easing of pressure and a letdown in activity.

In the five-year period 1946–1950 inclusive, immediately following the close of the war, exploration and development increased greatly, the construction of big-inch gas lines exceeded anything in the past, oil and products line facilities were expanded, and gas processing and secondary recovery operations moved forward, augmented by new advances in gas conservation and by the initial storing (in 1950) of liquefied petroleum gases in salt reservoirs.

During this period the total number of wells, both wildcat and development, completed in Texas more than doubled. This increase in wildcat activity reflected the return to normalcy of the search for new reserves, with adequate supplies of steel and necessary equipment and men to operate it. The results of exploration were evident in such discoveries as the reef areas of Scurry County, the Spraberry trend, and the first Texas offshore production, which was secured in 1949 in the Copano Bay and Corpus Christi areas of southern Texas by the Phillips Petroleum Company and The Texas Company. These developments, plus the discovery of new producing horizons in many districts, added seventeen new counties to the list of those producing oil in Texas. Also during this period a new producing depth of 13,300 feet was established in March, 1950, by General American Oil Company of Texas in Midland County.

That the demand for oil did not necessarily keep pace with the accelerated program of exploration and development during this period is shown by the fact that while statewide allowable producing days gradually increased to 366 in 1948 (a leap year), they then dropped to 230 for the year 1950.

The years of all-out war effort had demonstrated the need for the fullest utilization of material and men and for the greatest degree of conservation of natural resources. The lesson was well learned. Industry and regulatory bodies were becoming more conscious of natural gas. Chemical processing of the constituents of natural gas emerged during the war from a business of comparative obscurity to a prominent role, and the new methods and processes provided the motive for more effective conservation of this great resource.

In the years immediately following the war, advances in gas conservation in Texas paralleled, if indeed they did not exceed, the advances made in oil conservation during the early 1930s. Alarmed by the evident wastage of untold power through the flaring of tremendous quantities of gas, particularly casinghead gas, Governor Beauford H. Jester appointed a committee to investigate the matter and report on it. That committee, under the leadership of William J. Murray, Jr., was composed entirely of engineers from the oil industry. Following the committee's report, and as a result of the conditions set forth, the Railroad Commission issued a call for oil and gas operators in the eleven districts of the commission to meet and consider with the commission the problem of gas flaring as it was then being practiced.

This step marked the transition from the old era, when a well was not considered to be a high ratio one unless a four-inch gas riser could be heard screaming for three-quarters of a mile, to the new, in which maximum utilization is made of all gas.

The first of the hearings was held in Corpus Christi on February 6, 1946, and, following further investigation, the landmark order of the commission in the field of conservation of casinghead gas was issued on March 17, 1947. This order applied to the Seeligson Oil Field of Jim Wells and Kleberg counties, where some thirty-five to forty million cubic feet of gas were burned daily in flares. The order set forth certain beneficial uses for gas and stipulated that, unless the gas produced in the field should be so utilized, it was not to be produced. Paralleling the course of early oil conservation orders, legal proceedings against the commission and its order followed immediately. The order was stricken down in the trial court but was supported by the supreme court of the state which held, in effect, that the commission had the statutory authority to enter and enforce such an order, and that it would stand if the fact situation on which it was premised showed that the waste it sought to prevent was preventable. Following these initial steps, and after additional hearings on specific fields where large quantities of casinghead gas were still being flared, the commission entered orders similar to its Seeligson order on sixteen such fields in November of 1948. Again court action followed, but the net results are considered to be a general achievement of the conservation sought since the volume of gas reportedly flared dropped about 60 percent from 1948 to 1949. It is unquestionably true that such conservation action, initiated by the Railroad Commission of Texas, has promoted a usage for previously flared casinghead gas in the conservation of reservoir pressure in oil fields, which will result in an increased recovery of oil and in the subsequent sale of the gas. Additional revenue thereby accrues to the operators, to the royalty owners, and to the state.

It was during this five-year period, 1946–1950, that tremendous increases in gas-processing capacity were made, especially through such large plants as those at Carthage and Slaughter in 1949, at North Cowden in 1950, and at Old Ocean, which was unitized on August 1, 1948, and was then the largest voluntary domestic unit operation. It was also during this period that Governor Allan Shivers early in 1950, after consultation with members of the Railroad Commission, designated the recently formed Texas Petroleum Research Committee as the appropriate agency in Texas to aid in making a survey and in developing a program of research in petroleum engineering, with particular emphasis to be given to secondary recovery and the improving of primary recovery. The work of this committee has been outstanding.

In connection with its natural-gas investigations, the Federal Power Commission held hearings in Houston late in January, 1946. At these hearings, the governor, the members of the Railroad Commission, leaders in the oil and gas industry, royalty owners, consumers, research men, and representatives of the Petroleum Administration for War, and the attorney general, appeared and pointed out the necessity for the oil and gas business to remain in the hands of private industry and for problems of conservation and waste to be handled by proper state agencies if the industry was to continue to grow and to be a bulwark for democracy.

In the six years immediately past, 1951 through 1956, the oil industry of Texas has continued its steady growth, reaching new peaks in the production of oil and gas, attaining greater success in the field of conservation, and developing new techniques for more complete recovery of oil by both primary and secondary methods, as well as for a higher recovery of the end products of the oil and gas produced.

Exploration and development during these years, 1951–1956, have not been restricted to any particular district or districts, but have been widespread throughout the length and breadth of the state. These activities have resulted in important discoveries in West Texas in horizons ranging in age from Permian to Cambrian, in the discovery in McMullen County in 1953 and the subsequent development of deep Edwards lime horizons in southwestern Texas, in the discovery of Ellenberger production in Gary County in the Panhandle in 1955, in the discovery and development of production from horizons of Jurassic age in northwestern Texas, and in the development of deeper and new horizons on the flanks of old producing salt domes, which is evidenced by the wells along South Main Street in Houston on the flanks of Pierce Junction. This exploration and development also resulted in the first commercial production of oil from the Texas tidelands off the coast of Kleberg County by the Standard of Texas in

July, 1954. It will be recalled that the Supreme Court of the United States had ruled in June, 1950, that the federal government had paramount rights off both Texas and Louisiana coasts, that following congressional action President Dwight D. Eisenhower signed the tidelands bill in May, 1952, and that the first sale of Texas's tidelands oil leases after such action was on December 1, 1953.

A continuation of the increased interest in the prevention of waste and the conservation of oil and gas which had been evident in the preceding five years was particularly noticeable during the past six years. This is well exemplified in connection with the development of the Spraberry trend centering in the counties of Glasscock, Martin, Midland, Reagan, and Upton. Following discovery of production in the Spraberry horizon of Permian age in Dawson County on January 22, 1949, in Reagan County on January 29, 1949, in Midland County on February 24, 1959, and in adjacent counties shortly afterward, development expanded rapidly to 80 wells, with an average daily production of 8,576 barrels on January 1, 1951, to 462 wells in sixteen fields and a daily production of 53,078 barrels nine months later, and it continued to grow. To facilitate development of the trend and the supervision of operations, the Railroad Commission decided in August, 1951, to grant discovery allowables to any well in the Spraberry completed at a distance of three miles or more from known Spraberry production, and to adopt blanket spacing and production allocation rules. Development continued, with gas production becoming far in excess of capacity to move it until all wells were ordered closed in, effective on April 1, 1953, at which time it was estimated that the amount of such gas being flared amounted to nearly a quarter of a billion cubic feet per day—enough to serve a good-sized pipeline. This order of the Railroad Commission was a pioneer one in that it not only shut down the wells from which the gas was being flared, but also shut down the other wells to protect correlative rights in the field affected. The order was held void on June 10, 1953, by the supreme court of Texas, which pointed out that the statues permitted the shutting down of wells in order to prevent waste but not to protect correlative rights. A new order, effective July 16, was issued immediately by the commission permitting the production of a quantity of oil such that the amount of gas produced with it would not be in excess of facilities to handle it. Although many of the wells were off production for several months, such an order and the completion shortly afterward of more ample facilities to handle the gas had reduced materially the waste of gas formerly attendant upon the production of oil from this great area.

Another excellent illustration of the effectiveness of conservation is shown by the unitization agreement for the Canyon Reef production of the Scurry County area, which was approved by the commission on January 25, 1954. The approval was granted more than a year after the field had been unitized and after extensive hearings, at which about three thousand pages of testimony had been taken, in addition to many briefs by attorneys and engineers. The SACROC agreement, as it is commonly referred to, is a coordinated gas and water-injection pressure-regulation program for the entire unitized area of some 47,000 acres, and it is estimated by some engineers that it will result in the recovery of approximately 720,000,000 barrels more oil. This is an achievement of material significance to producers, to royalty owners, and to the state generally.

Additional steps in the program of gas conservation were taken by the commission in April, 1952, when it acted to require that reports be furnished on the amount of gas burned from every well in the state, and again on August 1, when it amended existing rules, adopted certain uniform terms respecting gas and its production, and ordered into effect new provisions designed to insure that the production and disposition of all gas produced in the state would be reported, regardless of its type, and regardless of whether it was actually used or whether it was flared.

Other phases of regulation and conservation enacted, adopted, or promulgated by agencies of the state during this period include: the creation by the legislature of a separate Liquefied Petroleum Gas Division of the Railroad Commission to regulate the distribution, storage, and sale of liquefied petroleum gases, which regulatory power had been handled by the Gas Utilities Division prior to 1951; additional legislation in 1955 (Article 6029-a) with respect to pollution of fresh-water sources by drilling and other operations; Rule 55 of the Railroad Commission, adopted on May 19, 1955, requiring the furnishing of the same information and reports with respect to such exploratory wells as slim holes and core holes as is required with respect to wells drilled for oil or gas; restriction of production from certain fields such as Fort Chadbourne, McElroy, Jigger Y, and others until facilities were adequate to handle increased casinghead gas resulting from intensive exploration, formation fracturing, and the like; and adoption by the commission, as Statewide Rule 24(b), of the requirements of senate bill 431 of the Fiftieth Legislature with respect to balancing periods to adjust over- and underproduction of gas from the fields of the state.

Another phase of regulation during this period was the ruling by the United States Supreme Court on June 7, 1954, that the Federal Power Commission had the power and authority to regulate sales of gas in interstate commerce. This was followed on July 16 by Order No. 174 of the Federal Power Commission blanketing all producers selling gas into interstate commerce, which order was supplemented by Orders 174-A and 174-B on August 6 and December 17, respectively. The future of the independent producer whose gas may find its way into interstate commerce is uncertain at this time, particularly following the veto of the Oren Harris-James William Fulbright bill in February of 1956.

Pipeline expansion during the past six years has not been confined to gas lines, although there has been considerable expansion and extension of such facilities, including those projected for the importation of gas into Texas from Mexico and for the delivery of additional gas to eastern areas. Oil pipelines have been looped and extended to increase outlets for both old and new areas, and new lines of importance have been constructed, including the West Texas Gulf 466-mile line from Canyon City to Sour Lake and the Rancho 457-mile line from McCamey to Houston. These two lines increased the pipeline capacity for transporting oil from West Texas to the Gulf Coast by over 600,000 barrels per day when they were placed in service during the first quarter of 1953. Facilities for the transportation of oil, however, are not yet extensive enough to enable the movement of all oil from lease tanks by pipelines, as was well illustrated at a hearing before the Railroad Commission early in April, 1957, but that is merely one of the many problems that are perennial with the oil industry.

Although generally thought of as the foremost producer and exporter of gas to other states in the nation, as indeed it is, Texas actually ranks first among the states in the nation in the quantity of gas it consumes. It is this convenient and clean fuel which heats more than a million Texas homes, accounts for the clean, new look of the buildings in Texas cities, and is a primary factor in industrial growth throughout the state.

Texas continues undisputed in first place in the oil industry of the United States. It produces oil or gas in 204 of its 254 counties; it has about 7,000 oil fields and 1,900 gas fields, and new ones are being discovered at the rate of about 45 per month; it has over 171,500 oil wells and 17,300 gas wells; and it has produced a total of 19,720,689,338 barrels of oil since 1886, which is about 36 percent of the total production in the United States since 1859. Within the state there are currently 85,000 miles of pipeline, exclusive of gas-distribution lines; 57 operating refineries; 205 gasoline plants; 30 cycling plants; and 150 pressure-maintenance plants. More than 6,000 individuals and companies are operating more than 42,000 leases.

The state is currently producing approximately 3,250,000 barrels of oil every day, with the major oil-producing capacity being restricted to about sixteen allowable producing days per month, and its proven reserves are estimated at approximately 15,000,000,000 barrels of crude oil, 3,000,000,000 barrels of natural gas liquids, and 113,000,000,000,000 cubic feet of gas. In connection with these estimated recoverable reserves, however, it should be pointed out that the results of exploration and development in Texas during the past five years have been able barely to maintain the reserves of liquid hydrocarbons at their previous level and to increase the reserves of natural gas only about 10 percent. This is significant indeed, in view of the constantly increasing demand for oil and gas and their products and in view of the fact that such reserves constitute less than a twenty-year supply at present rate of production.

In the fifteen years since Pearl Harbor, the oil industry in Texas has made outstanding progress in gas conservation and the development of the liquefied petroleum gas industry and in the fields of well-completion technique and secondary recovery; it has adopted such new methods as mud acids, miscible displacement "fracing," jet perforating, and lease automatic custody transfer of oil; and it has witnessed an increase in its producing depth record from approximately 11,500 feet to 15,000 feet. During this fifteen-year period, Texas has produced some 12,641,013,287 barrels of oil, an amount equal to the total production of the United States from the time of the Drake well in 1859 until shortly before the discovery of the great East Texas oil field. The Texas oil industry is now practicing and will continue to use the most advanced processes in its exploration for production, refining, and marketing of oil and gas to the end that coming years will witness the fullest utilization of the maximum recovery of these God-given resouces.

GEOLOGIC FORMATIONS PROVEN PRODUCTIVE IN VARIOUS COUNTIES SINCE JANUARY 1, 1942

Oligocene	Frio and Vicksburg		Bee, Newton
Eocene	Cockfield and Yegua		DeWitt, Jasper, Lavaca, San Jacinto, Starr, Walker (1946)*
	Cook Mountain		Austin
	Mt. Selman		Atascosa, Frio, Houston, Karnes, McMullen
	Wilcox		Atascosa, Austin, Bee, Brazos, Fayette, Goliad, Gonzales, Grimes (1951), Hardin, Karnes, LaSalle, Lee, Liberty, Live Oak, Madison (1946), McMullen, Newton, San Jacinto (1942), Waller, Washington, Wilson (1942)
Cretaceous	Navarro		Burleson, Cherokee, Robertson (1944)
	Austin		Atascosa, Wilson
	Eagle Ford		Anderson, Camp, Cherokee, Hopkins, Houston, Wood
	Woodbine		Hunt (1942), Kaufman, Madison, Trinity
	Washita	Buda	Bastrop, Bell, Falls, Gonzales, Madison, Maverick, Trinity, Wilson
		Georgetown	Falls, Houston, Madison
	Fredericksburg Edwards		Atascosa, Bastrop, Falls, Gonzales, Harrison, LaSalle, Lee (1948), Madison (1946), McMullen, Trinity
	Trinity	Paluxy	Bowie, Hunt, Kaufman, Red River (1949), Trinity, Wood
		Glen Rose	Angelina, Cherokee, Edwards, Franklin, Gregg, Hopkins, Hunt, Kaufman (1948), Leon, Limestone, Maverick, Nacogdoches, Navarro, Panola, Red River, Robertson, Rusk, San Augustine (1947), Shelby, Van Zandt, Wood
		Travis Peak	Cass, Franklin, Freestone, Gregg, Harrison, Henderson, Leon, Marion, Nacogdoches, Navarro, Panola, Rusk, Smith, Upshur, Van Zandt, Wood
Jurassic			Bowie (1944), Franklin, Limestone, Marion

Permian	Undifferentiated	Borden (1948), Callahan, Crosby, Culberson (1948), Cottle, Dickens, Floyd (1948), Hale (1946), Hansford (1951), Haskell, Kent, Knox, Lamb (1944), Martin (1944), Midland, Schleicher, Sterling (1948), Sutton
	Spraberry	Borden, Dawson, Glasscock, Howard, Martin, Midland, Reagan, Sterling, Tom Green, Upton
	Undifferentiated	Andrews, Hale, Hansford (1951), Martin, Midland, Ochiltree (1951), Sherman (1949), Upton
Pennsyl-vanian	Cisco-Canyon-Strawn	Borden, Coke (1942), Crane, Dawson, Ector, Floyd, Gaines, Garza, Hale, Hansford, Hardeman (1944), Hockley, Howard, Irion, Kent, King (1943), Knox, Lynn (1950), Midland (1945), Mitchell, Scurry, Sterling, Sutton (1948), Terry, Tom Green, Upton, Wise
	Bend	Baylor, Brown, Callahan, Cochran, Coke, Concho, Foard, Grayson, Haskell, Knox (1946), Reagan, Stephens, Wise (1942)
Mississip-pian		Archer, Baylor, Borden, Brown, Callahan, Comanche, Eastland, Gaines, Glasscock, Haskell, Howard, Jack, Lynn, Roberts (1949), Shackelford, Stephens, Sterling, Taylor, Throckmorton, Wilbarger, Winkler
Devonian		Andrews, Cochran, Crane, Crockett, Dawson, Ector, Gaines, Martin, Midland, Runnels, Terry, Upton, Ward, Winkler, Yoakum
Silurian		Andrews, Crane, Crockett, Dawson, Ector, Gaines, Howard, Midland, Pecos, Reagan, Terry, Upton, Winkler
	Viola	Montague
	Simpson	Clay, Cooke, Crane, Ector, Grayson, Montague
Ordovician	Ellenberger	Andrews, Archer, Borden, Callahan, Clay, Coke, Coleman, Crockett, Eastland, Ector, Fisher, Gaines, Gray, Grayson, Irion, Jack, Jones, Kent (1946), Martin, Midland, Mitchell, Montague, Nolan, Palo Pinto, Scurry, Shackelford, Schleicher, Stephens, Sterling, Stonewall, Taylor, Tom Green, Upton, Ward, Wainler, Wise
Cambrian		Coke, Nolan, Stonewall

* Discovery also constituted first commercial oil production for the county.

TOTAL PRODUCTION OF OIL IN TEXAS*
(In thousands of barrels)

Year	East and E. Central	Gulf Coast	North	Pan-handle	South-west	West	Texas Total	Cumulative	Allowable Producing Days†
To 1-1-42	2,204,215	1,395,798	1,115,518	407,384	758,924	1,197,837	7,079,676	.....	.....
1942	152,117	91,190	50,318	30,747	72,270	81,186	477,828	7,557,504	243
1943	171,800	139,174	50,392	33,352	94,875	98,096	587,689	8,145,193	249
1944	184,562	178,302	53,433	33,442	131,343	160,103	741,185	8,886,378	281
1945	179,573	174,396	54,478	31,436	135,379	175,406	750,668	9,637,046	277
1946	172,195	167,248	57,345	30,470	138,495	190,888	756,641	10,393,687	292
1947	173,063	175,555	62,303	31,347	153,932	220,421	816,621	11,210,308	324
1948	174,117	192,610	69,569	30,795	165,546	276,122	893,759	12,109,067	366
1949	139,547	139,312	70,235	33,034	126,807	227,692	736,627	12,845,694	238
1950	143,550	143,873	78,868	33,057	134,018	284,476	817,842	13,663,536	230
1951	160,358	171,690	87,485	30,977	163,624	377,848	991,982	14,655,518	278
1952	159,926	164,031	98,925	29,018	161,557	396,036	1,009,793	15,665,311	259
1953	152,624	161,205	109,841	27,260	161,647	387,001	999,578	16,664,889	236
1954	138,009	149,586	114,235	30,910	150,314	371,381	954,435	17,619,324	194
1955	140,931	155,212	126,593	33,015	158,021	408,708	1,022,480	18,641,804	194
1956	138,542	157,477	135,433	36,155	160,460	450,818	1,078,885	19,720,689	190
Total	4,585,129	3,746,659	2,334,971	882,399	2,867,512	5,304,019	12,641,013	19,720,689	

*Data are compiled from published reports of U.S. Bureau of Mines and Railroad Commission of Texas and from unpublished private files and reports.
†Statewide—for all fields not exempted or covered by special order.

WELLS COMPLETED IN TEXAS

Year	TOTAL (INCLUDING WILDCATS)				WILDCATS			
	Oil	Gas	Dry	Total	Oil	Gas	Dry	Total
1942	3,041	186	1,461	4,688	55	12	780	847
1943	2,373	140	1,908	4,421	135	17	1,021	1,173
1944	3,526	268	1,935	5,729	170	33	1,072	1,275
1945	4,036	714	2,445	7,195	228	44	1,280	1,552
1946	4,720	499	2,582	7,801	247	34	1,310	1,591
1947	5,814	537	2,950	9,301	355	80	1,460	1,895
1948	7,619	542	4,090	12,251	377	104	2,087	2,568
1949	8,613	746	4,306	13,665	440	112	2,239	2,791
1950	10,665	647	5,273	16,585	575	113	2,755	3,443
1951	10,086	726	5,843	16,655	802	133	3,473	4,408
1952	9,682	778	6,385	16,845	823	126	3,902	4,851
1953	9,380	978	6,648	17,006	904	169	4,172	5,245
1954	11,068	912	6,885	18,865	823	163	4,204	5,190
1955	12,476	603	6,902	19,981	883	132	4,109	5,124
1956	13,082	894	7,543	21,519	766	205	4,639	5,610
Total	116,181	9,170	67,156	192,507	7,583	1,477	38,503	47,563
%	60	5	35	100	16	3	81	100

COMPARATIVE DATA

	1942	1956
Field Activity		
Total Wells Drilled..............................	9,827	21,519
Wildcat Wells Drilled...........................	847	5,160
Total Footage Drilled...........................	57,317,700	92,620,000
Production		
Number of Oil Wells............................	99,185	171,500
Statewide Producing Days	242	190
Oil Production (Millions Bbls.).....................	478	1,079
Number of Gas Wells	3,685	17,339
Gas Production (Billions cu. ft.)	1,916	6,005
Reserves (Estimated)		
Oil (Including gas liquids)..........................	11,756 Millions Bbls.	18,163
Gas..	78° Trillions cu.ft.	113

°As of December 31, 1945 (first available).